The Politics of India under Modi

AN INTRODUCTION TO INDIA'S DEMOCRACY, ECONOMY, AND FOREIGN POLICY

Vikash Yadav & Jason A. Kirk

LEVER PRESS

ASIANetwork Books

Series Editors:
Erin McCarthy (St. Lawrence University)
Lisa Trivedi (Hamilton College)

ASIANetwork Books strives to publish high-quality, original monographs, edited collections, and translations that embody a rigorous liberal arts approach to Asian Studies. A collaboration with ASIANetwork, a consortium of Asian Studies faculty at 160 colleges, the series seeks to fill a space between works that address the critical pedagogical strategies of the Asian Studies classroom and works of specialized scholarship that engage a broad readership outside higher education. Manuscripts published in the ASIANetwork Books series, no matter how narrowly focused, are expected to raise broad questions of interest for the public and demonstrate classroom utility for Asian Studies.

Copyright © 2023 by Vikash Yadav and Jason A. Kirk

Lever Press (leverpress.org) is a publisher of pathbreaking scholarship. Supported by a consortium of higher education institutions focused on, and renowned for, excellence in both research and teaching, our press is grounded on three essential commitments: to be a digitally native press, to be a peer-reviewed, open access press that charges no fees to either authors or their institutions, and to be a press aligned with the liberal arts ethos.

This work is licensed under the Creative Commons Attribution-NonCommercial -NoDerivatives 4.0 International License. To view a copy of this license, visit http://creativecommons.org/licenses/by-nc-nd/4.0/ or send a letter to Creative Commons, PO Box 1866, Mountain View, CA 94042, USA.

The complete manuscript of this work was subjected to a fully closed ("double blind") review process. For more information, please see our Peer Review Commitments and Guidelines at https://www.leverpress.org/peerreview

DOI: https://doi.org/10.3998/mpub.12847233
Print ISBN: 978-1-64315-053-6
Open access ISBN: 978-1-64315-054-3

Library of Congress Control Number: 2023938833

Cover art: Photo 127192891 / Modi Mask © Dddube. Courtesy of Dreamstime.com.

Published in the United States of America by Lever Press, in partnership with Michigan Publishing.

Contents

Member Institution Acknowledgments	ix
Acknowledgments	xi
Preface	xiii
Introduction	1
India's Precarious Time	1
Studying the New India	2
Themes	3
Enigmatic Inertia	4
Bold Rhetoric, Weak Capacity	6
Puzzles	9
Chapter One: A Political Overview	11
Dramatic and Decisive Decisions; Poor Planning and Execution	11
System of Government	13
A Brief Biography of Narendra Modi	15
First Term Overview (2014–19)	21
Second Term Overview (2019–)	23
Chapter Two: Subnational Politics	33
Andhra Pradesh	38
Situating India's First "Linguistic" State	41

From Congress Party Dominance to Competitive Elections	43
Developmentalism and "Reform by Hype"	44
Telangana Goes Its Own Way	46
Confronting the Naxalite Insurgency	50
Capital Dreams and Coercive Developmentalism	51
Development Amid Democracy's Contradictions	53
Bihar	54
Developmental and Security	58
Intergovernmental Financial Support	61
The JD(U)–BJP Alliance	62
West Bengal	64
Big Sister's Party	67
The Clover and the Lotus	70
Employment and Investment	73
Education Reform	74
Secessionist Unrest and Security Concerns	75
Chapter Three: An Economic Overview	**95**
Introduction	95
Demographics	97
Poverty	98
Inequality	100
Employment	102
Locational and Sectoral Employment	103
The Smile Curve	105
Formal and Informal Employment	106
Income	110
Trade Flows	111
Global Value Chains	114
Investment Flows	115
Domestic Financial Sector	115
Foreign Direct Investment	118
Foreign Portfolio Investment	119

Economic Growth	120
Corruption	120
Chapter Four: India's Economic Policy under Modi	**129**
Domestic Economic Policies	130
Seeming Inclusive	130
Promising Techno-Modern Utopias	132
Blundering Market Intervention and Reform	135
International Economic Policies	140
Enduring Mercantilism	141
Exploring Alternatives	148
Going It Alone	151
Explaining the Boom	154
Chapter Five: India's Foreign Policy under Modi	**161**
The Modi Factor in India's Foreign Policy: Continuity and Change	166
India–China Relations under Modi: Economic Cooperation and Territorial Confrontation	168
India and the United States in the Modi Era	177
Redefining Strategic Autonomy and Non-Alignment	184
Defense Cooperation, Defense Spending, and Military Modernization	189
Relations with Pakistan and Afghanistan	194
Constructing an "Indo-Pacific" Region and Modi's "Act East" Policy	202
India's Regional Diplomacy: Soft Power, Hard Lines, and Vaccine Nationalism	206
Conclusion	223
Bibliography	231

Member Institution Acknowledgments

Lever Press is a joint venture. This work was made possible by the generous support of Lever Press member libraries from the following institutions:

Amherst College
Berea College
Bowdoin College
Carleton College
Central Washington University
Claremont Graduate University
Claremont McKenna College
Clark Atlanta University
College of Saint Benedict & Saint John's University
The College of Wooster
Davidson College
Denison University
DePauw University
Grinnell College
Hamilton College
Hampshire College
Harvey Mudd College
Hollins University
Iowa State University
Keck Graduate Institute
Knox College
Lafayette College
Macalester College
Middlebury College
Morehouse College
Norwich University
Occidental College
Penn State University
Pitzer College
Pomona College
Randolph-Macon College
Rollins College

Santa Clara University
Scripps College
Skidmore College
Smith College
Spelman College
Susquehanna University
Swarthmore College
Trinity University
UCLA Library
Union College
University of Idaho
University of Northern Colorado
University of Puget Sound
University of Rhode Island
University of San Francisco
University of Vermont
Ursinus College
Vassar College
Washington and Lee University
Whitman College
Whittier College
Whitworth University
Willamette University
Williams College

Acknowledgments

Our sincere thanks go to Lisa Trivedi at Hamilton College and Erin McCarthy at Saint Lawrence University, the ASIANetwork Series editors at Lever Press, for their support and encouragement with the prospectus that launched this project.

Jason would like to thank Deepa Kirk, my inspiration, greatest source of life wisdom, and best friend.

Vikash owes a deep debt of gratitude to Stacey Philbrick Yadav for long walks during our sabbaticals in which we each worked though our book projects. Her brilliance and kindness have always made my work stronger. Our daughters, Kieran and Lila, and our beloved little dachshund, Snickers, provided much-needed daily distractions with their countless shenanigans.

Preface

This book provides a detailed overview of India's political trends, economic prospects, and foreign policy in the twenty-first century. Since the right-wing government of Narendra Modi's Bharatiya Janata Party (BJP) came to power at the national level in 2014, and with its consolidation of power in the 2019 general election, India has witnessed a significant realignment of its national politics and a shift toward the right of the conventional political spectrum. Economically, despite the devastation of the COVID-19 pandemic, India is projected to be the fastest growing major economy in the world for the next several years—far outpacing its rival juggernaut, China. India is no longer a poor country, even though it continues to host one of the largest concentrations of entrenched poverty in the world. In terms of security policy, India is experiencing alarming confrontations along its Himalayan borders with China as well as its unending dispute with its fraternal enemy, Pakistan. At the same time, India has become a sought-after partner by global and regional powers in the "Indo-Pacific" region working to manage the rise of China to great power status. Our aim is to help undergraduate students "come up to speed" on these current issues and assess trends in the Indian republic.

This project grew out of student questions and concerns expressed in the classroom about India's political economy in the contemporary moment. As professors, we were frustrated by the lack of accessible academic texts designed for American undergraduates that provide a broad overview of the political and economic system in India along with a sober but critical analysis of specific policy initiatives in recent years.

This book is not meant to substitute for a history of India since its independence from Great Britain in 1947. A wide array of books is available to help students understand how the colonial encounter with Britain, which began in 1608, shaped the choices of institutions and style of politics adopted by India after it gained independence. Similarly, while our book examines the impact of India's economic liberalization after 1991 in the current moment, it cannot substitute for a history of that monumental shift in India's economic pathway.

INTRODUCTION

INDIA'S PRECARIOUS TIME

> In the 21st century, no obstacle can stop us from fulfilling the dreams and aspirations of India. Our strength is our vitality, our strength is our solidarity, our vitality is the spirit of nation first—always first. This is the time for shared dreams, this is the time for shared resolve, this is the time for shared efforts...and this is the time to move towards victory.
> And so I say once again –
> This is the time,
> This is the time...the right time!
> India's precious time!
> This is the time, the right time! India's precious time!
> —Prime Minister Narendra Modi[1]

The mesmerizing delivery of Modi's speeches projects the utmost confidence in India's destiny at a time when India's core political, economic, and security policies are all under severe strain. Standing only a quarter century from the centenary of its independence, India finds itself on a precipice. Despite immense progress across a range of metrics, India's political institutions are fraying from rank corruption and growing illiberal tendencies; its economy faces the daunting challenge of creating millions of labor-intensive jobs for a young nation, even as the window of opportunity for that development model is closing; and its mountainous northern borders are marked with flaring skirmishes and a growing sense of encirclement around its namesake ocean, threating the very basis of the state's hard won sovereignty.

STUDYING THE NEW INDIA

A new India has emerged. Political leadership is only one particularly visible manifestation of change. However forceful (and polarizing) Narendra Modi's leadership may be, India today is a quite different country from the low-income, socialistic, ecumenical, non-aligned, post-colonial state birthed by India's first prime minister, Jawaharlal Nehru. While two centuries of indirect and direct British imperial domination dramatically shaped the state's original choice of political institutions, economic framework, and foreign policy, understanding India in the twenty-first century requires apprehending dramatic changes in each of these areas.

As the fastest growing major economy in the world, with one of the largest populations, and as a nuclear power with significant capabilities in a restless continent, India demands global attention. India is a country capable of impressive technical feats, such as placing a satellite in orbit around Mars on its first attempt, but it also sustains one of the largest concentrations of absolute poverty in the world, despite significant poverty reduction in the last three decades (now significantly threatened by the COVID-19 pandemic).

India is at a pivotal moment in its history. The country needs to hurdle the "Middle-Income Trap"[2] and find new markets to expand its exports if it hopes to lift millions more out of destitution. The republic's fraying democratic institutions need mending. India's borders must be secured from encroachment and infiltration. Finally, India needs to find reliable partners to stabilize the

Indo-Pacific region.³ Tackling all of these daunting challenges hinges on the character of India's political leadership.

The election of Narendra Modi as the prime minister of India represents a new chapter in India's storied politics. Modi's Bharatiya Janata Party (BJP) swept to power in 2014, dealing a significant blow to the once hegemonic and venerable Indian National Congress (INC) party. Although the BJP, a party created in 1980, had held power momentarily in 1996 and then from 1998 to 2004 under the leadership of Atal Bihari Vajpayee at the head of the National Democratic Alliance (NDA) coalition, the election of Modi was widely viewed as a triumph of *Hindutva* (i.e., Hindu nationalism) as the BJP obtained an absolute majority in the lower house without relying on its coalition partners. The BJP further consolidated its hold on power and increased its majority in 2019.

THEMES

This book argues that two major themes emerge from a careful analysis of India's political economy and security policy since Modi came to power. First, for each step forward that India has progressed toward its collective ambition of creating a harmonious, prosperous, and secure society, India has had to take one step backward. Some of India's struggles are due to exogenous shocks (e.g., the COVID-19 pandemic), but others are due to strategic missteps and poor policy execution. This lack of clear momentum means that India does not fit comfortably into existing, dichotomous classificatory schemes (e.g., liberal vs. illiberal democracy). Second, the bold rhetoric and ambition of India's elite mask critical weaknesses in its capacities. Modi may be widely perceived as a "strong" (or strongman) leader, and India's diverse and endlessly resourceful society may possess its own myriad strengths, but the Indian *state*'s capacity to respond to the governing challenges of the twenty-first century remains an open question—at a time when the demands placed on it are rapidly intensifying.

Enigmatic Inertia

On the political front, we argue that India has emerged as neither an inclusive liberal democracy nor an "illiberal electocracy." India's politics today are somewhat akin to those of the United States in the century prior to its transformation into an inclusive democracy in 1965. In other words, India is characterized by a hierarchical (i.e., casteist and classist) and exclusive (i.e., communal and identity-based) society, with India's sizeable Muslim majority increasingly alienated and outcast from the political and economic mainstream at the national level. Nevertheless, alternative models of governance continue to percolate at the subnational level. Most prominent are the templates for neo-patrimonial and personalistic governments associated with chief ministers such as Mayawati in Uttar Pradesh and Mamata "Didi" (Big Sister) Banerjee in West Bengal, and the developmental/technocratic models associated with figures like N. Chandrababu Naidu in Andhra Pradesh and Nitish Kumar in Bihar.

On the economic front, India's economy is neither "neo-liberal" nor "developmental." The term "neoliberalism" has witnessed a dramatic inflation in its meaning and has become nearly synonymous with the "evils" of contemporary consumer-driven capitalism among certain academics. However, the actual ideology of the economic liberalism that began its revival in the mid-twentieth century is not an accurate description of Indian capitalism. The state certainly protects the right to private ownership of property, production is organized predominantly on the basis of market signals about consumer demand, and free labor is generally hired on the basis of formal contracts. But the state is not oriented toward allowing the market to allocate goods on the basis of efficiency alone. The market is still heavily regulated, foreign competition is limited in several areas, and the state provides a range of subsidies that distort market signals.

At the same time, India is not a developmental state on the East Asian model first pioneered by Japan (and later by South Korea,

Taiwan, Singapore, and others), although several of India's federal states seek to emulate the developmental state model. The Indian bureaucracy is unable to provide compelling, tutelary guidance to "national champion" industries or to create a disciplined and a flexible skilled-labor force. While there is a cozy relationship between politicians and business elites, the state lacks both the capacity to guide firms and the autonomy from the owners of capital to discipline their behavior. With a few exceptions (e.g., Narayan Murthy at Infosys), India's billionaire entrepreneurs tend to populate industries that benefit from access to state licensing or the privatization of formerly state-owned industries, as opposed to new sectors. Rent-seeking, family-owned, crony-capitalist firms predominate, rather than innovative, professionally managed firms. India is better characterized as a "mercantilist" economy that seeks to achieve national economic prosperity by using tariff barriers to limit imports and exploit the international liberal trade regime to expand exports—but this formulation may imply a more coherent and intentional national economic strategy than India actually exhibits. When India was a low-income country, it benefitted from a range of exceptions to international free trade rules. As a middle-income country, India has yet to shed its illiberal approach to the international free trade regime and to embrace global competition, although India is finding that it can deliver competitive, world-class goods and services in some sectors. Hence, India's confusing economic policy posture.

Prior to the onset of the COVID-19 pandemic, India had made dramatic progress in alleviating poverty. But India's growth trajectory was unconsolidated, many households were "one illness away" from economic crisis,[4] and the Great Pandemic threatens to undo years of progress. As will be discussed in detail, India is *not* on a path to provide labor-intensive employment to the millions of undereducated young workers who enter the job market annually. At the same time, income inequality has seen a dramatic surge since economic liberalization in 1991. In 1990, the bottom half of the population earned roughly a fifth of national pre-tax income, while the top decile earned roughly a third of national income. By 2014, the bottom half of the population had barely 13% of national income, while the top decile of earners received well over half (57%) of national income. More concerning, the top 1% of income earners commanded a fifth of national pre-tax income in 2014, whereas prior to liberalization it earned a tenth of the total.[5] While income inequality may not be as politically salient as many political observers imagine, it may have long-term consequence for the regime's legitimacy if social mobility ossifies.

Bold Rhetoric, Weak Capacity

The bold rhetoric and ambition of India's loquacious commentariat masks severe weaknesses in the state's capacity. Too often, talking about India's "great power" potential—and sometimes, nursing resentment that India still isn't receiving its "due"—substitutes for critical thought and grounded planning as befits a great civilization. As Aparna Pande explains in *Making India Great: The Promise of a Reluctant Global Power*,

> The sense of Indian exceptionalism that the country's founding fathers spoke about and that the average Indian believes in, comes from the seeming inevitability of its rise to great power status. For Indians, India's greatness is a given. The only question is when and how it will manifest itself on the world stage.[6]

But, Pande insists, "India's promise cannot be realized without acknowledging its failings"—and it seems too often of late an inward self-absorption, self-congratulatory nationalism, and "recent focus on religious and cultural disputes could end up reversing India's success in nation-building since Independence."[7]

In international relations, India is neither a pivotal great power, nor a pawn of greater powers. Though it faces real external threats and constraints on its ability to order the regional and global institutional and security environments according to its interests (as do all states, to varying degrees), the most significant current constraints on India's global potential may be self-imposed.

Politically, India prides itself in being the world's largest democracy, and each election is as a matter of course the largest in world history. The reality, however, is that while certain democratic values may be relatively robust, the regime that democracy delivers is relatively fragile. The first-past-the-post (or FPP) electoral system that has, of late, delivered strong parliamentary majorities to the BJP masks the thinner popular support for the ruling government (31% of votes in 2014; 37% of votes in 2019), despite the impression of strong electoral mandates. The underlying fragility and appearance of popular mandates may reinforce authoritarian tendencies of the government, particularly with regard to issues of free speech and freedom of the press. More broadly, there is a lack of a serious commitment to political liberalism among the current generation of political decision-makers—and, perhaps, among large and growing segments of the electorate.

Beyond the confines of the national capital, alternative models of governance that may challenge the consolidation of Hindu nationalism have emerged. From West Bengal's patrimonial politics and Bihar's developmentalism, to Andhra Pradesh's eclectic "reform by hype," state leaders with national ambitions and global economic interests are experimenting with new ways to rally their constituents. At the same time, the Modi government's recent administrative reorganization (read: division and diminution) of Jammu and Kashmir state into a union territory of the same name and a second union territory of Ladakh, while certainly a unique case, attests to the top-down nature of Indian federalism and the strong hand of the central (federal) government in circumscribing subnational political possibilities. The diversity of India's subnational state-level polities may hold the greatest potential to stand as a countervailing force to the centralizing tendencies of Modi and the BJP, but it will take some combination of state-level parties and personalities in coalition (as India has seen in the not-too-distant past) to check the BJP's ascendance, and not any single state satrap.

Economically, while India works diligently to attract foreign direct investment, its industrial strategy (e.g., a "Make in India" campaign) appears to simply ignore the fact that major global changes, shifting away from outsourcing, are underway. India is desperate to grow its economy, but it has made serious blunders (e.g., so-called demonetization, involving a hastily implemented paper banknote transition in 2016) under the Modi regime that have threatened its progress. India projects the image of a dynamic market economy despite a residual mercantilist outlook, autarchic aspirations, and a crony-capitalist framework. In essence, despite the hype that India has embraced free market capitalism, India shows a lack of serious commitment to economic liberalism.

In international relations, it is clear that India desires "great power" status despite inadequate power projection capabilities. With $72.9 billion in military spending in 2021, India is currently the third highest military spender in the world. And at nearly a tenth of global arms imports, India is the second highest importer of military equipment after Saudi Arabia. However, with few exceptions, India is extremely reluctant to project military power beyond its South Asian neighborhood. Even within South Asia, India has passively watched as its influence and investments are subverted by its smaller rival Pakistan in areas where India remains popular, such as Afghanistan. Moreover, even when it has a militarized border dispute with neighboring China, India is unable to exert any real leverage or to extricate itself from economic relations with Beijing. India also covets "soft power" or the ability co-opt foreign power rather than relying on military or economic coercion. And while India's culture (e.g., "Bollywood" cinema) is popular throughout Asia and Africa, its enduring images of poverty, corruption, military weakness, and bureaucratic intransigence hamper the attractiveness of its institutions. India too often remains a "dispensable power" in international relations, despite increasingly recognized potential.

PUZZLES

For students of India, these thematic observations listed above naturally pose a series of pressing puzzles:

1. *Do the alternative governance models found in the larger states have the potential to offset the rise of the BJP and "Hindu nationalism"?*
2. *Is India's high economic growth rate sustainable in a competitive global economy?*
3. *Given India's reluctance to project power, why has it been sought after (particularly by successive US administrations) as a counterbalance to a rising China?*

The following chapters will seek to answer these questions through explorations of India's federal and subnational politics, political economy, and foreign policy.

NOTES

1 Narendra Modi, "Sabka Saath, Sabka Vikas, Sabka Vishwas and Now Sabka Prayas Are Vital for the Achievement of Our Goals: PM Modi on 75th Independence Day" (75th Independence Day Speech, Red Fort, Delhi, India, August 15, 2021), https://www.narendramodi.in/text-of-prime-minnister-narendra-modi-s-address-from-the-red-fort-on-75th-independence-day-556737.
2 The Middle-Income Trap describes a pattern in which "middle-income countries" (i.e., World Bank member countries with a per capita gross national income between $1,026 to $12,475) stagnate because: 1) they are unable to maintain high rates of export-led industrial growth due to rising wages in labor-intensive industries relative to the low-income countries; and 2) they

are unable to innovate to compete with high-income countries in frontier technologies.
3 The Indo-Pacific is a mental map that reconceptualizes the littoral states of the Indian Ocean and the western Pacific Ocean as part of one strategic area. Although the parameters of the concept are contested, at its broadest it would include the littoral states of East Africa, West Asia, South Asia, South-East Asia, Australia, East Asia, and West coast of North America. For a detailed discussion of the concept, see Chapter 5.
4 Anirudh Krishna, *One Illness Away: Why People Become Poor and How They Escape Poverty* (New York: Oxford University Press, 2010).
5 World Inequality Database, "India," WID—World Inequality Database, accessed May 27, 2021, https://wid.world/country/india/.
6 Aparna Pande, *Making India Great: The Promise of a Reluctant Great Power* (Noida, Uttar Pradesh: HarperCollins India, 2020), ix.
7 Pande, xii, xv.

CHAPTER ONE

A POLITICAL OVERVIEW

DRAMATIC AND DECISIVE DECISIONS; POOR PLANNING AND EXECUTION

On the 24th of March 2020, with 519 officially confirmed cases of COVID-19 and ten officially acknowledged deaths, in a live prime-time broadcast across 201 television channels,[1] Prime Minister Modi ordered a three-week lockdown of the entire country. The order confined 1.3 billion people to their homes with only four hours' notice. In the days prior to the decree, the government had tried stringent measures to create social distancing but quickly recognized these measures were futile, particularly in densely populated urban areas. Long-distance train and air travel were suspended, but essential services, such as grocery stores, banks, and the media, were permitted to remain open. After the announcement, the government said it would draw up plans to provide emergency cash to citizens to provide food for the poor. The decision displayed the typical "decisiveness" that Modi supporters applauded, but also the lack of forethought and empathy for the impact of policy decisions on the marginalized that critics derided.

The impact on poor workers was swift, devastating, and highly counterproductive from a policy perspective. As migrant workers living in urban tenements streamed back to their villages on foot, the virus likely spread deep into the heart of rural India. Moreover, there were reports of police beating grocery store workers and journalists for violating the decree despite their exceptional status as essential workers. Prices of local food skyrocketed as panic buying set in.[2] Ultimately, the lockdown, for all its theatrical drama, had little effect on containing the virus. And despite highly discredited government statistics, India became a global epicenter and the site of a serious mutation in the virus. India's long neglected public health infrastructure buckled under the strain, and as crematoria filled to capacity, corpses were seen floating down the Ganga River. By June 2021, Arvind Subramaniam, the former chief economic advisor to PM Modi, estimated (using figures for excess mortality) that between 3.4 to 4.7 million Indians had died from COVID-19, numbers at least ten times greater than the official government tally.[3]

The decision to lock down a country the size of India, although not wholly irrational given the poor state of India's health system and the understanding of the virus' mode of transmission at the time, reflected a complete lack of planning and poor execution. The decree fit a pattern of making dramatic and decisive announcements without much forethought or mobilization of the instruments of the state for executing the policy. Nevertheless, despite the poor policy execution, Modi has managed to retain an enthusiastic base of support. In fact, with the exception of a brief dip in May 2021, Modi has consistently remained the most popular leader out of 13 major countries.[4] As the COVID-19 crisis has unfolded, Modi's popularity has declined from a high of 84% in May 2020, when India appeared to be turning a corner, to a low of 63% in May to June 2021, but he returned to over 70% approval by mid-August 2021. His disapproval rating dipped to 12% in May 2020 but has not exceeded 32% (May 2021).[5] To understand how this is possible, it is first necessary to understand the institutional and political framework within which the prime minister operates.

SYSTEM OF GOVERNMENT

India is a constitutional, parliamentary, democratic republic with a federal structure. The Indian Constitution provides a progressive, liberal framework for reforming Indian society and promoting economic development. The nominal head of state is the president, but actual, day-to-day political power resides in the office of the prime minister and their cabinet. With the exception of a brief period of Emergency Rule (1975–77), India has remained a functional democracy with universal suffrage and broad legitimacy since the inauguration of the Constitution in 1950 and the first general elections in 1951–52.

The British or Westminster parliamentary model fuses the legislative and executive functions of the state. Elections to hold one of the 543 seats in the lower house of parliament, the House of the People (or Lok Sabha), is on the basis of a "first-past-the-post" (FPP) electoral system for a single member district. In other words, as in the United States, the first candidate to win a plurality of votes wins the sole right to represent their district in Parliament. Nearly a quarter of the seats are reserved for candidates from the Scheduled Caste (*Dalit* or SC) and Scheduled Tribe (ST) communities. The party or coalition of parties able to form a majority in Parliament are appointed by the president to form a government. A full term for a government is five years, but elections may be held before that time if the government loses the confidence of the majority of the members of Parliament or if the ruling government believes it is advantageous to hold elections early.

The upper house of Parliament, the Council of States (or Rajya Sabha), has 233 members elected by state (or territory) legislatures. Twelve additional members, usually eminent and accomplished citizens, are appointed to the upper house by the president of India. The term of office is six years, and elections are staggered so that one-third of the elected members face election every two years.

The political spectrum in India ranges from revolutionary communism on the far left to fascistic organizations on the far right. However, the two largest mainstream national parties are the center-left, ecumenical Indian National Congress (INC) party and the right-wing, Hindu nationalist Bharatiya Janata Party (BJP). While ideology shapes the broad contours of politics at the national level, politics at the regional and state level is often concerned with patronage networks and the politics of collective dignity and identity.

The Indian judiciary adheres to the common law system inherited from British India. The Supreme Court of India is the apex court and has original and exclusive jurisdiction in disputes between the Centre and the states as well as disputes between the states. The Court has the power of appellate jurisdiction in any case pertaining to the Constitution or significant matters of law—as determined by the Court itself.[6] Its 34 members are appointed by the president of India. Unlike the British political system, the Indian Supreme Court has the power of judicial review over the constitutionality of any law passed by the national or state governments. However, the scope of judicial review in India's Supreme Court, which is confined to laws that violate the "basic structure" of the Constitution, is not as wide as that of the United States' Supreme Court. While India's Supreme Court has been relatively passive in the Modi era, there have been periods of judicial activism in cases of public interest litigation, in which any aggrieved party may file a case and seek direct redress from the Court.[7]

The civil service or Indian Administrative Service (IAS) serves at the executive branch's permanent bureaucracy. This is a meritocratic and politically neutral organization that administers the laws of the state and represents India in intergovernmental organizations. The service was reorganized to create nationally balanced recruitment and to ensure representation by minorities and women. The IAS is organized by regional cadres with half of the recruits coming from outside the region—the aim is to promote cross-regional linkages in the bureaucracy.[8] Although the civil service once retained a stellar image, it has been marked by growing corruption in recent years.

India is organized as a federal republic, in part to allay fears of separatism. India's federalism operates on the "union-state" model similar to the United Kingdom and the Kingdom of Spain. The union is constitutionally indestructible, but the constituent states may be subdivided by the central government.[9] The federal states were reorganized along ethno-linguistic lines in the 1950s, a decision that paradoxically but effectively strengthened national unity by sapping many ethno-linguistic grievances. New federal states continue to be created periodically in response to local agitation and the machinations of political parties at the federal level. Four additional states (Chhattisgarh, Uttarakhand, Jharkhand, and Telangana) have been created since 2000 and three new Union territories (Jammu and Kashmir; Ladakh; and Dadra, Nagar Haveli, and Daman and Diu) since 2019.

As the federal government maintains control over the collection and distribution of revenue (e.g., income tax, corporate tax, customs duties), it is ultimately in a stronger position vis-à-vis the states, which are economically dependent on transfers. States may collect some of their own revenue (e.g., land revenue, irrigation taxes), but these tax streams are not as lucrative as those controlled by New Delhi.[10] Nevertheless, the relationship between the center and the states varies greatly depending on the strength and popularity of the federal government and the corollary need or disdain for regional coalition partners, and the strength and popularity of state leaders.

A BRIEF BIOGRAPHY OF NARENDRA MODI

India's 14th prime minister was born to a humble, large, lower caste ("backward" or OBC) family in the village of Vadnagar, in the present-day state of Gujarat in 1950. Modi and his six siblings undoubtedly grew up in a home without electricity or a proper roof and with the most basic schooling and medical facilities. As a child, he helped his father sell tea from a small wooden tea stall next to the Vadnagar railway station.[11] To this extent, Modi represents a significant departure from the general background of Indian prime ministers, almost all of whom were drawn from the upper castes.

At the age of 8, he joined the local branch of the fascistic, paramilitary Rashtriya Swayamsevak Sangh (National Volunteers Organization or RSS), which would meet daily at the village parade ground for communal calisthenics and patriotic singing. The organization promotes the ideology of *Hindutva* (Hinduness or Hindu nationalism), which seeks to align Indian identity with Hindu identity. In the eyes of the RSS, the Hindu identity encompasses all those religions that originate in the Indian subcontinent (i.e., Hinduism, Buddhism, Sikhism, and Jainism). Islam and Christianity are therefore considered to be alien religions. Although as a cultural organization the RSS does not formally field candidates for political office, the organization would eventually give birth to the Bharatiya Janata Party (BJP) in 1980. The RSS, with 85,000 cells (*shakhas*) nationwide and 15 affiliated organizations, operates to mobilize support for the BJP at the local level.[12]

HINDUTVA AND THE BJP

Over 81% of Indian adults identify with the Hindu faith. *Hindutva* [Hinduness], an ideology that traces to the early twentieth century, represents the appropriation of Hindu religious identity for political purposes. Proponents of the ideology assert that India should be a nation-state reflecting the values of Hinduism and its offshoot religions: Jainism, Buddhism, and Sikhism. Followers of Islam and Christianity, which originate outside of the Indian subcontinent, are to be treated as tolerated minorities or second-class citizens as long as they show deference to the cultural values of the majority community. If they do not, as M. S. Golwalkar, a founding ideologue of the movement, wrote in 1938, the minorities must be "wholly subordinated" to the Hindu majority and may lay claim to "nothing...no privileges, far less any preferential treatment—not even citizens' rights."[13]

How widely *Hindutva*, as a political ideology, might resonate with the population can be ascertained through survey data. According to a Pew Research Center survey of 29,999 Indian adults published in 2021, Indians express a strong preference (91%) for religious freedom and tolerance. However, a large majority of Hindus (>65%) and Muslims (>76%) also oppose religious intermarriage.[14] A similar sentiment is also common among the majority of Sikhs and Jains surveyed. The Pew survey also found that over a third of Hindus (36%) would not be willing to have a Muslim as a neighbor. The composite image of India's social life that emerges from the survey is that while Indians value religious tolerance, they prefer to live in segregated communities for the most part.[15]

The imbrication of Hindu religious identity and Indian national identity, a central pillar of *Hindutva* ideology, is shared by a large majority of Hindus (64%).[16] The BJP as a political party particularly appeals to that subset of Hindu voters (i.e., 30% of all Hindu voters in 2019) who believed that being "truly Indian" is linked to both the Hindu religion and speaking Hindi as their "mother tongue."[17] It should be noted, however, that only 49% of Hindus voted for the BJP in 2019. While the proportion of Hindus voting for the BJP in north (68%), central (65%), and northeast (73%) India was very high, in southern India, the BJP did not have much appeal for Hindu voters (19%). In other words, being Hindu or even equating the Hindu faith with Indian identity does not automatically translate into support for the BJP. The BJP's political agenda has limited salience in certain regions of India such as the southern and eastern states. The Hindu vote is also fractured along caste lines in many areas.

SECULARISM AND EXCLUSION

Surprisingly, the BJP does not seek to attack directly the secular foundation of the Indian state. In fact, the BJP has consistently accused its rival, the INC, of being "pseudo-secular" and pandering to religious minorities. This rhetoric implies that the BJP is actually the more secular party. (American readers familiar with the phrase "owning the libs" [i.e., liberals], fashionable among conservative activists, will recognize the political style.) The implicit argument is that the institutions of the secular state in the context of an electoral majority are sufficient to establish and maintain a hierarchy between communities and to marginalize minorities.[18] This logic paints Muslims as communal and backward while leaving the majority community unmarked, undifferentiated, and modern.[19] In any case, the BJP is not a religious party with a specifically theological agenda; indeed, this would be difficult to articulate given the diversity of religious thought and regional traditions in Hinduism. Rather, the party and the broader Hindu nationalist movement promote cultural hegemony in the vernacular of nationalism.

Despite its officially secular posture, however, the BJP does not seek to create a shared republic. In 2019 the BJP passed the Citizenship Amendment Act, which stated that only non-Muslim refugees from majority-Muslim Afghanistan, Bangladesh, and Pakistan would be eligible for Indian citizenship. While the legislation shocked many liberal Indians, who saw it as a violation of the egalitarian provisions in the Indian Constitution,[20] the new law continues a tradition of questioning Muslim belonging and citizenship that can be traced at least to the Abducted Persons (Recovery and Restoration) Bill of 1949, which sought the return of Hindu women (regardless of the woman's own preferences) suspected of being abducted during the chaos of Partition by Muslim men, and to repatriate Muslim women suspected of being abducted to Pakistan.[21] A similar logic, albeit more classist than gendered, was at work in the creation of Non-Resident Indian (NRI) status after the Diaspora Report of 2001 for upper-echelon Indians who had migrated to the US, Canada, Australia, New Zealand, and Western Europe but not for those who had departed as indentured servants to the Caribbean, Oceania, or East Africa—as many in the latter group might be Muslim.[22] In essence, the BJP's anxieties about who constitutes a "real Indian" reflects a much broader question in India since the start of the struggle for independence. The main change, then, is that the BJP is more forthright in answering "the Muslim question."

Modi would eventually become a full-time volunteer for the RSS after moving to Ahmedabad. He rose quickly as a propagandist within the organization. The RSS delegated Modi to join the BJP in 1980. By 1995, Modi had risen to the position of Party Secretary for the BJP. In 2001, despite a lack of experience in government, Modi was selected by the BJP national leadership to run for the chief minister position.

In February 2002, a few months after taking office, nearly 60 Hindu pilgrims/activists were killed when a train car caught fire in the town of Godhra, Gujarat. The events would lead to a three-day pogrom against Muslims as Hindu mobs blamed Muslims for the Godhra incident. Over a thousand died in the ensuing carnage and over a hundred thousand were internally displaced. Modi's government was unable to terminate the violence. Modi would be officially cleared of any wrongdoing in the riots by the Indian court system in 2013.

Modi served as chief minister of Gujarat for 12 years, re-elected three times, before becoming prime minister of India in 2014. Modi's success is generally attributed to his shift away from identity politics to an emphasis on economic development and anti-corruption. Modi's 2014 campaign slogan, "*acche din*" (Good Days), tapped in to middle-class desire for economic reforms and national strengthening. The narrative of a "Gujarat Model" of economic development, which began to build around 2008 as Modi entered the national stage, helped Modi to secure a new template for the political right. The three main components of the new model could be summed up as:

1. Performance—an economic, performance-oriented style of governance that fetishizes rankings and prioritizes entrepreneurs;
2. Anti-corruption—leadership that rhetorically claims to reject both personal corruption and a permissive environment for corruption despite a crony-capitalist modus operandi;
3. Pro-business and physical infrastructure-led development— an emphasis on public–private partnerships (PPP) and the establishment of special economic zones (SEZs).[23]

The Gujarat Model was always more hype than reality. Despite high growth rates and a cozy relationship between business interests and the state, both of which preceded Modi's tenure,[24] Gujarat did not significantly outperform the more redistributive Kerala model on a range of indicators. Gujarat's inter-state Human Development Index ranking actually fell from 6th in 1991 to 11th in 2007–08. It is true that Gujarat's actual HDI score had improved, but the improvement mirrored the national average.[25] In any case, Gujarat was not the only model of development on offer in India's diverse political ecosystem. The main function of the Gujarat Model hype was to divert attention from the legacy of the Gujarat pogrom and rebrand Modi as a viable national candidate.

Modi's slogan of "minimum government, maximum governance" even led some commentators to confuse Modi for a "Thatcherite" neo-liberal.[26] It is import to understand, however, that support for economic reforms and development did not translate to an embrace of economic liberalism per se. The RSS had mainly endorsed liberal economic reforms in the previous decade as part of a tactical strategy to weaken the appeal of the Indian National Congress party among the middle class and to disassociate Hindu nationalism from the legacy of the anti-Muslim pogrom in Gujarat. However, there were other voices that emphasized an alternative, nationalist economic vision. For example, an offshoot of the RSS, the Swadeshi Jagran Manch (Forum for the Awakening of National Self-Sufficiency), argued for autarchic economic policies.[27]

Modi is transparently pro-business (for national elites at least) rather than pro-market. Nevertheless, he is careful not to alienate his core constituencies. (In this regard, Modi and the BJP's posture is not significantly different from the INC, which first began to tilt toward business elites in 1980.[28]) Thus, while there is support for attracting greater foreign direct investment (FDI), multi-brand retail is not welcome since petty merchants, a major source of support for the BJP, would be threatened by new competitors. Modi openly supported protectionism for Indian industries and converting India into a manufacturing hub so it could dump its products in other countries.[29]

First Term Overview (2014–19)

In the lower house of Parliament, the BJP won 282 out of 543 seats or a 52% absolute majority in 2014. When combined with their coalition partners in the NDA, the allies had 336 seats (a 62% majority). The rival INC party, under the leadership of Rahul Gandhi, was reduced to a humiliating 44 seats after losing 162 contests; even with their coalition, the United Progressive Alliance (UPA), the Congress party only held a total of 60 seats in the lower house. The BJP's performance represented a dramatic improvement from the 2009 election in which the BJP had won only 116 seats compared to the INC's 206. In terms of the popular vote, the BJP secured 31%, while the INC had 19.3%. Even though the BJP had the support of only a third of the electorate—with the balance of non-INC vote going to smaller national and regional parties—it was clear that the BJP was in a position to advance its agenda.

The NDA coalition was a minority in the upper house of parliament, the Rajya Sabha, holding only about a third of the seats. By itself this did not represent an implacable impediment to reforms. As Vijay Joshi writes,

> Though the government does not have a majority in the RS [Rajya Sabha], the latter cannot hold up money bills. Moreover, quite a lot can be done without new legislation, simply on the basis of "executive action." Lack of a majority in the RS was also not a completely new problem: other governments in the past have faced it quite successfully by using their negotiating skills. It was therefore widely expected that the new government would undertake a programme of sweeping economic reform.[30]

Nevertheless, the BJP did experience a few significant setbacks. For example, the BJP was unable to repeal or even amend the Right to Fair Compensation and Transparency in Land Acquisition, Rehabilitation, and Resettlement Act (LARRA) of 2013, a piece of legislation designed to protect landholders and their communities, which the business community viewed as a significant obstacle to business expansion in India.[31] Given that part of Modi's reputation in Gujarat had been shaped by his ability to acquire land for major projects faster than rival states,[32] the failure to overturn LARRA was a major blow.

In addition to a litany of economic policy initiatives (detailed in Chapter 4), the first term was marked by a remarkably vigorous effort to engage foreign heads of state and to project the image of India as a rising power. Alongside meetings with neighboring South Asian states and the littoral states of the Indian Ocean region (many of which have a significant Indian diaspora), Prime Minister Modi called several times upon heads of state from the United States, Japan, China, Germany, France, Russia, and Singapore. All totaled, the prime minister made 108 foreign visits to 60 countries from 2014 to 2019. Several of these trips were for multilateral organizations of which India is a member. India also hosted the India–Africa Forum in 2015 and the BRICS Summit in 2016.

Second Term Overview (2019–)

Modi started the 2019 campaign season with above 50% approval ratings. His popularity soared further after he ordered air strikes in Balakot, Pakistan, in response to a terrorist attack in the Pulwama district of Jammu and Kashmir that killed 40 Indian Central Reserve Police Force members. Even though Pakistan's retaliation to the airstrike led to the downing of an Indian fighter jet and the capture of the pilot, Modi did not suffer a significant loss in popularity. In fact, even though 68% of Indians surveyed believed job creation was the most important issue and that the PM had not created sufficient jobs in his first term, 64% still believed that Modi would be re-elected.[33]

In the ensuing 2019 general election, the BJP won in another landslide victory. The party picked up an additional 21 seats for a total of 303 out of 542 seats or a 56% majority. In terms of the popular vote, the BJP won 37.4% of electorate. Almost all of northern and central India is now represented in Parliament by the BJP or one of its coalition partners. Notably, in 191 head-to-head contests between the BJP and INC, the BJP won 175 times.[34] The INC did pick up 8 seats for a total of 52 seats. Despite their dismal performance overall, it is worth noting that the Congress held steady relative to the last election at 19.5% of the popular vote. For political analysts, the consolidation of the BJP's power signals a monumental realignment and the beginning of the "second dominant party system" in India, the original dominant party system being linked to the INC from 1952 to 1975.[35]

Despite these gains, the BJP's coalition still does not have a majority in the upper house. The NDA holds 115 out of 245 seats, while the opposition UPA holds 54 seats. At the federal level the BJP controls 12 out of 28 states, with an additional 5 states led by coalition partners.

The onset of the COVID-19 pandemic in India beginning in January 2020 upended much of the government's political and economic agenda. Moreover, the passage of three farm bills in September 2020 resulted in protracted farmer protests—one of the largest general strikes in history—and a stay by the Supreme Court on implementing the new laws. Negotiations between the Modi government and the farmer unions were generally unproductive until the government finally capitulated in late 2021 (see the "Farm Bills" discussion in Chapter 4 for more details).

In terms of foreign policy, there were no in-person foreign state visits in 2020; however, India did host a virtual BRICS Summit in September 2021. The prime minister physically visited Bangladesh in March and the United States on a state visit and to attend a meeting of the "Quad" and the UN General Assembly in September. Modi also attended the G-20 Summit in Rome in late October 2021.

POPULISM, NATIONALISM, AND SUBNATIONALISM

Hindutva should not be completely conflated with populism. A survey of Indian voters demonstrates that they consider Hindu nationalism and right-wing populism as distinct phenomena.³⁶ Populism generally implies the lack of a developed ideology (relying instead on direct appeals to mass emotions) and is deeply anti-elitist. In the Indian context, the rule of Indira Gandhi in the seventies is an example of leftist populism given her direct appeal to the impoverished masses and her anti-elitism toward the owners of capital (e.g., commercial banks and private industry) and the former rulers of princely states under the British Raj.³⁷ Nationalism is often framed by elites and aspires to become a routinized state ideology, while populism seeks a "relentless mobilization of popular energy."³⁸ Nationalism tends to be externally oriented, i.e., it seeks to find a place for its nation among the other great nations, except where it is secessionist or focused on scapegoating minorities for "disloyalty." Populism is generally internally delimited and focuses on the image of the authentic folk, except in situations where a cosmopolitan elite is alleged to be allied to internal minorities of foreign origin.³⁹ In essence, these are rather distinct types of politics—except when a minority is targeted for persecution.

While on the "supply side," PM Modi certainly deploys populist techniques such as seeking to appeal directly to his constituents (with his monthly radio broadcast), to speak on behalf of "the people," and to display hostility toward the non-elected institutions that buttress a democratic state (e.g., the free press and the judiciary) and the "Lutyens elite" of New Delhi. On the "demand side," however, Varshney et al. find that non-Hindu minorities are more populist than Hindus.⁴⁰ Populism is also more prevalent in rural areas than in cities; lower castes are more populist than Hindu nationalist, whereas the upper classes are more Hindu nationalist than populist.⁴¹

Regional parties, such as the Shiv Sena [Shivaji's Army] in Bombay/Mumbai and throughout the western state of

Maharashtra, have found ways of combining populism, nationalism, and regional chauvinism to their benefit by expanding from a linguistic chauvinism or nativism to an endorsement of Hindu nationalism since the mid-eighties.[42] Notably, Bal Thackeray, the notorious political godfather who founded the Shiv Sena in 1966, was trained by the RSS.[43] The party is currently led by Bal Thackery's son, the chief minister of Maharashtra, Uddhav Thackeray. The Shiv Sena adopted a Hindu nationalist framework as it sought to build a larger coalition of support beyond its municipal stronghold and undertake statewide politics. Thus, the Sena entered into a seat adjustment alliance with the BJP in 1990.[44]

The linkages connecting regional and national prejudices permit a party like the Shiv Sena to pivot more swiftly in limiting access to public goods to a narrower range of beneficiaries or to mobilize more bodies on the street and in the ballot box. Moreover, the violent resentment periodically whipped up by the party against a shifting host of enemies to the common man (particularly "seditious" Muslims and South Indian migrant workers) provides the party with an "authenticity" and an association with a "rougher plebian world" that has brought reliable gains at the polls.[45]

THE SANGH PARIVAR AND NEO-HINDUTVA

Hindu nationalists are organized in a "family" of heterodox organizations affiliated with the RSS known as the Sangh Parivar. This loose group includes a national political party (the BJP), pietistic organizations (Vishwa Hindu Parishad), student groups (Bajrang Dal, Akhil Bharatiya Vidyarthi Parishad), a farmers' union (Bharatiya Kisan Sangh), a labor union (Bharatiya Mazdoor Sangh), economic associations (Swadeshi Jagaran Manch), and many others—including affiliated organizations overseas, particularly in the US and UK. Within the Sangh are also organizations for "loyal" Muslims (Muslim Rashtriya Manch) and Tribals (Vanavasi Kalyan Ashram). The exact relationship between these organizations and the RSS is a matter of academic dispute.[46]

However, Hindutva ideology in the era of social media is no longer confined to the organizations loosely grouped within the Sangh Parivar. The concept of "neo-Hindutva" captures the notion of an ideology that has transcended the institutional and ideological boundaries of the RSS and its affiliated organizations.[47] Even the nominally secular-left-leaning Indian National Congress is not above using "soft neo-Hindutva" images and themes in its electoral strategies. In particular, transnational Hindu nationalism has evolved in a distinctive and hybrid manner, and the "laboratory of Hindutva" has shifted from Bombay/Mumbai to India's remote northeastern states.[48]

VIOLENCE AND VIGILANTISM

The BJP and its parent organizations are clearly not above instigating violence, inciting vigilantes and colluding with the police to look the other way, or generally using menace as a political tool to unite those Hindu voters who prefer to assert a rigid social hierarchy and to oppress targeted minorities. To this extent, the BJP is not dramatically different from other parties, including the INC. For example, in the immediate aftermath of the 1984 pogrom against Sikhs, following the assassination of PM Indira Gandhi by her Sikh bodyguards, PM Rajiv Gandhi flatly stated, "when a mighty tree falls, it is only natural that the earth around it does shake a little." This was widely interpreted as justifying the ethnic cleansing. In a similar manner, PM Modi has been accused of failing to stop the 2002 anti-Muslim pogrom in his home state when he was the chief minister. In 2013, when Modi was aspiring to become the prime minister, he finally spoke publicly about the events. He stated to Reuters, "Even If I am in the back seat of a car and a puppy (*kutte ka bachcha*) comes under the wheels, isn't it painful? It is. Whether I am a chief minister or not, I am a human being—I will be sad if something bad happens anywhere." The comparison of Muslim victims to dogs was widely viewed as insulting and callous. As prime minister, Modi has spoken out against the lynching of *Dalits* (as this group is viewed by the BJP as Hindu) but has maintained either a studied silence or blamed state governments for lynchings of Muslims.[49]

NOTES

1. Lata Jha, "Modi's Address on Covid-19 Lockdown Draws 197 Million TV Viewers," *Mint*, March 27, 2020.
2. Jeffrey Gettleman and Kai Schultz, "India Locks Down 1.3 Billion People for 3 Weeks: Foreign Desk," *New York Times*, 2020, Late (East Coast) edition.
3. Karan Deep Singh, "India Deaths from COVID May Exceed 3 Million," *New York Times*, July 21, 2021.
4. Australia, Brazil, Canada, France, Germany, India, Italy, Japan, Mexico, South Korea, Spain, the US, and the UK.
5. The daily poll on Modi's approval/disapproval from March 6, 2020, to September 7, 2021, is based on a sample of 2,126 adults in India with a margin of error of +/−2.2%. Political Intelligence Morning Consult, "Global Leader Approval Tracker," Morning Consult, September 13, 2021, https://morningconsult.com/form/global-leader-approval/.
6. Subrata Kumar Mitra, *Politics in India: Structure, Process and Policy* (London; New York: Routledge, 2011), 78.
7. Mitra, 79.
8. Mitra, 81.
9. Brendan O'Leary, "Federalism and Federation," in *The Princeton Encyclopedia of Self-Determination* (Princeton University Press), accessed August 17, 2021, https://pesd.princeton.edu/node/431.

10 Mitra, *Politics in India*, 92–93.
11 James Crabtree, *The Billionaire Raj: A Journey through India's New Gilded Age*, 2019, 117–19.
12 Kiran Bhatty and Nandini Sundar, "Sliding from Majoritarianism toward Fascism: Educating India under the Modi Regime," *International Sociology* 35, no. 6 (2020): 633, https://doi.org/10.1177/0268580920937226.
13 Madhavrao Sadashivrao Golwalkar, *We, or Our Nationhood Defined* (Nagpur, India: Bharat Publications, 1939), Chapter V.
14 Neha Saghal et al., "Religion in India: Tolerance and Segregation" (Washington, DC: Pew Research Center, June 29, 2021), 9.
15 Saghal et al., 10.
16 Saghal et al., 12.
17 Saghal et al., 13.
18 Peter Van der Veer, "What Transcends the Nation?," *Asian Ethnology* 80, no. 1 (2021): 23.
19 Cécile Laborde, "Minimal Secularism: Lessons for, and from, India," *The American Political Science Review* 115, no. 1 (2021): 8, https://doi.org/10.1017/S0003055420000775.
20 Shaikh Mujibur Rehman, "Subordinated Citizenship: Muslims in the Hindu Rashtra," *PS, Political Science & Politics* 54, no. 4 (2021): 634–35, https://doi.org/10.1017/S104909652100072X.
21 Itty Abraham, *How India Became Territorial: Foreign Policy, Diaspora, and Geopolitics*, Studies in Asian Security (Stanford, CA: Stanford University Press, 2014), 40.
22 Abraham, 100–01.
23 Salman Anees Soz, *The Great Disappointment: How Narendra Modi Squandered a Unique Opportunity to Transform the Indian Economy* (Gurgaon, Haryana, India: Ebury Press / Penguin Random House India, 2019), 45–47.
24 Christophe Jaffrelot, "Business-Friendly Gujarat under Narendra Modi: The Implications of a New Political Economy," in *Business and Politics in India*, ed. Christophe Jaffrelot, Atul Kohli, and Kanta Murali, Modern South Asia (New York, NY: Oxford University Press, 2019), 211–12.
25 Soz, *The Great Disappointment*, 44, 50.
26 Soz, 49.
27 Ravinder Kaur, *Brand New Nation: Capitalist Dreams and Nationalist Designs in Twenty-First Century India*, South Asia in Motion (Stanford, California: Stanford University Press, 2020), 152–54, 246–50.
28 Christophe Jaffrelot, Atul Kohli, and Kanta Murali, eds., *Business and Politics in India*, Modern South Asia (New York, NY: Oxford University Press, 2019), 8.

29 Soz, *The Great Disappointment*, 62–63.
30 Vijay Joshi, *India's Long Road: The Search for Prosperity* (New York: Oxford University Press, 2017), 278.
31 Rob Jenkins, "Business Interests, the State, and the Politics of Land Policy," in *Business and Politics in India*, ed. Christophe Jaffrelot, Atul Kohli, and Kanta Murali, Modern South Asia (New York: Oxford University Press, 2019), 125.
32 Jaffrelot, "Business-Friendly Gujarat under Narendra Modi," 215–17.
33 BW Online Bureau, "68% of India Feels PM Narendra Modi Failed to Create Jobs, yet 64% of India Feels He will be Re-Elected in May 2019, Says BW-Decode Survey," *Business World* (March 28, 2019).
34 Yamini Aiyar, "Modi Consolidates Power: Leveraging Welfare Politics," *Journal of Democracy* 30, no. 4 (2019): 78, https://doi.org/10.1353/jod.2019.0070.
35 Aiyar, 79.
36 Ashutosh Varshney, Srikrishna Ayyangar, and Siddharth Swaminathan, "Populism and Hindu Nationalism in India," *Studies in Comparative International Development* 56, no. 2 (2021): 197–222, https://doi.org/10.1007/s12116-021-09335-8.
37 Varshney, Ayyangar, and Swaminathan, 202–3.
38 Ashutosh Varshney, "Populism and Nationalism: An Overview of Similarities and Differences," *Studies in Comparative International Development* 56, no. 2 (2021): 131, https://doi.org/10.1007/s12116-021-09332-x.
39 Varshney, 134–36.
40 Varshney, Ayyangar, and Swaminathan, "Populism and Hindu Nationalism in India," 214–15.
41 Varshney, Ayyangar, and Swaminathan, 217–20.
42 Mary Fainsod Katzenstein, Uday Singh Mehta, and Usha Thakkar, "The Rebirth of Shiv Sena: The Symbiosis of Discursive and Organizational Power," *The Journal of Asian Studies* 56, no. 2 (1997): 371–90, https://doi.org/10.2307/2646242.
43 Christophe Jaffrelot, *Modi's India: Hindu Nationalism and the Rise of Ethnic Democracy*, trans. Cynthia Schoch (Princeton: Princeton University Press, 2021), 242; Crabtree, *The Billionaire Raj*, 319.
44 Katzenstein, Mehta, and Thakkar, "The Rebirth of Shiv Sena," 374.
45 Thomas Blom Hansen, "Whose Public, Whose Authority? Reflections on the Moral Force of Violence," *Modern Asian Studies* 52, no. 3 (2018): 1084, https://doi.org/10.1017/S0026749X17000282.
46 Edward Anderson and Arkotong Longkumer, "'Neo-Hindutva': Evolving Forms, Spaces, and Expressions of Hindu Nationalism," *Contemporary South Asia* 26, no. 4 (2018): 372, https://doi.org/10.1080/09584935.2018.1548576.

47 Anderson and Longkumer, "'Neo-Hindutva'."
48 Anderson and Longkumer, 373.
49 Varshney, Ayyangar, and Swaminathan, "Populism and Hindu Nationalism in India," 205–6.

SUGGESTED FURTHER READING

Corbridge, Stuart, John Harriss, and Craig Jeffrey, *India Today: Economy, Politics & Society* (Polity Press, 2013). ISBN: 978-0745661124.

Crabtree, James, *The Billionaire Raj: A Journey through India's New Gilded Age* (Tim Duggan Books, 2019). ISBN: 978-1524760076.

Jaffrelot, Christophe, *Modi's India: Hindu Nationalism and the Rise of Ethnic Democracy* (Princeton University Press, 2021). ISBN: 9780691206806.

Mitra, Subrata K., *Politics in India: Structure, Process, and Policy* (Routledge, 2011). ISBN: 978-0415585897.

CHAPTER TWO

SUBNATIONAL POLITICS

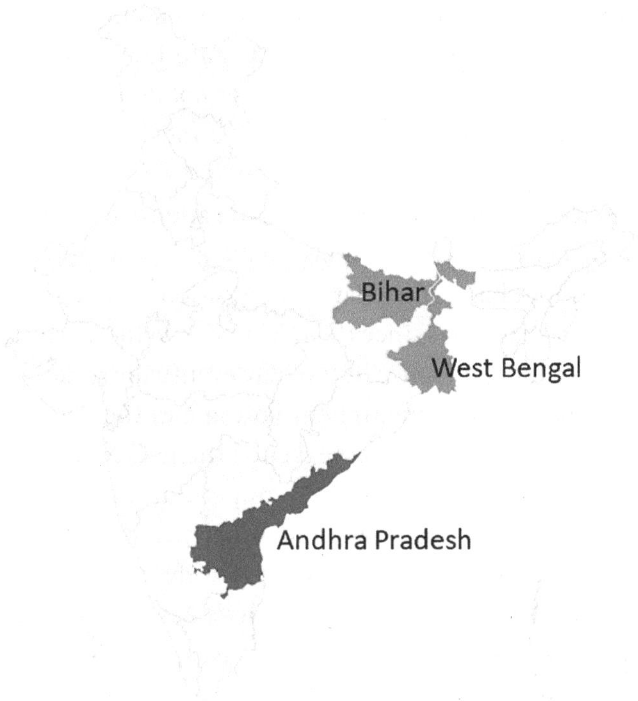

Map 1. Indian States—Case Studies

"India is a continent masquerading as a country," observed the *Economist* in 2015.[1] This assessment reflects the extraordinary diversity that India's states have always exhibited in the overlapping domains of culture, economics, and politics. It was worth reemphasizing this point in 2015 amid the new Modi government's accumulation of power at the center, given competing pressures from India's states to continue the devolution trend that has given many of the states considerably greater power and policy autonomy since the 1990s. This devolution has largely been a consequence of India's economic liberalization, which has not so much shrunk the role of the state in the economy[2] as shifted the domain of governance, and of fiscal and policy reforms, from the center to the states.

Even if understanding the different political contexts of each state requires a detailed familiarity not unlike that necessary to understand different countries across a region such as Europe, Latin America, or sub-Saharan Africa, state-level politics matter for national governance. Modi's BJP does *not* dominate politics in many of India's states, and the party is a much weaker presence in the state assemblies than it has been at the national level, even following its Lok Sabha majorities of 2014 and 2019. While its position at the center may look unassailable for now, and while the BJP under Modi has consolidated its position to a degree that no other political party has since the INC under Nehru in the first two decades after Independence, it too may eventually reckon with the strong impulse to anti-incumbent voting and the decentralizing political economy forces that weakened the INC over time. When Modi's BJP faces more significant competition than the faltering INC posed in 2014 or 2019—and it will, barring a truly transformational change in India's democracy—it is likely to come from political leadership at the state level, much as Modi himself parlayed perceptions of a "Gujarat miracle" into his ascendance to national frontrunner status in 2014.

To be sure, Modi has been a unique phenomenon and has personalized governance to a significant degree—arguably even more than his nearest antecedent in this respect, Indira ("India is Indira, Indira is India") Gandhi, at the height of her powers in the 1970s. It could be argued rightly that many prominent chief ministers lack the apparatus of a national party, not to mention the broader Sangh Parivar network of Hindu nationalist organizations, that enabled Modi to spring to national prominence. But this forgets how much the vote mobilization machinery Modi had built in Gujarat took over the existing BJP apparatus, and the degree to which Hindu nationalist themes co-mingled in his campaign with the populist Vikas Purush ("Development Man") narrative of a decisive and dynamic leader who could bring the Gujarat Model to the rest of India. "Throughout the entire campaign," Christophe Jaffrelot observes, "Modi repeatedly contrasted the mediocre performance of the rest of India with that of his state, systematically claiming that the Congress Party was to blame."[3] As prime minister, if anything, Modi has only sought to deepen the perception that his government and party deserve credit for India's overall economic performance—even as he has so far managed to avoid electoral consequences for negative impact of demonetization, high youth unemployment, farmer protests, and other issues.

It is far too early to predict how the major economic and social disruption of the COVID-19 pandemic could shape elections to come. Since the pandemic "lockdown" and its economic impact began to be felt in March 2020, the BJP's experience in state legislative assembly elections in 2020 and 2021 has been mixed, making it difficult to forecast what the next general election, due in 2024, may have in store. In Delhi's February 2020 election—before the pandemic already spreading globally from Wuhan, China, was yet perceived as a major issue in India—the BJP modestly improved its seat share, but the incumbent Aam Aadmi Party easily retained power. In Bihar's fall 2020 election, the BJP picked up 21 seats and eclipsed its ally the Janata Dal (United), but the latter retained the chief minister's position held by incumbent Nitish Kumar since 2015. Kumar, Bihar's chief minister five times previously, has repeatedly shifted alliances to maximize electoral potential in this historically unpredictable state (see the Bihar discussion below).

In 2021, the BJP led the NDA to victory in Assam, in the country's northeast, but it fell short in a major state-level contest in neighboring West Bengal (also discussed below). The BJP was held to 77 seats of the 294-seat assembly—and this after Modi's lieutenant Amit Shah, the Union Home Minister, had predicted a sweep of 200 seats for the party.[4] West Bengal's incumbent chief minister, Mamata Banerjee of the All-India Trinamool Congress (AITC) party,[5] ran a successful populist and sub-nationalist campaign to defend against the rising BJP tide, emphasizing "Bengali pride" and casting rivals as non-Bengali invaders and interlopers.[6] She and her party retained power with a two-thirds majority but only gained 4 new seats. Meanwhile, the CPI(M) and INC folded and most of the gains went to the BJP, which added 74 new seats to its previous base of 3 seats. To the south, in the politically distinctive state of Kerala, the BJP marginally increased its share of the vote, but not enough to offset declining support for its NDA allies. In the small union territory of Puducherry, the BJP and allies won a one-seat majority, capitalizing on defections from Congress (INC) legislators that had felled its government in 2020.

Even a major state power broker like West Bengal's Banerjee cannot duplicate Modi's mobilization-through-polarization strategy at quite the same scale of what he has achieved with the BJP. But with allies in other states forming a new "third front" coalition, they could still prevent a third national victory for Modi. As noted in the Introduction, for all the strength the BJP possesses in the 543-seat Lok Sabha, its share of the *popular* vote—while the highest of any single party in three decades—was just over 37% in 2019. A significant voter shift away from the BJP in even one major state would weaken the party's position in the Lok Sabha. A coalition of parties from several states could certainly threaten the BJP's ability to pull off a "three-peat" in 2024 (conceivably earlier should an earlier general election date be called before then, as parliamentarism permits).

Moreover, support for the BJP among those voters who identify as Hindu varies widely by region. Pew Research Center's 2021 survey of nearly 30,000 Indian voters found that just under half (49%) of Hindus supported the BJP in 2019, with the party receiving as much as two-thirds of the Hindu vote in northern and central parts of India. But support among Hindus falls to 46% in the east and craters at just 19% in the south, according to the survey. In the south, a slightly greater share of Hindus (20%) supported the INC, and another 11% supported various regional parties. Nationally, nearly two-thirds (64%) of Hindus agreed that "being Hindu is important to being truly Indian," with the share rising as high as 83% in the central region—and falling to 42% in the South.[7]

Of course, using the organizational resources of the Sangh Parivar, Modi has built a formidable fundraising machine for the BJP. He has used the advantages of incumbency to introduce "electoral bonds," a controversial but apparently legal instrument that critics say allow corporations and other anonymous contributors to "funnel unlimited amounts of money to political parties."[8] Significantly, the southern states have higher per capita incomes and have experienced faster economic growth than most other parts of the country. Were business sentiments to turn against Modi and the BJP, it is conceivable that a well-financed challenger could emerge out of one of the states where the BJP is less popular.

Surveying key developments in state-level politics, coalitions, and "rapid system change in India" during the 1990s and early 2000s, Virginia Van Dyke observes,

> First, in terms of the coalition at the Center, the regional parties continue to tend towards forming a third front that cannot be written off, even though the members of that front are transient. That is, it is not so clear that India is moving towards a permanent

two-front [i.e. BJP-led/NDA versus INC-led/UPA] system at the Center, despite the fact that it has been the pattern since 1998 [until the BJP's majority victory in 2014]. Second, regional parties are crucial at the Center, but participate there largely to extract benefits and support at the state level where their interests essentially lie.[9]

Simply put, India's states are worth attending to analytically not only because they are major polities in their own right—some would be among the largest countries in the world by population, if ranked independently—but also because of the potential for state-based parties and state-level issues to mobilize voting behavior in ways that tip national outcomes.

To beat Modi's BJP, state leaders will need to limit the consolidation of the Hindutva project, promote an alternative economic development model, institutionalize new identity politics to enhance governance, and overcome security challenges (e.g., the Maoist or Naxalite insurgency present in the rural areas of several states). This chapter conducts three state-level case studies that represent alternative models of governance: Andhra Pradesh (AP), Bihar, and West Bengal. Notably, two of these states, AP and West Bengal, are now led by parties that broke off from the once hegemonic INC. Bihar's Janata Dal (United) traces its roots to the Janata Party, which defeated the INC in the post-Emergency period to elect the first non-Congress prime minister in India's history. In other words, while these leaders appear confined to their respective states and regions in an era of BJP dominance, the parties they lead could be the building blocks of a broader platform to challenge Modi.

ANDHRA PRADESH

Andhra Pradesh is an instructive first case study in subnational political development in India. No single Indian state can be taken as representative of India's myriad subnational dynamics,

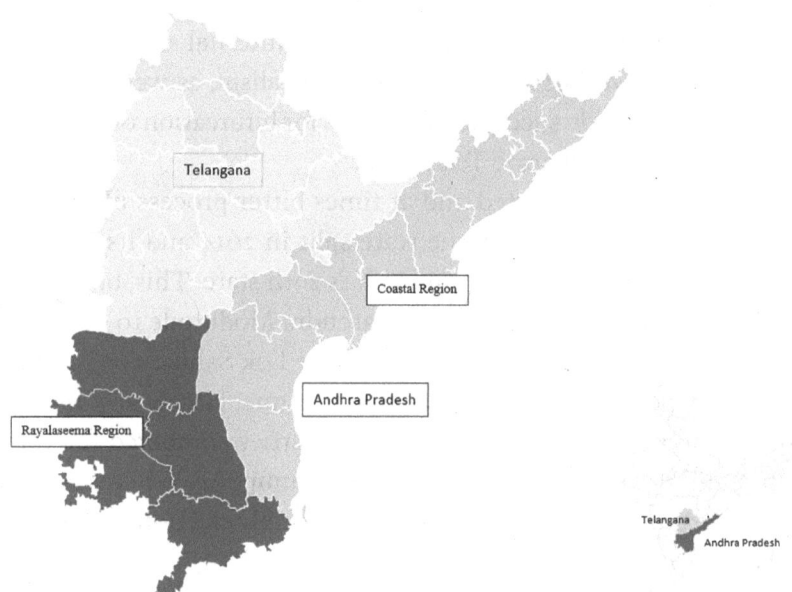

Map 2. Andhra Pradesh

but Andhra Pradesh (AP) to a remarkable degree exhibits within a single state many of the various political patterns seen in other states. These include language-centered, subnational identity politics that have given the state a distinctive history, but also interregional economic disparities and caste divisions that have made its history contentious. The Congress Party dominated the state for decades, but perceptions of the central government's interference in the state's affairs encouraged the rise of the Telugu Desam Party (TDP) in the 1980s, which ushered in a new period of two-party competition.

Since the 1980s, the TDP and Congress (and, more recently, a Congress offshoot) alternately have put forward distinctive leaders with different developmental priorities. These have ranged from broad-based welfare programs—popular with voters but straining to the state's finances—to more growth-oriented strategies seeking to raise incomes and reduce poverty by making the state attractive to international investors. At the same time, the state has seen challenges to law and order and internal security posed by the insurgency of militant, Maoist Naxalism, as well as recurring and ultimately successful demands for bifurcation of the state itself to create a separate Telangana.

Following a protracted and at times bitter process ultimately directed from New Delhi, the state split in 2014 and its interior subregion of Telangana became India's 29th state. This, of course, was the same year the BJP led by Narendra Modi rode to power at the center with a historic majority in the Lok Sabha. But Andhra Pradesh's politics marched to a different tune, largely around the bifurcation issue as the main political parties competed for vote shares in the smaller but still significant "rump" AP. While the TDP won a majority in the state legislative assembly election of 2014, its leadership of the first government for post-split AP was marred by controversy surrounding the development of a new capital city. In 2019, the Yuvajana Sramika Rythu (Youth Labor Farmers) Congress Party, or YSRCP, won a commanding majority in the second post-bifurcation state assembly elections. This regional, rebel offshoot of the national Congress Party is a largely personality-driven organization, led by the son of a beloved former Congress chief minister known by his initials, "YSR," who died in a helicopter crash after winning reelection in 2009, and whose visage is given pride of place at the center of the newer party's flag.

What makes AP especially interesting to consider, from the perspective of this book, is that the BJP has been unable to make inroads in the state, even as the original Congress Party organization in AP has been broken over an extended period, amid defections first to the TDP and more recently to the YSRCP and other new, smaller parties.[10] Prime Minister Modi's party "has virtually no presence in the state" and won less than 1% of the vote in the 2019 state assembly elections. The TDP under Andhra Pradesh Chief Minister N. Chandrababu Naidu was a key member of the NDA governments at the center, headed by the BJP, during the coalition's 1998–2004 turn in power, but the parties fell out after the state's bifurcation. In 2018, Naidu withdrew the TDP's support from the NDA over the central government's refusal to grant Special Category status to the state after bifurcation, which would have meant a large infusion of central funds to help build its new capital city, Amaravati.[11] State BJP leaders have since called for a "merger" with the TDP, but there is little trust between the parties, and some speculate that the BJP actually seeks to cut into the vote share of its erstwhile ally—which fell to under 40% in the state's 2019 assembly election. Meanwhile, the Congress Party (INC) won less than 2% of the vote in the state assembly and Lok Sabha elections, whereas the YSRCP not only won a landslide victory in the state (151 of 175 seats) and half the popular vote but also tied for fourth place among *all* parties in the national Lok Sabha, with 22 seats.

Situating India's First "Linguistic" State

Andhra Pradesh spans much of India's southeastern coast along the Bay of Bengal. Before its bifurcation in 2014, AP was India's fourth largest state by land area and fifth largest by population; it now ranks seventh and tenth, respectively. At around 50 million people, even the downsized AP has a population roughly equal to that of South Korea. AP has experienced faster economic growth than India overall in recent years, and even in estimates for the pandemic year 2020–21 it logged nearly 1.6% growth in gross state domestic product (GSDP), compared to an overall GDP contraction of –3.8% for India as a whole. Still, AP has remained a middle-income state, with a per capita income (around US$2,268 in 2020–21) only modestly above the all-India average.[12]

Before it acquired the global image of a leader in economic growth around the turn of the century, Andhra Pradesh was a lower middle-income state best known in India as the first "linguistic" state—that is, a state formed on the basis of a regional language, Telugu, which a majority of its people claim as their "mother tongue." Like its southern neighbor Tamil Nadu, it was also a state in which a language-as-identity politics eventually gave rise to a formidable regional political organization, in this case the Telugu Desam Party, as a challenger to the Congress Party. (Telugu *Desam* translates approximately as "Telugu Country.")

Telugu speakers comprise one of the largest first-language groups in India, at nearly 7% of the population in the 2011 Census—ranking behind only Hindi, Bengali, and Marathi. At Independence in 1947, Telugu ranked second only to Hindi, and demands for a state corresponding to the Telugu-speaking area were quick to emerge. Nehru's government at the center resisted, contributing to the INC's poor performance in Telugu-speaking constituencies in the first general election in 1951–52. In 1952, an activist named Potti Sriramulu undertook a hunger strike for the statehood cause. When he died on the 56th day of his fast, statehood demonstrations turned violent, and the central government relented, creating a new Andhra State in 1953 out of the Telugu-speaking regions of the former Madras presidency. The British had ruled this area directly amid competition between Tamil speakers and Telugu speakers for political influence.

In 1956, under a broader reorganization of India's states, the Telugu-speaking part of the former Hyderabad princely state, Telangana, was added. The state was renamed Andhra Pradesh (*pradesh* being the word for "province" or "territory" in multiple Indian languages). As political economists Arvind Panagariya and M. Govinda Rao observe, "Ironically, the [pre-2014] movement for the separate state of Telangana sought to split the state precisely along the lines of its original formation."[13]

From the outset, Telangana was poorer than the Coastal Andhra and Rayalaseema regions of the former Madras presidency. It also had a history of unrest, with the Indian Army repressing a "peasant uprising" in the area not long before Independence. But having consolidated Telugu speakers into one state, the INC built a broad electoral base in Andhra Pradesh, holding on to power in the state even in the 1967 elections, in which it suffered significant losses elsewhere (marking the first real challenge to its post-Independence dominance of India's electoral arena).

From Congress Party Dominance to Competitive Elections

In the 1980s, following the Emergency (1975–77) that alienated many Indian elites and voters from the INC under Indira Gandhi, there was a further fragmenting of the party system. In Andhra Pradesh, the charismatic former film star N. T. Rama Rao ("NTR") founded the Telugu Desam Party (TDP) on a platform of Telugu "self-respect" and opposition to Delhi's "interference" in the state's affairs. Tollywood (a play on Bollywood) is the state's lively niche in the burgeoning Indian film industry, and on its silver screen NTR was literally a larger-than-life figure, playing epic heroes and demon-slayers. Such was the cinematic backdrop to his game-changing foray into state politics, and more than a subtext to his personalization of power as his TDP took advantage of the Congress Party's declining popularity. As Atul Kohli observed in 1988, conditions had been ripe for political change in the state, because "Indira Gandhi's repeated intervention in Andhra politics and the factionalized nature of her party in the state [had] also contributed to Congress's delegitimization and to the emergence of an organizational vacuum within the region." NTR, Kohli explains, filled this vacuum by "offering a political alternative that stressed the twin themes of populism and regional nationalism."[14] What NTR did not do was break the state's tradition of leader-dominated political parties. To the contrary, he leaned even further into this tendency. Consequently, both organizations in this newly competitive two-party environment were (and remain) weakly institutionalized beyond personalities.

Another important subtext, involving caste competition, became more prominent in the state's politics with the rise of

NTR and the TDP. Amid AP's many other local caste (*jati*) groups, the Kamma and Reddy communities are two dominant "rich peasant" castes. The Reddy caste is prominent in the Rayalaseema region, and the Kamma caste is prominent in Coastal Andhra (as is the Kapu community, another rich peasant caste). These castes rose to prominence through landholding arrangements and benefitted historically from state policies, from the colonial period and continuing after Independence into the modernization of India's agriculture.[15]

As a widespread perception held, "From its creation in the 1950s, the state was ruled by Reddys, till that pattern was broken by the rise of NT Rama Rao, who belonged to the Kamma caste."[16] In fact, NTR more inclusively "put together a coalition of groups that had not benefited from earlier Congress rule."[17] Even so, a new perception emerged that Kammas were the major beneficiaries of TDP rule—and that the Congress vs. TDP electoral rivalry was, to a significant extent, a proxy for Reddy–Kamma competition.

The TDP held power in the state from 1983 to 1989, with NTR serving as chief minister for two terms (and in 1984 fending off a challenge from his own finance minister to return as chief minister, following temporary removal from the office for open heart surgery). After losing narrowly to the INC, the TDP led the Opposition from 1989 to 1994, when it returned to power in an alliance with left parties. NTR, now 71 and ailing, began a third term as chief minister, but he was pushed aside in a revolt led by his son-in-law N. Chandrababu Naidu, who took over as chief minister in 1995.

Developmentalism and "Reform by Hype"

Naidu took a few years to define himself in NTR's shadow, but his strategy came into focus ahead of the state's 1999 elections. On the one hand, he presented himself as "the laptop chief minister" and projected an image of efficient, results-oriented governance, in contrast to the patrimonialism and melodrama associated with his film-star father-in-law. Naidu courted loans and development assistance from the World Bank and foreign direct investment from major multinationals including Microsoft, promising to improve infrastructure and restructure the state's faltering power sector. He pledged to make government more responsive to both business and the public, even as he committed to reduce the state's large fiscal deficit, accumulated over years of indiscriminate welfare spending: a generous rice subsidy enacted under NTR was equal to half of the state's total spending on education and health. Naidu produced a *Vision 2020* plan, largely written by McKinsey & Company, for transforming the mainly agrarian state into a global center for information technology and IT-enabled services, centered in Hyderabad, and using technology to modernize government and "e-service" provision. On the other hand, Naidu continued to spend lavishly on welfare programs clearly designed to enhance the TDP's electoral prospects, including a scheme just months before the 1999 election to provide one million households with liquified petroleum gas connections for cooking. This was widely seen as a bid for rural women's votes.

The late Jos Mooij, a Dutch political scientist and a leading analyst of AP politics in the early twenty-first century, thus characterized Naidu's style as "reform by hype"—overselling his commitment to fiscal discipline to secure external support. This, Mooij observed, stood in contrast to the "reform by stealth" that another scholar, Rob Jenkins, had observed in other states where leaders typically sought to deflect popular attention *away* from reform policies that reduced public spending, fearing electoral backlash.[18] Though the "reform by hype" strategy worked to secure the TDP's 1999 election victory and Naidu's second term as chief minister, Naidu's self-promotion and constant media presence apparently wore thin with voters. In the state's 2004 election, despite (or partly because of) the World Bank's continuing championing of his agenda, Naidu lost out to a resurgent Congress Party led by

Y. S. Rajasekhara Reddy ("YSR"), a more charismatic figure reminiscent of NTR. Naidu blamed the loss on a drought before the election. But YSR led the Congress to victory on the more fundamental criticism that Naidu's reforms had been too focused on urban sectors and had deprioritized rural poverty reduction.

Once in office, YSR

> surprised the business community by not only leaving all of Naidu's economic reforms intact but also significantly improving the pace of execution of the projects. At the same time, he placed added emphasis on rural development programs and social spending... In a nutshell, YSR efficiently continued the pro-growth economic agenda, whose foundation was laid by his predecessor Chandrababu Naidu, but at the same time he took the benefits of growth proactively to socially and economically backward sections of society.[19]

Both Naidu and YSR, though fierce rivals, have been credited as "two excellent successive chief ministers"[20] who set AP on a path of sustained growth in per capita income and poverty reduction, enabling it to outperform other states such as India's largest, Uttar Pradesh. YSR's tenure especially has been hailed as a "golden age," and while he won reelection in 2009, he died only months later in a helicopter crash. The state's politics entered a more tumultuous phase.

Telangana Goes Its Own Way

As noted, the state's Telangana subregion, comprising 10 of its 23 districts, from the outset was less developed economically than the Coastal Andhra and Rayalaseema regions, and its late colonial history was restive. Though it may seem paradoxical, the state's economic development under Naidu appears to have given new momentum to the regional discontent behind the movement for a separate Telangana state. Hyderabad, which is in the Telangana region, long has been an important regional power center; its Chowmalla Palace was the seat of the Asif Jahi dynasty and the seat of the Nizams of Hyderabad during their two-century rule (1724–1948). The capital's rapid development in the early 2000s unfolded against entrenched perceptions of competition between locals and Coastal Andhrans, who had invested in the city over the decades and especially during the Naidu and YSR years. Caste politics also played a role in the resurgence of Telangana statehood demands: the Sri Krishna Committee on Telangana, appointed by the central government in 2010 and headed by a former chief justice of India, observed that "the regional distribution of upper castes varies with Coastal Andhra having the highest proportion at 32%, followed by Rayalaseema at 24% and Telangana having the smallest proportion at only 11%."[21]

In 2001, a former TDP cabinet member for both the NTR and Naidu governments, K. Chandrashekar Rao, founded a new political party, the Telangana Rashtra Samithi (TRS), on the single-issue agenda of Telangana statehood. The TRS won 26 seats of 294 seats in the state legislative assembly and five parliamentary seats in the 2004 elections, leading to an alliance with the Congress Party (INC) and its joining of the UPA at the center. The TDP, originally opposed to the state's bifurcation, switched its position in 2008 to give support for Telangana statehood—first as it sought to siphon back TRS voters, and later as it perceived that its electoral prospects could be significantly enhanced in a smaller AP consisting of districts in the Coastal and Rayalaseema regions. A new regional party, the Praja Rajyam Party, was founded in 2008 by another actor-turned-politician, K. Chiranjeevi, against Telangana statehood in the view that AP's bifurcation would adversely impact Hyderabad's development. But it, too, pledged to support Telangana statehood if the central government decided on it.

With the state's two main parties now courting its supporters, the TRS lost seats in 2009 in both the state assembly and the parliament. The TRS won only ten assembly and two parliamentary seats, and switched allegiance to the BJP and its NDA. Employing a new but time-tested Indian tactic, Rao undertook an 11-day hunger strike. This sparked demonstrations by Telangana statehood supporters and clashes with police; though the tumult subsided after several weeks, the confrontational dynamic continued for several more years. The state assembly building in Hyderabad and its iconic statue of Mahatma Gandhi—which had just undergone restoration during Naidu's focus on beautifying the capital city—now became ringed by police barricades and wire.

In a further sign of the capriciousness of party positions on issues when coalition-building is at stake, the Congress Party-led UPA at the Center, hoping to improve its position in Telangana in alliance with the TRS, came out in support the creation of Telangana—even as the Congress Party leadership in AP itself remained divided on the issue. In 2013, the Congress Working Committee and the UPA government at the Center approved the creation of Telangana. In early 2014, the state's Congress Party chief minister, Kiran Kumar Reddy, staged a last-ditch sit-in in New Delhi to oppose a bill dividing the state, but to no avail. Six Congress Party members of Parliament (MPs) from AP's Coastal and Rayalaseema regions were expelled for moving a no-confidence motion against the UPA government; 16 MPs were suspended for disorderly conduct after the bifurcation bill was introduced, including one who used pepper spray inside the Parliament house.[22] Kumar ultimately resigned from both the chief minister's office and the Congress Party.[23] Amidst the chaotic atmosphere, the Lok Sabha passed the Andhra Pradesh Reorganization Act in February, and Telangana became India's 29th state on June 2, 2014.

This process may surprise observers more familiar with "bottom-up" federalism, as it originated in the United States, in contrast to the much more "top-down" Indian variant. Louise Tillin, a scholar who has written incisively on India's post-2000 "new states and their political origins," explains,

> Article 3 of India's Constitution, often described as its least federal provision, places the full responsibility for the creation of new states in the hands of Parliament. State division or boundary change is not a matter that can be decided by state governments alone, nor is there any constitutional provision for local referenda. Central legislation mandating the creation of a new state must be referred to the relevant state legislative assembly but states possess no right to veto a change to their borders, nor an ability to make binding amendments to provisions for the placing or borders of division of assets and liabilities consequent of the creation of any new state.[24]

Tillin observes, "despite such centralized provisions, debates about statehood have tended to have a profoundly decentralized character." In the runup to the creation of three new states in 2000—when Chhattisgarh, Uttaranchal, and Jharkhand were carved out of Madhya Pradesh, Uttar Pradesh, and Bihar, respectively—the NDA government "took action to create new states only where the BJP had already laid roots, the state assembly had already passed a resolution agreeing to statehood and where major BJP allies agreed to the bifurcation of their states."[25] The Telangana case was very different, Tillin observed, in that the UPA central government, led by the Congress Party, "actively intervened before any such state assembly resolution was tabled or passed." This made the political stakes higher for all involved.

As we have seen, perceptions of central "interference" by past Congress Party governments were a key driver in the formation of the TDP in the 1980s; thus, there were also strong historical reasons for the mobilization of popular sentiment *against* statehood for Telangana, both within the region and across Andhra Pradesh before the bifurcation. The passions and resentments aroused in the run-up to the 2014 separation have not been resolved in the aftermath, as administrative, logistical, and political challenges consequent to the center's decision have confronted AP ever since (and the new Telangana as well).

Confronting the Naxalite Insurgency

Perhaps surprisingly, given all this political upheaval, one challenge the state (now states) managed to surmount is the threat posed by militant Naxalism, a Maoist-inspired movement across a "Red corridor" spanning much of eastern India that originated in rural West Bengal in 1967 and peaked around 2009, when it had an active presence in as many as 180 districts across several states. Much of the movement's senior leadership in this early-2000s phase was drawn from the Telangana region.[26] Amidst an intense campaign by AP state police to defeat the Maoists—one faction's moniker, People's War Group (PWG), gives a sense of the struggle's intensity—officers told *India Today*, "They are not like the dreamy Naxalite intellectuals of yore such as Charu Mazumdar [the movement's founder, who died in 1972]....These Maoist leaders back ideology with hardcore military skills." In 2003, then-Chief Minister Naidu narrowly escaped a deadly attack on his motorcade by PWG insurgents. The conflict claimed around 8,000 lives across eastern India in the decade between 2003 and 2013, when a combination of aggressive policing, better coordination among the central government and affected states, and government programs to promote rural development and poverty reduction gradually began to turn the tide.[27]

The Telangana movement's original association with the 1940s "peasant uprising" long had contributed to fears of destabilizing violence around the statehood issue,[28] and in 2010 Chief Minister Reddy told Congress Party leaders in Delhi that statehood for Telangana would "aggravate" the insurgency. He pointed out that both Chhattisgarh and Jharkhand, ten years after their creation, "were in the grip of Naxalism."[29] The Maoists themselves also viewed a separate Telangana as an opportunity, according to a report of the movement's central committee meeting held in 2013 that was seized by security forces.[30]

But in this case, the state's fears and the militants' aspirations have not been borne out. Electoral politics have even given some former Telangana Maoists a new outlet for activism: in late 2018, the 69-year-old revolutionary and poet Gummadi Vittal Rao, who had boycotted elections for almost 40 years, stepped onto a stage at a TDP campaign rally in Telangana's Khammam district to embrace AP chief minister Chandrababu Naidu ahead of the new state's second assembly election following the bifurcation.[31]

Capital Dreams and Coercive Developmentalism

By contrast, the process of developing a new capital city for Andhra Pradesh has been bitterly contentious. Under the terms of the bifurcation, AP and Telangana would share Hyderabad until 2024, to give AP ample time to transition to a new capital. Eager to move forward after returning to power in 2014 in downsized AP, Naidu's TDP government announced major development plans for a new "greenfield" capital at Amaravati, to be a planned city with state-of-the-art infrastructure—a technologist's utopia, all glass and greenery and with a 125-foot Buddha statue on the banks of the Krishna River. The World Bank, again embracing its onetime favorite chief minister, prepared a $500 million loan to support development of the capital city, with co-financing from the Chinese-led Asian Infrastructure Investment Bank (AIIB) for another $300 million. The remaining $215 million of the project's $715 million price tag would come from the state government.

However, Amaravati's development would require the state's acquisition of many small parcels of land from local landowners, mostly farmers, and in 2016 a group of impacted stakeholders brought a complaint to the World Bank's independent Inspection Panel alleging coercive practices and inadequate compensation under the state's "land pooling" scheme. After a prolonged inquiry marked by process delays, as the Panel repeatedly gave the World Bank's management more time to respond to the complaint, it finally issued a third report and planned to recommend a full investigation of the World Bank's involvement in the project. Ultimately, in a face-saving move, the Government of India withdrew its loan request, ending the World Bank's and AIIB's involvement in the project.

There were also allegations of caste bias in the land acquisition process, with supposedly more favorable arrangements for landowners from the Kamma caste (a key TDP constituency) and opposition from the Reddy community.[32] And, in the campaign for the 2019 state assembly election, Naidu's chief opponent Y. S. Jagan Mohan Reddy, son of the late former chief minister YSR, charged that Naidu's Kamma community had enriched themselves through shady land speculation deals around Amaravati in advance of the site's selection.[33] Jagan Mohan Reddy painted Amaravati as the "Kamma capital," and seemed intent on not only tainting Naidu personally but sowing discontent within Kamma and TDP ranks over the capital fiasco.[34] Naidu and the TDP were voted out, once again, as Reddy led the YSR Congress Party to victory in the second post-bifurcation election in AP. The new party is a split-off from the state's Congress Party; the YSR of its name stands for Yuvajana Sramika Rythu (Youth Labor Farmers) but clearly evokes the famous former chief minister. Politics in Andhra Pradesh, it would appear, remain as personalized as ever.

The new government initially said that it would not move the capital from Amaravati, but it also said that building the city was not its priority. It has since halted construction, pending inquiries into the land acquisition process during Naidu's term. Jagan Mohan Reddy subsequently put forward a plan for three capitals, with justification from an appointed expert panel and the Boston Consulting Group, which said the capital envisioned by Naidu is "not feasible." Under the new plan, the Legislative Assembly will remain in Amaravati, but the government's executive administration will be from Visakhapatnam (Vizag) in Coastal Andhra and the judiciary will be in Kurnool, Rayalaseema.

Development Amid Democracy's Contradictions

It is remarkable that in the face of so much political turbulence and uncertainty, Andhra Pradesh has continued to experience annual economic growth ranging from 11 to 15% between 2014-15 and 2019-20,[35] surpassing India as a whole. This trajectory is a testament to the resourcefulness of its people, but also to the soundness of policies enacted by Naidu's earlier TDP governments from around 1998 to 2004 and improved upon by YSR during the Congress Party's return to power from 2004 to 2009. Though nothing should be taken for granted, this suggests that AP may have come through a take-off phase and into an era of sustained economic growth. The state has also dramatically reduced poverty, from 45% in the 1990s to 9% in 2016, though rural poverty at 11% remains higher than urban at 6%.[36]

Ironically, given the TDP's founding theme of autonomy from Delhi, the central government has continued to play a significant role in the state's economic and political development. After 1997-98, which coincided with Naidu's TDP joining the NDA at the center, AP received a disproportionate share of the center's Plan outlays to states—much higher than Bihar, for example—with the difference only widening in the early 2000s and 2010s. In 2008-09, AP received three times the Plan outlay for Bihar, which has twice its population.[37] The state's bifurcation in 2014 was by an act of Parliament, as we have seen, following the central government's commitment to the cause. And since the bifurcation, both the Naidu and Reddy governments have sought (so far, unsuccessfully) to hold the central government to a commitment made by then-Prime Minister Manmohan Singh to designate AP as a Special Category Status, which would make it eligible for a larger share of central budgetary support. Prime Minister Modi has rejected the idea, citing advice from the 14th Finance Commission.[38]

As the case of Andhra Pradesh demonstrates, democracy at the state level in India reflects many of the complexities and contradictions that characterize India as a whole, at a smaller scale and with distinctive local ingredients. The state's elections have been competitive, and they have not necessarily rewarded incumbents for generally strong economic performance when voters have perceived misplaced ambitions and unresponsiveness toward vulnerable groups—and especially when urban development has been given higher priority than rural interests. But elections alone do not ensure justice for those harmed by state policies undertaken in the name of development. Even after the TDP had been voted out of power again in 2019, one woman at a 2020 protest over ill-fated land acquisition process for Amaravati told a reporter, "The smallest farmer with just half an acre also came forward trusting the government." Another, surveying the halted, half-finished construction, said there was no way they could farm their land again even if it was returned: "How do you sow paddy on a place with three inches of concrete underneath?"[39]

BIHAR

The politics of the plains state of Bihar during the Modi era demonstrates the challenges in stabilizing identity politics and advancing a developmental agenda in the context of internal security challenges. Against all odds, Bihar has begun to turn away from its reputation of lawlessness and violence and emerge as one of the fastest growing economies in the country.

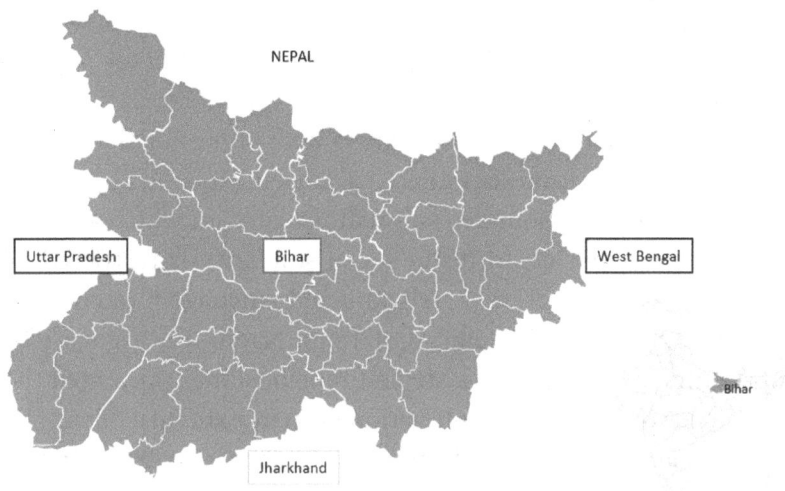

Map 3. Bihar

Bihar's renaissance has been skillfully engineered by Chief Minister Nitish Kumar of the Janata Dal (United) party. Kumar had been chief minister briefly in 2000 and again from 2005 to 2014. Kumar resigned as chief minister in 2014 after taking responsibility for a poor electoral performance and handed power to an associate, Jitan Ram Manjhi. Kumar returned to power in 2015 after Manjhi was forced by the JD(U) to resign as Chief Minister.

With roughly 128.5 million inhabitants, Bihar is India's third largest state in terms of population after Uttar Pradesh and Maharashtra. Its population size is roughly comparable to that of Mexico or Japan; in other words, if Bihar were a country, it would be the 12th most populous country in the world. Despite being the poorest Indian state in per capita terms, Bihar is now one of the fastest growing economies in the country, with a compounded annual growth rate of the gross state domestic product at 13.27% from 2016 to 2020.[40] In the same period, the per capita growth rate has also matched the aggregate economic growth rate, which suggests an alignment of the economic growth rate with the fertility rate. Nevertheless, it is still heavily agrarian and 90% of the population live in areas classified as rural.[41]

Bihar's poor social outcomes, along with other northern states like Uttar Pradesh and Rajasthan, have been explained by Prerna Singh's concept of "bounded sub-nationalism," in which a strong local identity that could foster social solidarity is restricted by the social divisions of caste, religion, and language.[42] In contrast to southern states like Kerala and Tamil Nadu, it is argued that intra-elite divisions along caste and religious lines prevented the emergence of an inclusive sub-nationalism in states like Bihar. The rapid turnaround in Bihar's fortunes since 2005 is explained in this argument by pointing to Nitish Kumar's efforts to create a Bihari subnational identity.[43] Evidence for the creation of a Bihari identity include state sponsorship of celebrations on the occasion of "Bihar Diwas" (Bihar Day) and "the promotion of a range of cultural and literary activities."[44]

The explanation in the case of Bihar is not compelling, particularly since Bihar Diwas was first celebrated in 2010,[45] five years after Nitish Kumar came to power and began Bihar's economic growth acceleration. In fact, the celebration of Bihar Diwas was established by Nitish Kumar precisely to celebrate Bihar's economic revival under his administration.[46] It is likely, as Singh contends, that Kumar began to espouse an inclusive Bihari identity on the campaign trail in 2004 to distinguish himself from the caste politics of the incumbent.[47] But the widespread embrace of a Bihari identity is unlikely to have preceded Bihar's economic acceleration and may be an effect of recent growth rather than a cause.

Another problematic explanation for Bihar's poor social outcomes in the nineties and its recent revival focuses on finally hitting the "sweet spot" in a "complex and fluid" party system. Banerjee and Hankla explain that when there are either too few political parties or too many political parties, or when political parties are too temporally volatile, there is little incentive for incumbent governments to provide public goods. In their model, the best developmental results are delivered when there is balanced competition and the risks of party fragmentation are relatively contained. Thus, Bihar's rise from the ashes of dysfunction is attributable, at least in part, to the decline in the effective number of parties and, relatedly, in electoral volatility since 2005:

> The slow consolidation of Bihar's party system, and especially the willingness of Bihari voters to reward Kumar for good performance, could therefore be another reason for its improved performance.[48]

The explanatory power of the theory weakens, however, if the political space becomes too consolidated but economic performance continues unabated. This is exactly the situation in Bihar. Kumar has been in office for a decade and a half, and political power has grown increasingly stabilized and consolidated around three political parties without a decline in economic performance or the provision of public goods. Thus, Banerjee and Hankla's "sweet spot" theory also struggles to explain Bihar's continued economic performance. This trend leaves Banerjee and Hankla to speculate that there may be problems in the future if the consolidation trend continues:

> That said, Kumar's ability to hold onto power almost uninterrupted for twenty years might signal future problems for Bihar. While the JD(U) has had to form precarious coalition governments, notably with the BJP, to retain power, having a single politician holding power for so long may indicate a less-than competitive party system, one that is failing to incentivize public goods.[49]

The use of a speculative argument to save a theory is not convincing. In fact, as Banerjee and Hankla concede, Bihar appears to be becoming similar to the state of Gujarat, which has had strong economic performance but is one of the country's least competitive political arenas as it has become a "bastion for the BJP."[50]

A more compelling explanation for the improvement in Bihar's social outcomes requires an exploration of its development agenda.

Developmental and Security

Kumar is commonly credited with turning around the image of the "Republic of Bihar" as a failed state.[51] The state's rapid growth is remarkable because its reputation for lawlessness and insecurity had previously deterred investment; its poverty created limited effective demand; its neglected infrastructure hindered commerce; and its rampant corruption eroded the efficacy of federal transfers.[52] In 2000, the state was internally partitioned and the mineral rich Jharkhand region became a new state in India's federal system.

The ratio of Bihar's per capita GDP relative to India as a whole had steadily deteriorated from 1990 to 2005, with only small improvements in 1991 and 2002. Bihar's ratio of per capita GDP relative to India as a whole fell from over half in 1990 to less than a third by 2005.[53] The compounded annual growth rate from 1980 to 1998 was only 1.1%.[54] Beyond income statistics, Bihar scored poorly along every measure of human development relative to the national average.[55] While the partition of the mineral rich districts of Jharkhand in 2001 did not help matters, Bihar also failed to capitalize on the economic liberalization ushered in at the beginning of the 1990s. The politics of this period was focused on redistribution of public goods to the economically underprivileged or "backward" castes and outright corruption under chief ministers Lalu Prasad Yadav and his wife, Rabri Devi.

Beneath the muscular atrophy, however, Bihar's economy was undergoing a structural transformation. From the 1980s onward, Bihar's service sector (including construction) as a share of the state's domestic product began to grow more rapidly than the industrial sector.[56] In other words, while Bihar remained a heavily agrarian economy in terms of employment, the rise of the service sector meant that its structure was similar to India as a whole. However, the services and industrial sector failed to continue their expansion in the 1990s.[57]

Nitish Kumar, although reliant on a lower caste and minority vote base like his predecessor, focused on assembling a (nominally) secular coalition that prioritized economic transformation (*parivartan*) and development (*vikas*) over subsidies and patronage.[58] In part, it was a shrewd strategy for Kumar to develop a broader coalition with a development agenda since his own caste group, the Kurmis, constitute only 2 to 4% of Bihar's population.[59] Kumar did forge an alliance between the Kurmi and (the more numerous) Koeri caste groups in the nineties as a counterweight to the dominant Yadav–Muslim alliance in Bihar. However, moving beyond caste coalitions helped Kumar attract support of the upper caste groups and those for whom caste identity is less politically salient.

Kumar's administration focused first on improving the court system and the police. Given that Bihar had acquired a reputation for entrenched corruption, brutal violence, kidnappings, home invasions, general lawlessness, organized crime, private caste militias, and even a Maoist insurgency in rural areas, creating law and order—based on a corrupt, demoralized, and understaffed police force and judiciary—was no small feat. Kumar empowered senior police officers to recruit, train, and professionalize the force. Police officers and senior bureaucrats who had migrated away from Bihar were lured back with prestige postings. Retired Army infantrymen were brought in as a Special Auxiliary Police force on a contract basis. The police were mandated to uphold human rights protections and to find innovative policy solutions to control the crime rate. Fast-track procedures were developed to expedite the handling of criminal cases relating to politicians and bureaucrats under the Bihar Special Courts Act of 2008. Police emphasized ensuring that witnesses actually testified in court. An obscure provision in the

Indian Arms Act was also invoked to target illegal firearms possession, resulting in thousands of convictions within a few months.[60]

Next, the administration attempted to reduce corruption by increasing transparency and accountability of government officials through the implementation of the federal Right to Information Act and Right to Public Services Act.[61] Legal provisions to entrap low-level bureaucrats suspected of taking bribes were also used, and a special unit was authorized by the chief minister to entrap corrupt senior bureaucrats.[62] Although an increased emphasis on vigilance and swift punishment for corrupt government employees may not have improved welfare provision, the state's reputation ameliorated.[63]

Kumar's policies paid rapid dividends. Crime statistics, although only marginally reliable in Bihar, and media reports both indicated a dramatic reduction in most types of violent crime[64] and the conviction of 26,000 individuals, including over a dozen state and federal legislators, in the first three years of Kumar's administration.[65] Bihar's compounded annual growth rate jumped to 8.6% from 2005 to 2010. From 2010 to 2012, the compounded annual growth rate was almost 14%.[66]

The Bihar government also made significant progress against the Naxalite (Maoist) insurgency, which enjoyed broad popular support in rural areas in the eighties. The insurgency reached its peak in 2011 with 316 incidents and 63 deaths. By 2017, the number of incidents was reduced to 99 incidents and 22 deaths.[67] Kumar created a 400-member Special Task Force to supplement the Special Auxiliary Police force and improved surrender and rehabilitation policies for the insurgents. These policies in conjunction with counter-insurgency assistance, resource transfers, and concessions to tribal communities from the federal government appeared to have a dramatic impact. Whereas previously 22 out of 38 districts had an insurgent presence, by 2021 only four to ten districts were still affected.[68] While the Maoist insurgency is by no means extinguished, economic growth and anti-corruption policies have sapped some of their appeal in rural areas.

Moreover, Kumar benefitted from a series of policy changes at the federal level that forgave state debt to the central government in exchange for implementing the Fiscal Responsibility and Budget Management (FRBM) Acts. The policies made greater resources available for state governments to redistribute. Reforms to the tax code also increased tax revenues, including the states' share in central taxes. The Kumar administration contained the state's fiscal deficit to 3% by fiscal year 2008/09 and raised non-tax revenues.[69] This is a notable accomplishment since Bihar's deficit had doubled from 1999 to 2005.[70]

Improvements in fiscal management were matched by improved spending on development aided by the World Bank.

Intergovernmental Financial Support

A significant portion of the Kumar government's reform agenda was funded by the World Bank.[71] Since 2005, there have been 41 World Bank projects in Bihar worth a total of $15 billion. There are currently 17 active World Bank projects in Bihar worth a total of $5.6 billion in commitments.[72] A World Bank concept note from 2005 clearly indicated that the Bank associated Nitish Kumar with a reformist agenda:

> The state election of November 2005 brought into power a new reformist government that has showed a strong commitment to increase public spending (with fiscal adjustment), strengthen governance, and improve social services delivery as means to accelerate economic growth and overcome the political and structural obstacles that have historically hampered the state's development. Policy reforms undertaken by the GoB since it came into power include key legislation to manage its fiscal deficit responsibly, modernize financial and procurement procedures, strengthen

police services, promote rapid clearance procedures for establishing enterprises and issuing required licenses, and introduce a standardized and decentralized system to recruit teachers based on their academic credentials, among others.[73]

By contrast, the World Bank associated his predecessor, Lalu Prasad Yadav, with lawlessness and a failure to develop the state's economy:

> One of the impediments to economic development that carries over from the period in which Lalu's party was in power is lack of progress in developing basic infrastructure. In addition, the State failed to shake off a reputation as being—in the throes of economic chaos and unprecedented social tension.[74]

World Bank support for Bihar has advanced Kumar's development agenda and contributed to high rates of economic growth.

The JD(U)-BJP Alliance

Despite Kumar's ideological roots as a socialist, his tactical alliance with the Hindu nationalist BJP helped him secure the support of upper caste Biharis, particularly Brahmins and Banias (merchants), in the mesmerizingly fractious and fluid political space of Bihar. The awkward alliance had its roots in the factional and internecine "socialist" politics of the mid-nineties.

In 1994, Nitish Kumar projected himself as a leader of the Kurmi caste group in distinction to his former friend and rival who championed the Yadav caste group, Lalu Prasad Yadav, within the left-leaning Janata Dal party. Unable to garner significant support within the Janata Dal, Kumar created an offshoot party with the famous socialist leader George Fernandes. The new party was known as the Janata Dal (George). In 1995, the Janata Dal (George) was rebranded as the Samata Party after more politicians joined the party. In 1996, the Samata Party joined into the BJP-led NDA in order to challenge the Indian National Congress Party, and the United Front, which was made up of Yadav's Janata Dal and other left-leaning parties. The Samata Party won eight seats in the national elections: six seats from Bihar, one from UP, and one from Odisha.

In the subsequent months, Yadav lost supporters within the Janata Dal because he faced serious accusations of massive corruption. In response, Yadav created his own party—the Rashtriya Janata Dal (RJD) in 1997. Symmetrically, Kumar created the Janata Dal (United) party or JD(U), a party formed by the fusion of the Samata party and defectors from the Janata Dal.[75]

In 1999, the JD(U)–BJP alliance performed very well at the national parliamentary elections, propelling Kumar to become a plausible candidate as the chief minister of Bihar in the 2000 state assembly election. Unfortunately for Kumar, the alliance did not have a majority of seats in the Bihar assembly and thus could not successfully retain power. Yadav's RJD, supported by the Congress party, was able to engineer Yadav's wife, Rabri Devi, as chief minister since Yadav faced arrest for corruption.

Nevertheless, the emergence of a stable BJP government in Delhi led by PM Atal Bihari Vajpayee pulled Nitish Kumar into the cabinet ranks and thus greater national prominence.[76] Meanwhile, the BJP passed the Bihar Reorganization Act in August 2000 and partitioned the state of Bihar and Jharkhand. Undoubtedly, the benefits of an alliance with the NDA shaped the JD(U)'s decision to join the NDA again in 2003.

The relationship between the national and the regional party has been rocky and personalized. In fact, Kumar vacated his support for the BJP from 2013 until 2017. Kumar claimed he would rather withdraw his support for the NDA than endorse Narendra Modi as the nominee for prime minister—although the real reasons probably had more to do with upper caste/right-wing agitation within Bihar against Kumar and his alleged land reform plans[77] and his own ambition to become the NDA candidate for prime minister.

In the 2015 Bihar Legislative Assembly elections, Kumar's JD(U) joined forces with Yadav's RJD and the INC in an alliance that came to be known as the Mahagathbandhan (Grand Alliance) to fight against the BJP and the National Democratic Alliance. The strange bedfellows were united primarily in pressing for the Indian census to include an enumeration of caste. The BJP government has issued conflicting statements on the issue but is widely viewed as opposed to asking about caste affiliation in the Census as it may entrench social divides among Hindus.[78] An enumeration of caste is pivotal to legitimating the patronage strategies of both the JD(U) and the RJD. The Grand Alliance won and Kumar retained his position as the chief minister. However, shortly after the election victory the two major parties began squabbling and the JD(U) returned to working with the BJP from 2017 onward.

Overall, the JD(U)–BJP alliance has helped the BJP to expand its foothold in Bihar and allowed Kumar to forge a winning coalition between the upper castes and the (mainly) non-Yadav middle caste groups. Moreover, Kumar's (nominally) secular politics and economic growth strategy helped to attract Muslims and other economically underprivileged constituencies.[79] Of course, beneath the surface, tensions with the BJP simmer on key issues that might alienate Muslims from supporting the JD(U), such as the building a controversial Hindu temple in Ayodhya, eliminating separate civil courts for Muslims, and revoking the special status of the state of Jammu and Kashmir.[80] Nevertheless, the ability of a popular regional party to form a relatively durable alliance with the ruling national party has created support for development-oriented policy solutions.

WEST BENGAL

In 2011, the Communist Party of India (Marxist) or CPI(M) was finally voted out of office in West Bengal after a tenure of almost three and a half decades. Having become ideologically hollowed

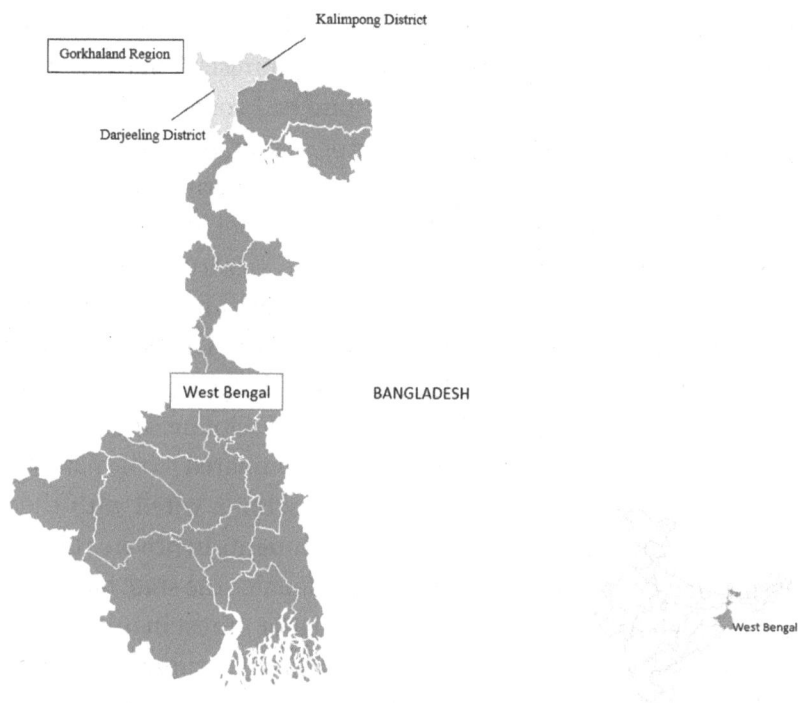

Map 4. West Bengal

out, the CPI(M) came to be synonymous with empty socialist slogans; a habitually violent, rent-seeking, patronage network; and public policy initiatives aimed at economic liberalization on the model of contemporary China or Vietnam.[81] To their credit and despite their patronage network, the CPI(M) was one of only a few ruling parties to successfully devolve a share of political power to the local level in accordance with the 73rd and 74th amendments to the Indian Constitution.[82] The party also oversaw land reform in rural areas, increased agricultural growth, and contributed to a remarkable decline in the rate of poverty.[83] In comparison to other states, West Bengal by 2011 was "average" in terms of per capita income, poverty, and human development. For critics of the CPI(M), however, the remaining high levels of poverty and low levels of human development after nearly three and a half decades in power revealed the emptiness of their grandiose promises.[84] Supporters of the CPI(M) pointed to how far the state had come over the years and blamed their lack of additional progress on the hostility of and insufficient fiscal transfers from the federal government.[85]

The new ruling party, the All-India Trinamool [three-leaf clover] Congress (AITC or TMC) party, was led to victory by its founder, Mamata Banerjee, who became West Bengal's first female chief minister. Along with the mixed record of the CPI(M), Banerjee inherited a state with several serious challenges, particularly in the areas of job creation, education, labor discipline, and security. The urban unemployment rate was 24% compared to the national average of 15%. In terms of education, parents voted with their feet by enrolling an astonishing 76% of students in private tuition, more than double the national average. Finally, the state had a history of high fiscal deficits and crippling labor unrest in urban areas and, like Bihar and Andhra Pradesh, a Maoist insurgency in rural areas.[86] Banerjee's proposed solutions appeared incongruous and amorphous relative to the scale of the problems—she promised to promote small and medium enterprises, she defended the teachers' union, she had a history of calling for wildcat strikes and squelching industrial investments in the state, and she did not initially appear to have a plan for tackling the insurgency. Her main virtue in the eyes of many voters had been simply that she was not associated with the CPI(M).

Although it was unclear how the new chief minister would tackle the problems, she was a seasoned politician. Banerjee had become politically active in her youth and was first elected to Parliament in 1984. After a brief setback in 1989, she would return to office and serve from 1991 to 2011 when she became the chief minister. She had previously served as the railways minister from 1999 to 2000 and the minister of coal and mines in 2004 in the BJP-led National Democratic Alliance government. Banerjee rose to prominence for her outspoken activism against the CPI(M)'s efforts to acquire rural land for a Tata Motors plant in Singur (2006) and the creation of a special economic zone in Nandigram (2007). In 2009, she once again became the railways minister after she allied with the Congress-led UPA.

Big Sister's Party

Banerjee, often referred to simply as "*Didi*" or "Big Sister," quickly set about creating a neo-patrimonial power base and a cult of personality to consolidate her position—a remarkable shift for a state that had been associated with "social-democracy" under the Communist party.[87] The familiar neo-patrimonial and charismatic mode of governance, in which the affairs of state are managed as an extension of the ruler's household, is particularly associated with politicians who head regional or state parties, such as Jaya Jayalalitha of the All-India Anna Dravida Munnetra Kazhagam (AIADMK) party in Tamil Nadu; Mulayam Singh Yadav of the Samajwadi Party (SP), and Mayawati of the Bahujan Samaj Party (BSP) in Uttar Pradesh.

Like many political parties in India, the AITC is blatantly transactional; the party gains voter support in exchange for welfare provisions (i.e., patronage). For example, in her 2021 election platform, Banerjee announced that if her party were re-elected, the government would provide ₹500 ($6.68) to the senior-most female in each household every month. Members of Scheduled Castes (i.e., *Dalits*), Scheduled Tribes (*Adivasis*), and Other Backward Castes (OBCs) would be eligible for double that amount. Students would be issued credit cards worth ₹1 million (or $13,363) in loans at 4% interest. Citizens eligible for rations from the state would now have their rations delivered to their doorstep, etc.[88] There is little, if any, attempt at ideological persuasion or detailed public policy discussion.

The AITC, like its Communist predecessor, is also a corrupt and violent organization. Banerjee and the AITC have done little to curb the influence of "black money" (illegal campaign contributions and money laundering) or to combat corruption more broadly. In fact, Banerjee herself has used a creative loophole to raise funds for her re-election campaigns:

> An amateur painter, she claimed to have persuaded various friendly business leaders to donate as much a Rs2 million (about $31,000) to buy each of her works, creating an artful means of legally raising large sums.[89]

Several AITC Members of Parliament and Members of the West Bengal Legislative Assembly have also been linked to the Saradha Financial Group scam, a massive multibillion-dollar Ponzi scheme and international money laundering scandal. Although the financial group had connections to politicians in other parties, key positions in the organization were held by AITC politicians. For example, the CEO of the Saradha Media Group was Kunal Ghosh, an AITC member of the Rajya Sabha. The scheme collapsed in 2013, prompting a multi-agency federal investigation. The federal government's Central Bureau of Investigation (CBI) told the Supreme Court that Mamata Banerjee was directly implicated in the scandal for using the Chief Minister's Relief Fund to pay the salaries of workers at a media company owned by the Saradha financial Group for 23 months after the scheme collapsed.[90] The CBI also informed the Supreme Court that the chief minister's government showed "constant, deliberate and willful non-cooperation" in the investigation in "a concerted effort to evade, avoid and escape the process of law."[91]

The party has also been implicated in the misallocation of relief funds for the victims of Cyclone Amphan, which caused widespread damage in West Bengal in 2020. Over two thousand complaints allege that relief funds went to local AITC officials whose homes were not damaged and actual victims were left uncompensated.[92] These corruption allegations were only the most recent following a slew of other accusations levelled at AITC officials, including protests related to the distribution of rations during the height of the COVID-19 pandemic in 2020, state-wide protests over the "cut-money" scam (i.e., siphoning of aid funds) meant for housing grants to the poor in 2019, a coal smuggling scam allegedly involving the chief minister's nephew, the Rose Valley Ponzi scheme of 2013, etc.[93]

Like its predecessor, the AITC is not above systematically using violence to defend its turf and advance its influence. For example, supporters of Banerjee and her nephew, Abhishek Banerjee, a member of Parliament who is also currently the general secretary for the AITC, were accused of using excessive force against a man who slapped him during a political rally in 2015.[94] AITC supporters also attacked the media and ransacked a police station after the incident, blaming the police for lax security. Derek O'Brien, a member of the Rajya Sabha and the national spokesperson for Trinamool, speculated that the attack on Abhishek Banerjee may have been an attempted assassination.[95] Other AITC members ventured that the assault was at the behest of the BJP. The man who was roughed up by AITC party members, Devashish Acharya, did go on to join the BJP in 2020. Subsequently, Acharya died in June 2021 under suspicious circumstances after being left at a hospital emergency room in critical condition. For critics of the AITC, the entire arc of murky incidents points to the party's reliance on thuggery. Prime Minister Modi has used the prominence of Mamata's nephew to highlight the party's nepotism and corruption. At a campaign rally in March 2021, Modi stated:

> She was supposed to be everyone's "didi", but Mamata had been "bua" (aunt) to only one nephew. People of Bengal had chosen you to be their didi. But why have you chosen to be the aunt of only

one nephew? Instead of addressing the hopes and aspirations of lakhs [hundreds of thousands] of nephews in the state, why are you fulfilling the greed of only one nephew?[96]

The animosity between the rival parties has gone well beyond personalized rhetoric. Workers from the BJP and AITC clashed violently in April 2021 after the elections were held and again in September 2021 after a special election. The BJP claims that over 50 of their workers have been killed by the AITC.[97] The election-related violence in April led the prime minister to call the West Bengal governor to express his concern at the law-and-order situation in the state.

Regardless of growing corruption and violence, Banerjee's government was re-elected in 2016 and 2021. In fact, in 2021, her party won a two-thirds majority of seats; Banerjee did lose her own seat in the election, although that result is being contested in court. Nevertheless, by shifting to a vacated seat, Banerjee was chosen to lead a third term as chief minister.

The Clover and the Lotus

Although the rise of the AITC in the citadel of the Communist party has been impressive, the AITC now appears embattled as the right-wing BJP has overcome its "political untouchability" in the state and made dramatic gains.

At the federal level, the AITC has changed alliance partners relatively frequently since its creation in 1998. Ironically, given the recent heightened tensions between the AITC and the BJP, Trinamool was originally allied to the BJP-led National Democratic Alliance (NDA) for general (i.e., national) elections in 1998, 1999, and 2004. After losses in the 2004 general elections and the 2006 West Bengal state assembly elections, the party began to have doubts about its partnership with the BJP. In 2007, the AITC quit the alliance and switched its support to the Congress-led UPA ahead of the 2009 election. The AITC stayed with the UPA until September

2012, when it left due to disputes over economic policies. In the 2014 general election, the AITC won 33 seats in the Lower House of Parliament. After the 2019 general election, the AITC held on to 22 seats (or 4% of total seats) in the Lower House and 13 seats (5%) in the Upper House. The AITC is the fourth largest party in the country; it is not currently part of either major alliance group.

At the state legislative level, since the 2021 election, the AITC controls 214 out of 294 seats (or a 73% majority) in West Bengal. Notably, the CPI(M) and the INC did not win a single seat in the state assembly in 2021. The only other major party left at the state level is the BJP. In other words, the old political parties have been vanquished and the Hindu nationalists are now the main opposition.

How has the right-wing BJP managed to make "inroads" in a state once synonymous with the Communist party? And why are relations between the BJP and the AITC so contentious given their former alliance?

Christophe Jaffrelot argues that the BJP, under PM Modi and party leader Amit Shah, have emphasized ethno-religious identity as an election strategy. The BJP strategy clearly paid off as they went from 2 to 18 seats from West Bengal in the 2019 national parliamentary elections, and from 3 to 77 seats in the 2021 state elections.[98] Banerjee has responded to the "saffron surge" by urging voters not to be divided along communal lines.[99] Simplifying her message, she told her supporters that the symbol of the BJP, the white lotus flower, was "a rotten, bloodied flower...do not vote for it. Vote for 'joraphool' [the three-leaf clover, the symbol of the AITC]."[100]

For his part, Prime Minister Modi argued that it was Banerjee who was dividing Bengalis along communal lines:

> I have known Didi for long. She is not the same person who raised her voice against the Left. Today she speaks in someone else's language, and is being remote controlled. You (Mamata) have divided people on religious lines, and thus the lotus is blooming.[101]

Historical Context

The notion that the BJP is making "inroads" in Bengal ignores a broader historical perspective. Calcutta was the home of a nationalist intellectual movement in the late nineteenth century that, along with European fascism, inspired the emergence of Hindutva ideology in Bombay. Moreover, the demands of the Hindu Mahasabha, a right-wing political party, in 1947 to partition Bengal and create a Hindu-majority province in the Indian union resonated with the sentiments of the RSS on the western coast of India.[102] In other words, the ideology of Hindutva is not alien to the soil of West Bengal. Though the predecessor of the BJP, the Bharatiya Jan Sangh (BJS), never fared above 6% of the vote in general and state elections in West Bengal, it did capture two Lok Sabha seats in 1952 and nine state assembly seats.[103]

Not long after the creation of the BJP in 1980, the party strategically decided to enter West Bengal's political scene at the village level. The BJP aimed to build a base of authentic support in rural areas. The BJP began to gain traction the 1990s with the efforts by Hindutva organizations to destroy the Babri Masjid in Uttar Pradesh, a mosque built by the first Mughal emperor in 1528 CE, and replace it with a temple to the Hindu deity Lord Ram.[104] Although the BJP failed to win any seats from West Bengal in Parliament or in the state assembly, it did gain 11% of the vote in 1991. The BJP would win its first seat in Parliament representing West Bengal in 1998. At the time, the BJP was allied to the AITC. The two parties were united in their opposition to the incumbent parties, i.e., the Communists and Congress. By joining forces, they were able to conserve resources by agreeing on which party would contest seats in particular districts. Moreover, the AITC gained links with a national party, and the BJP gained acceptability in state-level politics.

The BJP in West Bengal has also clearly benefitted from the sensational popularity of Narendra Modi in 2014, at which time the BJP held only two seats in the state legislature. In 2016, the BJP won three seats. Five years later, the BJP was the main opposition party with 77 seats.

A major tension between the BJP and the AITC that could only be temporarily papered over was always related to the latter's Muslim support base. Muslims constitute 30% of West Bengal's population. Given the BJP's hostility toward undocumented Muslim immigrants from Bangladesh, and the BJP's support for the destruction of the Babri Masjid, the party was bound to alienate Muslim voters. As the Modi government gained popularity, Hindutva organizations increased their activities in West Bengal. Their main themes were to promote "reconversion" of Muslim and Tribal Christians "back" to Hinduism.[105]

Although the two parties ended their alliance in the mid-2000s, the BJP leadership refrained from attacking the AITC and Mamata Banerjee. Pralay Kanungo argues that once the allies were separated, Mamata Banerjee realized in 2014 that even the perception that the AITC was sympathetic to the BJP would cause Muslim voters to shift their support from the AITC back to either the INC party or the CPI(M). The CPI(M) had already begun insinuating that Banerjee's studied neutrality about the rise of a firebrand like Modi in the BJP was due to underlying sympathy with the Hindutva ideology. This led Banerjee to denounce the BJP, and Modi in particular, publicly.[106] Modi, in turn, retaliated and denounced Banerjee. The ensuing tit-for-tat mudslinging has polarized the two parties ever since. Bengalis threatened by the growing strength of Hindutva ideology at the national level have turned to Banerjee; those fed up with corruption, political violence, and lack of economic growth and development in Bengal have turned to the BJP.

Employment and Investment

Despite its electoral success, the AITC government has failed to change the business investment climate.[107] Of course, changing the business climate in a large state is complicated, but Mamata Banerjee's rhetoric and policies have not helped. Although a quarter of the state's gross domestic product is from industry and less than a fifth is from agriculture, the agrarian economy employs a large swath of the population. As a state with a very high population density (owing in part to waves of refugees from neighboring Bangladesh), parcels of rural land tend to be very small (0.77 hectares on average) and almost all (96%) farmers are classified as small and marginal.[108] Acquiring even a few hectares of land to promote capital investment is politically contentious.[109] In fact, it was in organizing against land acquisition that Mamata Banerjee rose to national prominence. And yet, the only way for West Bengal to improve its productivity is to shift its population from marginal agriculture into labor-intensive industry. When this problem is coupled with a long history of labor unrest supported by activist politicians, first under the CPI(M) and now under the AITC, few investors see West Bengal as an attractive site for green field investment. At the same time, the AITC has not sought to attract business:

> The AITC has never tried to acquire land for industry, nor was it ever serious about connecting with big business, given its Left politics.[110]

In fact, Banerjee has repeatedly made populist demands for "free gas" and an end to privatization of state-owned enterprises.[111] Although the AITC rose to power challenging the incumbent Communist party, the AITC is fundamentally a left-populist government that is hostile to corporations.

Education Reform

Education reform under the AITC has been heavily politicized and oriented toward election-related gimmicks; hence, there has been little progress in reversing trends in public education. Banerjee's response to increased defection from the state's public education system has been to promise English medium education "on every block." The policy is a challenge to Prime Minister Modi's New Education Policy, which advocates education in each state's mother tongue. The CPI(M) had banned English language education at the primary level in the eighties in order to stem dropout rates in rural areas, but abandoned the project in 2004 as the policy proved counterproductive since families tend to associate English medium education with greater rigor and employment opportunities.

During a campaign for the state assembly elections in 2020, Banerjee announced that she would transfer ₹10,000 (or $133) to each Class 12 student in a government school or madrassah, but not for students in private schools. The money could be used by students to purchase a tablet or mobile phone to take classes online.[112] Given that the announcement was in the midst of the COVID-19 pandemic, the policy was rational albeit a stopgap measure for a more systemic problem.

Secessionist Unrest and Security Concerns

The AITC has subdued both the Gorkhaland secessionists and the Maoist rebels, greatly enhancing stability and security in the state. However, the failure to reach a viable solution to separatist aspirations has strengthened the appeal of the BJP. Moreover, the pacification of the Maoists has not yielded a peace dividend.

Gorkhas

Since the early twentieth century, the Nepali-speaking Gorkha peoples, who live in the northern Himalayan foothills of West Bengal, have been agitating for a separate state, most recently under the moniker of "Gorkhaland." This area, which is historically famous for its colonial-era tea plantations, is also a significant tourist destination and a strategic chokepoint that links the subcontinental diamond with the far-flung northeastern states of India. The West Bengal government has responded to separatist demands over the years by alternatively using force or granting increased levels of autonomy to the region, including the creation of a semi-autonomous administrative entity, the Darjeeling Gorkha Hill Council in 1988 and the Gorkhaland Territorial Administration (GTA) in 2011.

From June to September 2017, agitation for the partition of West Bengal and the creation of Gorkhaland led to a 104-day strike in Darjeeling. The strike was provoked by the decision of the AITC government to make learning the Bengali language a compulsory school subject, even in non–Bengali-speaking areas such as Darjeeling. In response to the government of West Bengal attempting to force businesses to remain open, strike organizers asked the residents of Darjeeling district to voluntarily confine themselves in their own homes. All aspects of ordinary life were disrupted and even the fabled tea plantations closed shop. Violence resulting from the strike led to the death of 13 individuals, including a West Bengal police officer.[113] Although the BJP had formed an electoral alliance with the separatist movement in 2009, when the separatists helped elect a senior BJP leader from Rajasthan, Jaswant Singh, to represent Darjeeling, the Modi government did not support the strike and thus the agitation failed to bear fruit.[114]

The leadership of the Gorkhaland movement, particularly since the 2017 strike, has succumbed to petty factionalism and alliances of convenience. The leader of the Gurung faction of the Gorkha Janmukti Morcha (GJM) is Bimal Gurung. In 2020, the Gurung faction switched its support from the BJP and offered to enter into an alliance with Mamata Banerjee's Trinamool Congress. Ironically, Gurung had fled the state after the AITC cracked down on the GJM for organizing the 2017 strike. The Tamang faction of the GJM was led by the party's president, Binay Tamang. Tamang also allied with the AITC in the 2021 Legislative Assembly elections but ran separate candidates from the Gurung faction. After a resounding defeat, Binay Tamang resigned as party president. In September 2021, a former general secretary of the Tamang faction and the former chairman of the board of administrators of the Gorkhaland Territorial Administration (GTA), Anit Thapa, announced plans to form a separate party from the GJM. He hoped to attract supporters from both the Gurung and the Tamang factions of the GJM.[115] Thapa has argued for leaving the demand for Gorkhaland to technocrats and intellectuals. He has urged politicians to work for more pressing issues, such as land rights for the Nepali workers in tea plantations.[116]

Meanwhile, the BJP has become a major force in northern Bengal.[117] The BJP presents itself as a powerful connection to the federal government and a peaceful alternative to the AITC, which used violence to break up protests in 2017. Embracing Hindutva ideology also provides the Gorkhas, who are descended from Nepali migrants to the region over the last two centuries, a route to claim national belonging rather than merely regional minority status. The martial values of hyper-nationalism also appeal to a community that became world famous for its gallant mercenary troops. Even though the British imperialist discourse on the "martial races" was orientalist and racializing, there is still strong attachment to military service among Nepali Indians.[118]

Naxalites

The Darjeeling District is also home to the village of Naxalbari, the site from which a Maoist revolutionary movement began in 1967. The "Naxalite" movement, as it came to be called, aimed to redistribute land to landless peasant laborers, originally in accord with the unenforced Land Ceiling Act of 1953.[119] The movement quickly became violent after villagers used arms against the state police to prevent an arrest and police forces retaliated with lethal force in subsequent protest demonstrations. Although the CPI(M) would join the United Front government in 1967 and become the largest political party in West Bengal by 1969, the ultra-radical, revolutionary Maoists faction of the CPI(M) viewed "establishment Communists" as sellouts. The Naxalites would form a new party, the Communist Party of India (Marxist-Leninist or CPI(M-L)) and wage attacks on the "parliamentary communists" of the CPI(M). The Naxalite movement was mainly "subdued" within West Bengal by 1972, but the insurgency spread to rural areas of other states, where it continues to flare up spasmodically. Although the Naxalite movement splintered into a vast number of different parties as it spread across India, left-wing extremism has continued to haunt the eastern half of India to the present.[120] The two most prominent militant factions to emerge from the insurgency in the eighties were the Maoist Communist Centre (MCC) and the People's War Group (PWG); the former operated in areas near Nepal and the latter, as noted previously in this chapter, was associated with the southern states of Andhra Pradesh and Telangana. These two parties merged in 2004 to form the Communist Party of India (Maoist), the largest insurgency group operating in India.[121] A third faction, which had split off from the CPI(M-L), the "CPI(M-L) Liberation," has returned to parliamentary politics.

By the 2000s in West Bengal, the CPI (Maoist) had emerged in 18 districts. The Maoists were particularly active in the Nandigram and Singur land acquisition protests that brought down the CPI(M) and paved the way for the AITC. Banerjee was accused of working alongside the CPI (Maoists) in these protests; however, the Maoists would eventually turn on the AITC once the latter came to power.[122] In recent years, the AITC has sought to 1) create an elite police force to pursue insurgents; 2) incentivize left-wing insurgents to surrender by enrolling them in a "special home guard" and providing financial incentives, housing, medical, and child education; and 3) create confidence-building measures in "Maoist-infested" districts. Since 2014, there have been almost no deaths from incidents of insurgent violence in West Bengal—this is in sharp contrast from 2010 when 425 deaths (328 of which were civilians) occurred from left-wing extremist violence.[123] The BJP, however, has accused the AITC of "sheltering" the Naxalites.[124]

While security and secessionist concerns have both been brought under control, the AITC still has not charted a way forward for attracting investment, increasing employment, and helping youth to acquire the skills necessary to propel the economy forward. The AITC has destroyed the CPI(M) but also become no better than their old foe in terms of corruption and thuggery. Meanwhile, the BJP has coalesced into a formidable opposition within the state. Surprisingly, while the BJP could have exploited the Gorkhaland protests in 2017 to create a separate state, it chose not to do so. Now, having lost its Gorkha allies and fearing defections after seven members of the West Bengal Legislative Assembly switched parties or resigned following the 2021 elections, the BJP is under pressure again to grant statehood to the Gorkhas.[125]

JAMMU AND KASHMIR AND THE LIMITS OF ASYMMETRIC FEDERALISM

Unlike the federal states in which the struggle for power between the center and regional parties is very much constantly in play, the politics of Jammu and Kashmir highlight the potential and limits of the central government's asymmetric power—and, in the extreme, its ability to impose its will on states.

A unified Indian national state was an unprecedented achievement when it came into being, with some caveats, in the decolonization and Partition of August 1947. But from India's postcolonial beginnings, there were also gaps on the map,[126] reflecting historical developments and the circumstances of Britain's hasty exit. The former "princely state" of Jammu and Kashmir, often referred to simply as Kashmir, is at the heart of India's enduring conflict with Pakistan (see the foreign policy chapter). It also presents an essential and unique challenge to the Indian national state and its intermixture of federal and unitary elements.

At Independence in 1947, the princely state of Jammu and Kashmir (J&K) was ruled by a Hindu monarch, Maharajah Hari Singh. The state's population was (and still is) majority Muslim, but with subregional concentrations of Hindus (in the Jammu area) and Buddhists (in Ladakh), as well as smaller communities of Sikhs, Christians, and others. The maharajah, who desired independence and sovereignty for the kingdom, initially acceded neither to India nor Pakistan as they negotiated to incorporate British India's nearly 600 other princely states. (Most of these were much smaller than J&K; another significant and sizeable holdout was Hyderabad in the central south, encompassing present-day Telangana state and parts of neighboring Karnataka and Maharashtra.) Two months after Independence, when confronted with Pashtun tribal forces from the west (backed by Pakistan), the unsettled monarch signed an Instrument of Accession to join the Indian union, which India demanded as a condition for providing security assistance. By October, India and Pakistan were fighting their first war, and the conflict soon became internationalized at the new United Nations. India and Pakistan both claim the entirety of the former princely state. Since 1949, they have administered portions on their respective sides of a UN ceasefire line, later recharacterized as the Line of Control in the bilateral Simla Agreement of December 1971. Pakistan controls the northwestern one-third of the territory and India most of the remaining two-thirds, including Srinagar and the

Kashmir Valley or "Vale." In a separate dispute, China controls an eastern part of Kashmir called Aksai Chin, which India claims as part of Ladakh.

India has sought to govern J&K with a view to delegitimizing Pakistan's claim to the territory on the basis of religious identity, as it is (or rather, was) India's only majority-Muslim state. Until 2019, India's Constitution under Article 370 granted J&K a special semi-autonomous status, unique even among the other "special category" states (those designated until 2015 by the National Development Council to receive special development support, in view of geographic and socio-economic disadvantages). J&K had its own state constitution, its own flag, and for a period, even its own prime minister (until 1965, when the position became chief minister, in keeping with other Indian states). The state's special status gave it "the privilege of not having any Indian law automatically applicable to its territory," since "Indian laws had to be specifically permitted by its [Legislative] Assembly" (Nagaland enjoys similar but more limited privileges, under the Constitution's Article 371).[127] Further, under the Constitution's separate Article 35A, only permanent residents of J&K could own real estate therein—a potent territorial symbol of the state's being set apart from the rest of India.

But the central government also imposed President's Rule several times and blatantly interfered in the state's elections, giving rise to a Kashmiri insurgency beginning in the late 1980s.[128] India maintains a massive security presence in J&K, and its forces allegedly have committed human rights abuses including rape, torture, and extra-judicial killings. In 2016, the deadly cycle of insurgency by disaffected Kashmiris and the repression by Indian forces intensified further, marking a bitter new phase. The precipitating event was the killing of a young militant named Burhan Wani in a shootout with police. Thousands attended the funeral for this "freedom fighter" folk hero, a "young, social-media-savvy separatist" who had posted photos and videos online while in hiding from the security forces.[129]

The BJP's election platforms long have decried J&K's special status, lumping it in with other issues involving what it calls "pseudo-secular" Nehruvian state institutions, such as the separate civil code for Muslim marriage and family matters. On August 5, 2019—less than three months after the BJP's decisive victory in India's general election—the Modi government delivered on the party's promise to nullify Articles 35A and 370 and thereby strip J&K of its special status. Jammu and Kashmir was split into two union territories (UTs), with one UT retaining the J&K name and a locally elected legislative assembly, albeit with drastically curtailed powers, and the other established for the state's distinctive subregion of Ladakh, to be administered by New Delhi directly. Just before the government's unilateral announcement, additional security forces flooded into the state, tourists (mostly Indian) were evacuated, phone and internet services were cut off, and journalists were prevented from reporting. Around 7 million Kashmiris were confined to their homes: the world's largest detention, imposed by the world's largest democracy. The Modi government swiftly secured Parliament's approval for the unprecedented action of demoting an Indian state to a union territory,[130] and the move was generally popular in the rest of India.

As Modi has done in other contexts, he sought to frame the draconian unilateral action as really being about the promotion of economic development. In a national address to explain the abrogation of Article 370, he invited tourism, filmmaking, and industrial investment in the new J&K and

Ladakh. The writer Arundhati Roy, a frequent critic of the Indian state, warned that Kashmir "being open for business" meant for Kashmiris "being swept away by a tidal wave of triumphant Indians wanting a little home in their sylvan valley."[131] Conversely, Pratap Bhanu Mehta, a prominent political scientist, suggested that the BJP's move to impose the central government's writ on Kashmir could portend the "Kashmirization of India" writ large. He explained, "There are times in the history of a republic when it reduces itself to jackboot. Nothing more and nothing less. We are witnessing that moment in Kashmir. But this moment is also a dry run for the political desecration that may follow in the rest of India. This is a state for whom the only currency that matters is raw power."[132]

These stark assessments should be kept in perspective. It is precisely India's massive security presence in Kashmir, which the government does not (and could not) deploy across a larger number of states, that has enabled it to impose an unprecedented change in what was, in any case, a uniquely asymmetrical arrangement under Article 370. As scholar Sumantra Bose explains, Article 370 originally was not intended to be a permanent arrangement. Lord Louis Mountbatten, the last British viceroy and India's first governor general, said in accepting Singh's signature on the Instrument of Accession that the monarch's decision should be ratified by the people of Kashmir through a plebiscite or referendum, offering the choice to join either India or Pakistan. Prime Minister Nehru also accepted this commitment and spoke of it on several occasions into the early 1950s. The article basically limited the central government's jurisdiction to external defense, foreign policy, and currency and essential communications—not unlike the agreements British India had held with the hundreds of princely states.

But over time, though Article 370 survived "on paper," it became "increasingly hollowed out and irrelevant," in Bose's characterization, as the central government sought to integrate J&K into the Indian union as a normal state, albeit with what Bose calls "symbolic tokens of autonomy," even as it imposed repression backed by the heavy security force presence. Thus, the 2019 abrogation of Article 370, while symbolically important, ultimately may have fewer practical consequences than the Modi government's other moves, namely the simultaneous scrapping of Article 35A (on land ownership rights) and the "dismembering" and "abolishing" of the state in favor of the two new union territories.[133]

Nor is it clear that the Kashmir issue resonates deeply with Indian voters beyond the BJP's most devotedly nationalist base. Particularly in the south, even those who are paying attention to Kashmir may be most interested in how its representation and share of central tax revenues could impact their states. Critiquing a recent proposal by a central commission to increase the Jammu subregion's seat share in J&K's legislative assembly (a transparent effort to empower Hindu and pro-India voters) and imagining that the BJP may seek to do the same in the Lok Sabha if it wins the 2024 general election, one analyst warned, "This over-centralized approach of the BJP can, in the long run, trigger strong anti-New Delhi emotions in some southern states and lead to Balkanisation of the mind in parts outside of Kashmir."[134]

In any case, that the aftershocks of the Modi government's moves in 2019 could well run in both directions—with Indian central government policy changing Kashmir, and developments in Kashmir carrying broader implications for India's state and society—says much about the unique but central role of Kashmir in India's political development.

NOTES

1 The Economist, "How to Run a Continent," *The Economist*, May 21, 2015.
2 Baldev Raj Nayar, *The Myth of the Shrinking State: Globalization and the State in India*. (New Delhi: Oxford University Press, 2009).
3 Jaffrelot, *Modi's India*, 90.
4 Anilesh S. Mahajan, "Assembly Election Results 2021: Lessons for the BJP," *India Today*, May 17, 2021.
5 The "All India" element of the party's full name is usually omitted, and is misleading: the TMC is active mainly in West Bengal and has a scattered presence in not more than half a dozen other states.
6 Sandipan Deb, "The Triumph of 'Bengali Pride' and the BJP's Mistakes," *Mint*, May 4, 2021, sec. Opinion, https://www.livemint.com/opinion/columns/the-triumph-of-bengali-pride-and-the-bjp-s-mistakes-11620072906394.html.
7 Jonathan Evans, "In India, Hindu Support for Modi's Party Varies by Region and Is Tied to Beliefs about Diet and Language," *Pew Research Center* (blog), August 5, 2021, https://www.pewresearch.org/fact-tank/2021/08/05/in-india-hindu-support-for-modis-party-varies-by-region-and-is-tied-to-beliefs-about-diet-and-language/.
8 Nitin Sethi, "Electoral Bonds: Seeking Secretive Funds, Modi Govt Overruled RBI," *HuffPost*, November 17, 2019, sec. News, https://www.huffingtonpost.in/entry/rbi-warned-electoral-bonds-arun-jaitley-black-money-modi-government_in_5dcbde68e4b0d43931ccd200.
9 Virginia Van Dyke, "State-Level Politics, Coalitions, and Rapid System Change in India," in *Routledge Handbook of South Asian Politics: India, Pakistan, Bangladesh, Sri Lanka, and Nepal*, ed. Paul Brass (New York: Routledge, 2010), 67.
10 Rekha Diwakar, "The Origins and Consequences of Regional Parties and Subnationalism in India," *India Review* 20, no. 1 (January 1, 2021): 68–95, https://doi.org/10.1080/14736489.2021.1875701.
11 Nidhi Sethi, "5 Reasons Why Chandrababu Naidu Exited NDA Government," *NDTV.Com*, March 16, 2018, https://www.ndtv.com/andhra-pradesh-news/5-reasons-why-chandrababu-naidu-pulled-out-of-nda-government-1824561.
12 M.D. Illyas, "Survey Finds Andhra Pradesh Did Better in GSDP Growth Compared to India," *Deccan Chronicle*, May 20, 2021, sec. Current Affairs.
13 Arvind Panagariya and M. Govinda Rao, eds., *The Making of Miracles in Indian States: Andhra Pradesh, Bihar, and Gujarat* (Oxford University Press, 2015), https://doi.org/10.1093/acprof:oso/9780190236625.001.0001.
14 Atul Kohli, "The NTR Phenomenon in Andhra Pradesh: Political Change in a South Indian State," *Asian Survey* 28, no. 10 (1988): 992, https://doi.org/10.2307/2644703.

15 For a detailed discussion of the state's complex caste dynamics, see K. Srinivasulu and Overseas Development Institute, *Caste, Class and Social Articulation in Andhra Pradesh: Mapping Differential Regional Trajectories* (London: ODI, 2002). For discussions that give particular attention to the caste context behind the Telangana movement, see Gautam Pingle, "Reddys, Kammas and Telangana," *Economic and Political Weekly* Vol. X LVI, No. 46 (September 3, 2011): 19–21, and N. Purendra Prasad, "Agrarian Class and Caste Relations in 'United' Andhra Pradesh, 1956–2014," *Economic and Political Weekly* 50, no. 16 (2015): 77–83.

16 Abheek Barman, "Congress' Andhra Pradesh Policy Includes Weighing of Caste Equations," *The Economic Times*, November 22, 2013. According to a 2010 report by a committee convened by the central government to study the Telangana statehood case, from 1956 to 1980, the Reddy caste accounted for 26% of state cabinet positions in successive governments, compared to 8% for Kammas, 7% for Brahmins, and 28% for Kapus and all the various Other Backward Classes; cited in Pingle, "Reddys, Kammas and Telangana," 19.

17 Kohli, "The NTR Phenomenon in Andhra Pradesh," 992.

18 Jos Mooij, "Hype, Skill and Class: The Politics of Reform in Andhra Pradesh, India," *Commonwealth & Comparative Politics* 45, no. 1 (February 2007): 34–56, https://doi.org/10.1080/14662040601135771. See also Rob Jenkins, *Democracy and Economic Reform in India* (Cambridge, UK: Cambridge University Press, 2000).

19 Mudit Kapoor and Rahul Ahluwalia, "Part I: Andhra Pradesh," in *The Making of Miracles in Indian States*, ed. Arvind Panagariya and M. Govinda Rao (New York: Oxford University Press, 2015), 27.

20 Kapoor and Ahluwalia, 25.

21 Cited in Pingle, "Reddys, Kammas and Telangana," 19.

22 Deepthi Reddy, "Telangana Statehood: A Timeline of Events," *The Hans India*, May 31, 2018, https://www.thehansindia.com/posts/index/Latest-News/2018-05-31/Telangana-statehood-A-timeline-of-events/385650.

23 Reddy rejoined the INC in 2018, as the national party under Rahul Gandhi sought to rehabilitate its organization in AP.

24 Louise Tillin, "Statehood and the Politics of Intent," *Economic and Political Weekly* 46, no. 20 (2011): 34–38. See also Louise Tillin, *Remapping India: New States and Their Political Origins* (London: Hurst & Company, 2013).

25 Tillin, "Statehood and the Politics of Intent," 36.

26 Sandeep Unnithan, "Majority of the Maoist Leadership Hail from a Single District of Telangana, a Legacy That Haunts Its Demand for Statehood,"

India Today, July 29, 2013, https://www.indiatoday.in/magazine/india/telangana/story/20130729-maoist-leadership-hails-from-a-single-district-of-telangana-764751-1999-11-30.

27 Niranjan Sahoo, "From Bihar to Andhra, How India Fought, and Won, Its 50-Yr War with Left-Wing Extremism," *The Print*, June 26, 2019, https://theprint.in/opinion/from-bihar-to-andhra-how-india-fought-and-won-its-50-yr-war-with-left-wing-extremism/254462/.

28 Sumana Ramanan, "Why the Creation of Telangana Offers Maoists New Opportunities," *Scroll.In*, March 18, 2014, http://scroll.in/article/658486/why-the-creation-of-telangana-offers-maoists-new-opportunities.

29 Unnithan, "Majority of the Maoist Leadership."

30 Ramanan, "Why the Creation of Telangana Offers Maoists New Opportunities."

31 Rohini Swamy, "In Telangana, Naxal Poet Gaddar Embraces the Ballot & Old Foes to Fight 'Fundamentalists,'" *The Print*, December 4, 2018, https://theprint.in/politics/in-telangana-naxal-poet-gaddar-embraces-the-ballot-old-foes-to-fight-fundamentalists/157909/.

32 See Sruthisagar Yamunan, "They Gave up Farmland for New Andhra Capital. Now They Are Crippled with Uncertainty," *Scroll.In*, February 6, 2020, https://scroll.in/article/951454/they-gave-up-farmland-for-new-andhra-capital-now-they-are-crippled-with-uncertainty; Rohini Mohan, *Amaravati: The Price of a Dream City*, YouTube video, The News Minute, 2017.

33 On the "before" phase, see Sanam Roohi, "Anticipating Future Capital: Regional Caste Contestations, Speculation and Silent Dispossession in Andhra Pradesh," *Journal of Contemporary Asia* 50, no. 5 (n.d.): 723–42.; on the "after" phase, see C. Ramachandraiah, "Making of Amaravati: A Landscape of Speculation and Intimidation," *Economic and Political Weekly* 51, no. 17 (April 23, 2016): 68–75.

34 Venkatsha Babu, "Five Reasons Why Jagan Reddy Scuttled Amaravati as Andhra Pradesh's Capital," *Hindustan Times*, January 20, 2020, https://www.hindustantimes.com/opinion/five-reasons-why-jagan-reddy-scuttled-amaravati-as-andhra-pradesh-s-capital-opinion/story-5qepGlkZ4So2evcg9ihKBP.html.

35 According to "GDP Growth of Andhra Pradesh" data from the Ministry of Statistics and Programme Implementation, Government of India.

36 Planning Department, "Socio-Economic Survey 2016–17," Annex 9.1 (Government of Andhra Pradesh, 2017). The first figures combine rural and urban poverty. The 1990s rate is as per the Tendulkar Committee Report methodology, and the 2016 rate is as per the Lakdawala Methodology, which calculates state-specific poverty lines. For a detailed discussion of methods of

measuring poverty in India, see C. Rangarajan and S. Mahendra Dev, "Poverty in India: Measurement, Trends and Other Issues" (Mumbai: Indira Gandhi Institute of Development Research, December 2020), http://www.igidr.ac.in/pdf/publication/WP-2020-038.pdf.

37 Seyed Hossein Zarhani, *Governance and Development in India: A Comparative Study on Andhra Pradesh and Bihar after Liberalization* (London; New York: Routledge, 2019).

38 Srinivasa Rao Apparasu, "After BJP Promises Special Status to Puducherry, Demands Rise for Andhra Pradesh," *Hindustan Times*, April 1, 2021.

39 Yamunan, "They Gave up Farmland for New Andhra Capital."

40 IBEF, "Bihar," PowerPoint, India Brand Equity Foundation, March 2021, 3, https://www.ibef.org/download/Bihar-March-2021.pdf.

41 World Bank, "Banks and Community Institutions Partner to Create an Ecosystem for Sustainable Financial Inclusion in Bihar, India," Text/HTML, World Bank, March 27, 2013, https://www.worldbank.org/en/news/feature/2013/03/27/banks-community-institutions-partner-create-sustainable-financial-inclusion-bihar-india.

42 Diwakar, "The Origins and Consequences of Regional Parties and Subnationalism in India," 71.

43 Diwakar, 72.

44 Prerna Singh, "Subnationalism and Social Development: A Comparative Analysis of Indian States," *World Politics* 67, no. 3 (2015): 551 (fn.#165).

45 Times of India, "Bihar Diwas at Pragati Maidan on Mar 22," *Times of India*, February 21, 2010.

46 Arun Kumar, "Bihar Plans Statewide Celebrations to Mark Its Economic Revival," *Hindustan Times*, March 16, 2010.

47 Prerna Singh, *How Solidarity Works for Welfare: Subnationalism and Social Development in India*, Cambridge Studies in Comparative Politics (Cambridge: Cambridge University Press, 2015), 187–89.

48 Sayan Banerjee and Charles R. Hankla, "Party Systems and Public Goods: The Dynamics of Good Governance in the Indian States," *India Review* 19, no. 5 (October 19, 2020): 513–14, https://doi.org/10.1080/14736489.2020.1855015.

49 Banerjee and Hankla, 514.

50 Banerjee and Hankla, 514.

51 Arvind N. Das, *The Republic of Bihar* (New Delhi; New York: Penguin Books, 1992); Ashutosh Kumar, "Development Focus and Electoral Success at State Level: Nitish Kumar as Bihar's Leader," *South Asia Research* 33, no. 2 (July 1, 2013): 106, https://doi.org/10.1177/0262728013487630.

52 Kumar, "Development Focus and Electoral Success at State Level," 108.
53 Panagariya and Rao, *The Making of Miracles in Indian States*, 132–33.
54 Panagariya and Rao, 134.
55 Panagariya and Rao, 136–38.
56 Panagariya and Rao, 135.
57 Panagariya and Rao, 135.
58 Kumar, "Development Focus and Electoral Success at State Level," 109.
59 Ruchir Sharma, "The Rise of the Rest of India: How States Have Become the Engines of Growth," *Foreign Affairs* 92, no. 5 (2013): 79.
60 Rohan Mukherjee, "Clearing the Jungle Raj: Bihar State, India, 2005–2009," Innovations for Successful Societies (Princeton, N.J.: Princeton University, 2011), 1, 4–5.
61 Kumar, "Development Focus and Electoral Success at State Level," 109–10.
62 Mukherjee, "Clearing the Jungle Raj: Bihar State, India, 2005–2009," 5–7.
63 Rajiv Verma, Saurabh Gupta, and Regina Birner, "Can Vigilance-focused Governance Reforms Improve Service Delivery? The Case of Integrated Child Development Services (ICDS) in Bihar, India," *Development Policy Review* 36 (September 2, 2018): O786–802.
64 Panagariya and Rao, *The Making of Miracles in Indian States*, 176–81.
65 Mukherjee, "Clearing the Jungle Raj," 8.
66 Panagariya and Rao, *The Making of Miracles in Indian States*, 146.
67 Sahoo, "From Bihar to Andhra"; H. K. Verma, "Rajnath Lauds Nitish Govt for Tackling Left-Wing Extremism," *The Times of India*, 2018.
68 Sahoo, "From Bihar to Andhra."
69 Panagariya and Rao, *The Making of Miracles in Indian States*, 174.
70 Juliette John, Rushda Majeed, and Pallavi Nuka, "Modernizing the State, Connecting to the People: Bihar, India, 2005–2012," Innovations for Successful Societies (Princeton, N.J.: Princeton University, 2015), 2.
71 Kumar, "Development Focus and Electoral Success at State Level," 110–11; World Bank, "World Bank to Support Bihar Government's Initiative to Rebuild Flood-Affected Areas with $220 Million," Text/HTML, World Bank, January 12, 2011, https://www.worldbank.org/en/news/press-release/2011/01/12/world-bank-to-support-bihar-governments-initiative-to-rebuild-flood-affected-areas-with-220-million.
72 World Bank, "World Bank Maps," Database, World Bank Maps, 2021, https://maps.worldbank.org/#.
73 World Bank and Ernesto Sanchez-Triana, "Bihar Social and Environmental Analysis Concept Note," Concept Note, Bihar State Social and Environmental

Analysis (Washington, DC: World Bank), 1, accessed July 7, 2021, https://documents1.worldbank.org/curated/en/718661468040753838/text/698510ES WoP1050t0Note0SanchezTriana.txt.

74 World Bank and Sanchez-Triana, 6.
75 Panagariya and Rao, *The Making of Miracles in Indian States*, 171–72.
76 Panagariya and Rao, 171–72.
77 Awanish Kumar, "Nitish Kumar's Honourable Exit: A Brief History of Caste Politics," *Economic and Political Weekly* 48, no. 28 (2013): 15–17.
78 Anju Grover, "BJP's Doublespeak on Caste Census: Manoj Jha," *India Currents*, August 30, 2021.
79 Kumar, "Development Focus and Electoral Success at State Level," 112.
80 Bhavdeep Kang, "Is the JD(U)-BJP Honeymoon in Bihar Over," *Free Press Journal*, August 5, 2021, Mumbai, India edition.
81 Stuart Corbridge, John Harriss, and Craig Jeffrey, *India Today: Economy, Politics and Society*, Politics Today (Cambridge, UK; Malden, MA: Polity Press, 2013), 132–33; Abhijit Banerjee, "Food for Thought: Parties Should Reward Their Foot Soldiers Amply," *Hindustan Times*, January 1, 2015.
82 Corbridge, Harriss, and Jeffrey, *India Today*, 168–76.
83 Atul Kohli, *Poverty Amid Plenty in the New India* (Cambridge; New York: Cambridge University Press, 2012), 194.
84 Kohli, 193.
85 For a brief history of West Bengal's political economy, see: Suvojit Bagchi, "Bengal through the Decades: The More Things Change, Have They Stayed the Same?," Occasional Paper (New Delhi, India: Observer Research Foundation, April 2021).
86 Mihir Sharma, "The Change That Bengal Needs," *Indian Express*, May 21, 2011.
87 Kohli, *Poverty Amid Plenty in the New India*, 192–209.
88 Joydeep Thakur, "Jobs, Subsidised Food in Mamata Manifesto," *Hindustan Times*, March 18, 2021.
89 Crabtree, *The Billionaire Raj*, 181.
90 IANS, "Saradha Scam: Salaries Paid from CM Relief Fund, Says CBI," *Business Standard*, December 27, 2020.
91 Atri Mitra and G. Ananthakrishnan, "Saradha Scam: CBI Plea in SC on Mamata Govt 'Links', Says It Is Scuttling Probe," *Indian Express*, December 27, 2020.
92 Madhuparna Das, "Mamata Govt Now in Trouble Over Amphan Relief 'Scam', After Cut-Money and PDS Corruption," *The Print*, June 30, 2020, https://theprint.in/india/mamata-govt-now-in-trouble-over-amphan-relief-scam-after-cut-money-and-pds-corruption/451774/.

93 PTI, "'Cut Money Means Chief Minister': Opposition Leaders' Protest On 'Scam,'" *NDTV.Com*, June 24, 2019; Times Now, "Fresh ED Summons to Mamata Banerjee's Nephew for Questioning in Coal Scam," *Times Now*, September 11, 2021.

94 Hindustan Times, "'He's Still Alive': TMC Justifies Assault on Slapper," *Hindustan Times*, January 6, 2015.

95 Hindustan Times, "Mamata's Nephew Slapped, TMC Sees BJP Hand," *The Hindustan Times*, January 5, 2015.

96 Santu Chowdhury, "Modi Targets Mamata: TMC Game of Corruption Over, Time for Real Change," *Indian Express*, March 8, 2021.

97 Indian Express, "This Puja, BJP Thinking of Slain Workers: Dilip Ghosh," *Indian Express*, October 10, 2021.

98 Jaffrelot, *Modi's India*, 315–17, 342.

99 ANI, "Mamata Banerjee Promises to Ensure Safety, Education for All," *Asian News International*, April 4, 2021.

100 ANI.

101 Chowdhury, "Modi Targets Mamata."

102 Pralay Kanungo, "The Rise of the Bharatiya Janata Party in West Bengal," ed. Christophe Jaffrelot, *Studies in Indian Politics* 3, no. 1 (2015): 51, https://doi.org/10.1177/2321023015575213.

103 Kanungo, 52.

104 Kanungo, 53.

105 Kanungo, 56.

106 Kanungo, 57.

107 Bagchi, "Bengal through the Decades," 6.

108 State Government of West Bengal, "Bengal Surges Ahead—Agriculture," West Bengal Agriculture Department, January 2021, https://wb.gov.in/departments-details.aspx?id=D170907140022669&page=Agriculture.

109 Bagchi, "Bengal through the Decades," 8.

110 Bagchi, 8.

111 ANI, "Mamata Banerjee Promises to Ensure Safety, Education for All."

112 Indian Express, "Mamata to Give Rs 10k to Students Ahead of Polls; Here's What Her Counterparts Announced in Their States," *Indian Express*, December 23, 2020.

113 Debarati Sen, "Subnational Enterprise: Militarized Mothering, Women's Entrepreneurial Labour and Generational Dynamics in the Gorkhaland Struggle," *Journal of South Asian Development* 15, no. 3 (2020): 317, https://doi.org/10.1177/0973174120987094.

114 Miriam Wenner, "Trajectories of Hybrid Governance: Legitimacy, Order and Leadership in India," *Development and Change* 52, no. 2 (2021): 281, https://doi.org/10.1111/dech.12624.

115 Jayatri Nag, "Chaos Reigns in GJM as Top Leaders Float Own Parties," *The Economic Times*, August 28, 2021.

116 Vivek Chhetri, "Gorkhaland No Poll Plank," *The Telegraph*, December 27, 2020.

117 Vasudha Venugopal, "With Shah's Visit, BJP Hopes to Boost North Bengal Tally," *The Economic Times*, April 12, 2021.

118 Sen, "Subnational Enterprise," 317, 320.

119 Pritha Sarkar, "Patriarchy, 20th Century Bengal and the Naxalbari Movement: Tracing the Roots through Lives of Others," *Journal of International Women's Studies* 22, no. 9 (2021): 161.

120 Paul Staniland, "Leftist Insurgency in Democracies," *Comparative Political Studies* 54, no. 3-4 (2020 2021): 536-37, https://doi.org/10.1177/0010414020938096.

121 Siddharthya Roy, "Half a Century of India's Maoist Insurgency," *The Diplomat* (Tokyo: Tribune Content Agency LLC, September 2017).

122 Sahoo, "From Bihar to Andhra."

123 Bikash Singh, "Mamata Banerjee Claims Achievement in Dealing with Naxalites," *Economic Times*, May 2, 2017; Sahoo, "From Bihar to Andhra."

124 Namrata Agarwal, "Mamata Banerjee Providing Protection to Terrorists, Naxalites in West Bengal: Kailash Vijayvargiya," *Zee News*, September 28, 2020.

125 Indian Express, "Bypoll Wins Bolster TMC Strength in Bengal Assembly; Mamata Eyes 2024 with Return of 'Prodigal Sons', Import of New Faces," *Indian Express*, October 5, 2021.

126 In the case of Jammu and Kashmir, this literally was true; see Riley D. Champine, "The 'Cartographic Nightmare' of the Kashmir Region Explained," *National Geographic*, February 2021, https://www.nationalgeographic.com/magazine/graphics/the-cartographic-nightmare-of-the-kashmir-region-explained-feature.

127 K. Venkataramanan, "Explained: India's Asymmetric Federalism," *The Hindu*, August 11, 2019, sec. National, https://www.thehindu.com/news/national/the-forms-of-federalism-in-india/article28977671.ece.

128 For a recent authoritative history, see Sumantra Bose, *Kashmir at the Crossroads: Inside a 21st Century Conflict* (New Haven: Yale University Press, 2021).

129 Annie Gowen, "Indian Kashmir Suffers Worst Violence in Years after Militant Leader's Death," *Washington Post*, July 12, 2016, sec. Asia & Pacific,

https://www.washingtonpost.com/world/asia_pacific/indian-held-kashmir-suffers-worst-violence-in-years-after-militant-leaders-death/2016/07/12/c44ed4b8-482a-11e6-8dac-0c6e4accc5b1_story.html.

130 For a comparison of the new union territory of Jammu and Kashmir to the unique contexts and origins of three other UTs—Delhi, Chandigarh, and Puducherry—and a general discussion of the "union territory model" in India's quasi-federal system, see Rekha Saxena, "Constitutional Asymmetry in Indian Federalism," *Economic and Political Weekly* 56, no. 34 (June 5, 2015): 7–8.

131 Arundhati Roy, "Opinion | The Silence Is the Loudest Sound," *New York Times*, August 15, 2019, https://www.nytimes.com/2019/08/15/opinion/sunday/kashmir-siege-modi.html.

132 Pratap Bhanu Mehta, "The Story of Indian Democracy Written in Blood and Betrayal," *Indian Express* (blog), August 8, 2019, https://indianexpress.com/article/opinion/columns/jammu-kashmir-article-370-scrapped-special-status-amit-shah-narendra-modi-bjp-5880797/.

133 Nicholas Gordon, "'Sumantra Bose, "Kashmir at the Crossroads: Inside a 21st-Century Conflict" (Yale UP, 2021)'," *New Books in South Asian Studies* (podcast), January 13, 2022, newbooksnetwork.com.

134 Saba Naqvi, "Delimitation Double Standards: One Rule for J&K, Another for South India," Deccan Herald, December 24, 2021, https://www.deccanherald.com/opinion/delimitation-double-standards-one-rule-for-jk-another-for-south-india-1064017.html.

SUGGESTED FURTHER READING

Bose, Sumantra, *Kashmir at the Crossroads: Inside a 21st-Century Conflict* (Yale University Press, 2021). ISBN: 978-80300256871

Mitra, Subrata and Harihar Bhattacharyya, *Politics and Governance in Indian States: Bihar, West Bengal and Tripura* (World Scientific Publishing Co Pte Ltd, 2018). ISBN: 978-9813208223.

Singh, Prerna, *How Solidarity Works for Welfare: Subnationalism and Social Development in India* (Cambridge University Press, 2015). ISBN: 978-1107697454.

Swaminathan, Siddharth, and Suhas Palshikar, editors, *Politics and Society between Elections: Public Opinion in India's States* (Routledge India, 2020). ISBN: 978-1003120483.

Vaishnav, Milan, *When Crime Pays: Money and Muscle in Indian Politics* (Yale University Press, 2017). ISBN: 978-0300216202.

Zarhani, Seyed Hossein, *Governance and Development in India: A Comparative Study on Andhra Pradesh and Bihar After Liberalization* (Routledge, 2019). ISBN: 978-8153-6831-1.

CHAPTER THREE

AN ECONOMIC OVERVIEW

INTRODUCTION

India, which began its lurching transition from a quasi-socialist/autarchic system to a free market/globally integrated economy (arguably) four decades ago, is currently best characterized as possessing a crony-capitalist economic structure with an expansive but weak regulatory state. The state and politicians are oriented toward a "pro-business" posture[1] rather than either a "state-led" or a "pro-market" outlook. In other words, the state seeks to enhance economic growth of large private firms with ties to politicians and political parties rather than either discipline and guide firms in the manner of an idealized developmental state (e.g., Japan) or enforce the neutral rules characteristic of a vigorously competitive market arena in an idealized liberal state (e.g., the United States). Even if the Indian state possessed the will and wisdom to either govern the market or enforce a competitive market, the state lacks the capacity to enforce its rules effectively and efficiently. Corruption, opportunism, and incompetence gnaw away at the ability of the state to either provide tutelary guidance or enforce uniform rules in the marketplace. While the quasi-socialist/autarchic era has receded in the rear-view mirror, India has yet to arrive at the destination of a competitive free market/globally integrated economy.

Thus, large, family-owned, rent-seeking[2] conglomerates dominate the formal economy alongside lumbering state-owned enterprises (the relics of the quasi-socialist era), and a few foreign joint-venture firms in the formal sector. Naturally, in a crony-capitalist context, there is a strong nexus between the rent-seeking conglomerates, politicians, and the regulatory state. In other words, although India's economy is conventionally understood as capitalist,[3] it is not characterized by firms that compete primarily on productivity and innovation. Rather, links to politicians forged through campaign contributions in exchange for access to state permitted areas of economic activity are crucial for many firms in the formal economy seeking a competitive advantage. Of course, these family-owned firms use a veneer of professional management to disguise their convoluted governance structures, shell firms, shady deals, and the use of political favors to hamstring competitors, evade accountability, or gain a first-mover advantage.[4]

Meanwhile political entrepreneurs, operating in the context of a vibrant democratic republic, have perfected the art of exchanging votes for patronage (e.g., government employment, access to supposedly universal welfare services, in-kind payments, or just cash) from ever shifting "vote banks" of the aspiring classes; and large campaign contributions for access to rents or political favors from wealthy businessmen.[5] An increasing portion of political entrepreneurs have also become businessmen themselves and vice versa in order to cut out the middleman.[6]

Despite its corruption and dysfunction, India has become one of the fastest growing emerging markets in the world. The growth acceleration started in the 1980s, a period of deregulation that preceded economic liberalization. Since 1991, India has managed to achieve on average above 6% annual growth in its real (i.e., accounting for inflation) gross domestic product (GDP).[7] Even as late as April 2021, the IMF was predicting that India's GDP would grow at

12.5%, surpassing China for 2021. However, the mismanagement of the second wave of the COVID-19 pandemic has severely impacted growth and damaged the economy.

Thus, although major development and pandemic-related challenges remain, India is a rising market economy. The World Bank has classified India as a "lower middle-income" country since 2009. The 47 lower middle-income countries had an average annual gross national income (GNI) per capita of $1,026 to $3,995 in 2020. In other words, India with an annual GNI/per capita of $2,120 (in 2019)[8] is no longer a poor country in relative terms, but it still has a long way to go before it is re-classified as an upper middle-income country.[9]

In 2021, India's economy constitutes 7.19% of the World's GDP in terms of purchasing power parity (PPP).[10] India ranks third after China (18.78%) and the United States (15.97%).[11] Indian firms are also well integrated into global value chains (GVCs), particularly in business services. However, as global market integration has stalled in recent years, India's level of integration with GVCs has declined.

DEMOGRAPHICS

Much of India's heft in the global economy is a function of its demography. In a few short years, India will surpass China for the largest population.[12] India's population is already larger than the population of every other continent except for Asia. Thus, India should be mentally conceptualized not as a statistical outlier or even as just a part of the South Asian sub-continent, but as a continent all its own. India's population constitutes 18% of humanity. Its larger federal states have a greater population than most of the countries in the world.

India also has a young population, particularly in comparison to high-income countries. Only 6% of the population was over age 65 in 2019 compared to 16% for the United States, 20% for the EU, and 28% for Japan. Children aged 0–14 made up just over a quarter of the population (26.6%) in India; while those aged 15–64 constitute 67% of the population.[13] Although this distribution implies that a large number of young workers can help to support a small elderly population; it also means that India needs to create a massive number of jobs each year.

According the consulting firm McKinsey & Company, India will need to create between 90 million to 145 million non-farm jobs by 2030 to absorb 60 million new workers and 30 million farm workers transitioning out of the agricultural sector as well as 55 million women potentially joining the formal labor force. McKinsey argues that after the COVID-19 crisis, India's real GDP will need to grow at 8% to 8.5% annually and create 12 million gainful non-farm jobs annually.[14] It is worth noting that India only created 4 million non-farm jobs annually between 2012 and 2018 and its economy was stalling and weakening before the COVID-19 pandemic.[15]

POVERTY

Despite the overall rise of the national economy to middle-income status, India still contains one of the largest concentrations of extremely poor individuals in the world. In April 2017, the most recent year for which reliable data is available, there were between 109 million to 152 million people living below the international poverty line (defined as living with less than the purchasing power of US$1.90 [in 2011] per day per person for all consumption items, e.g., food, housing, clothing, etc.).[16] Using India's national poverty line, there were 273 million poor in 2011 or 21.9% of the population.[17]

Beyond the extremely poor, it is worth noting that in 2015 approximately 660 million people or 50% of the population lived on less than the purchasing power of $3.20 per day per person,[18] which is the World Bank's poverty line for lower middle-income countries. If the poverty line for upper middle-income countries (i.e., the purchasing power of $5.50 per day per person[19]) were

Table 1. Poverty Headcount Ration (International Poverty Line)

Poverty Headcount Ratio **International Poverty Line** ($1.90 / per day poverty line; 2011 PPP)				
	1996	2011	2015	2020
% of Population	45.9%	21.2%	13.4%*	10.7%**

Note: *World Bank Data; **Proportion of employed population.
Source: Asian Development Bank; World Bank.

Table 2. Poverty Headcount Ratio (National Poverty Line)

Poverty Headcount Ratio **National Poverty Line**				
	1993	2011	2015	2020
% of Population	45.3%	21.9%	—	—

Note: The national poverty estimates are based on household consumption expenditure surveys conducted by the National Statistical Survey Office (NSSO). Comparable data after 2011 is unavailable; the NSSO carried out a survey in 2014/15 but the methodology shifted.
Source: World Bank.

applied, then 1,078 million people or 82% of the population in India lived in poverty in 2015. The outbreak of the COVID-19 crisis is likely to hurl many of those who had recently escaped from extreme poverty back into a precarious existence.[20] This is likely because in April 2021, the labor forced dropped 60 million workers compared to the previous two years.[21]

From a historical perspective, however, there has been a remarkable decline in poverty associated with dramatically increased economic growth rates since economic liberalization, particularly in comparison to India's autarchic phase in the sixties and seventies. There is still higher poverty in rural areas (12% lived below the international poverty line in 2017) relative to urban centers (7%),[22] but poverty alleviation has been greater in rural areas.[23] Moreover, poverty alleviation has also impacted marginalized groups, particularly the Scheduled Castes (i.e., the *Dalit* community once known as "untouchables") and Scheduled Tribes. Levels of poverty among tribal communities remained at double the national rate in 2011, but that disparity can partly be explained by the fact that these communities are predominantly rural and have higher rates of poverty. Nonetheless, the rate of poverty alleviation for tribal groups since 1993 is slightly greater than the nation as a whole. Poverty among Dalits is rapidly converging toward the national poverty ratio.[24] The disparity in poverty between men (10% lived below the international poverty line in 2017) and women (11%) is roughly equal.[25] Children below the age of 14 are the group with the highest concentration of poverty as well as those over age 16 with no formal education (15% for both groups).[26]

INEQUALITY

The distribution of wealth in India on a national scale is highly inequitable despite rapid economic growth and poverty alleviation. It is indisputable that inequality, as measured across a range of indicators, has increased dramatically over the last three decades. Similar to the United States or Russia, the top 1% of the population in India earned more than 20% of all pre-tax national income in 2014 and greater than 30% of net personal wealth in 2012.[27] Meanwhile, the bottom 50% of the population earned only 13% of all pre-tax national income in 2014 and 6% of net personal wealth in 2012. The middle 40% of the population has seen the greatest squeeze as its share of all pre-tax income dropped from 45% in 1990 to 30% in 2014.[28]

For the last year in which data is available, it was clear that the Gini Index was increasing from 31.7 in 1993 to 35.7 in 2011,[29] indicating a more unequal distribution of consumption among households. While the Gini Index is not without flaws,[30] the general portrait of the trend in inequality seems correct.

However, as income inequality can be partially addressed through poverty alleviation, the situation in India is not bleak. There is intergenerational mobility in social status.[31] And the national pre-tax income per adult grew 122% from 2000 to 2018. Even the bottom two-fifths of the population witnessed a 58% growth in income in the same period.[32] Moreover, India pulled 271 million citizens out of poverty using a conservative multidimensional, non-monetary index.[33] Of course, persistent obstacles to a better life remain for key minority groups, but even these groups have witnessed significant poverty alleviation.

It is unclear how politically salient income inequality and wealth inequality is on a national basis in Indian politics. Arvind Panagariya argues,

> in all likelihood, citizens of the country themselves are hardly exercised by what happens to their well-being relative to all other citizens of the country. Their welfare is much more likely to be impacted by changes to their position relative to others within the group with which they socially and professionally interact on a regular basis.[34]

The wage ratio between skilled and unskilled workers is politically salient in high-income countries but is apparently less salient in low- and middle-income countries where a large mass of predominantly unskilled workers is concentrated in rural areas. In other words, the rural–urban divide may be more salient politically:

> ... in the Indian parliamentary elections in 2009, virtually no political party or politician mentioned skilled-unskilled wage inequality, which by all accounts has risen in recent years. Instead, the common theme of the ruling coalition, which won the election, was that the reforms pushed by its predecessor government had largely helped urban India and neglected the rural poor. Those commenting in the Indian press also rarely complain about the

relative rise in wages of the skilled. Instead, they reserve their concern for urban-rural and, especially, regional inequality.[35]

Of course, locational inequality is more likely to spur migration than policy action to mitigate inequality. As Panagariya argues,

> In India, Bihar is the poorest state and Kerala is one of the richest. Going by the Gini coefficient, Bihar is among the states with the least inequality and Kerala among those with the highest inequality. If people truly cared about inequality as measured by the Gini coefficient, we should expect them to migrate from Kerala to Bihar. Of course, the reality is quite the opposite: much of the migration is from Bihar to Kerala.[36]

Migration from rural to urban areas might be a welcome development if urban infrastructure and services could be upgraded to accommodate the influx and political deregulation of industries would remove the biases against large industrial employers. Similarly, regional migration and income remittances can help to create more equitable outcomes.

In any case, a redistributive solution to inequality, even if it were politically salient, would not be implemented effectively. The Indian state is officially committed to social justice, poverty eradication, and economic development but lacks strong transformative capacity despite affirmative action laws and targeted pro-poor programs. Furthermore, corruption and political polarization increasingly hamstring the state.

EMPLOYMENT

A curiosity about India's dramatic economic growth in recent decades is that this growth has had only a modest impact on employment in the formal sector. India's National Sample Survey Office (NSSO) stated that employment was essentially flat from

2013 to 2018. In other words, while 22 million jobs were created from 2013 to 2018, a similar number of individuals left the agricultural sector.[37] Despite a massive surplus of unskilled and low-skilled labor in rural areas that could spur industrial development, India's growth remains capital intensive and service-sector oriented.[38] The majority of firms are in the informal sector but the informal economy, while accounting for a significant share of employment, does not generate tax revenues or exports.[39] What accounts for this curious economic structure?

Locational and Sectoral Employment

India's population and workforce remain predominantly rural, but not all rural inhabitants work in the agricultural sector. According to the United Nations Population Division, 65% of India's population lived in areas classified as rural in 2019. The International Labor Organization (ILO) estimates that 42% of national employment (39.6% of all male workers nationally and 54.7% of female workers) was in the agricultural sector in 2019.[40] This figure can be contrasted with a high-income country like the United States in which only 1.4% of the total population (1.9% male; 0.8% female) worked in the agricultural sector in 2019. Despite India's relatively large agricultural workforce, the contribution of the agricultural sector to national wealth is limited. The agricultural sector (along with forestry and fishing) constitutes approximately 16% of the value-added to the GDP, compared to 24.8% for industry and 49.4% for services.[41]

The data implies that the agricultural sector is not highly productive—particularly per capita—and hence it is not surprising that the sector is characterized by low wages and entrenched poverty.[42] Wages in rural areas (although still quite low relative to non-agricultural wages) have improved substantially, in part due to the creation of the Mahatma Gandhi National Rural Employment Guarantee Act (MGNREGA) in 2005. The act provides 100 days of unskilled manual labor employment to each household at a minimum wage during the year. The government also supplies subsidized fertilizer, minimum price supports for crops, free electricity for farmers, free education, free primary health care, heavily subsidized food grains for the poor, and several other schemes. The effect of all of these programs is to incentivize individuals to remain in rural areas and stay employed in agriculture despite low productivity and low wages. In fact, between 2000 and 2005 there was actually an unexpected increase in agricultural employment by 22 million workers.[43] Nevertheless, the long-term trend is toward urbanization and a shift toward services and manufacturing even though the transition is not keeping pace with changes in each sector's contribution to GDP. From 1991 to 2019, employment in agriculture as a share of total employment dropped from 63.3% to 42.6%.[44] Meanwhile, the percentage of the population living in urban areas increased from 25.8% to 34.5% in the same period.

Thus, just over a third of the population lives currently in urban areas, which is a nearly 10% increase from 30 years ago and 15% over a half century.[45] Moreover, there is substantial high-density population growth in areas that are still officially classified by the government as rural but in which a substantial proportion of the population is engaged in non-agricultural occupations.[46] Conversely, a small portion of the urban workforce is engaged in work related to the agricultural sector (6.1% in 2017/18),[47] but the vast majority work in services or industry. Of course, urbanization has not always meant an improvement in living standards. India accounts for nearly half of all slum dwellers in Southern Asia.[48] Residents of slums, although not always officially classified as poor, often face daily social discrimination, spatial exclusion, and hardships in obtaining basic human resources. If India is to generate inclusive growth and prosperity, it must work to make its urban areas more accommodating for those transitioning out of the agricultural sector.

Similar to the agricultural sector, employment in the services and industrial sectors is often characterized by low productivity and low wages. A major reason for the lack of greater productivity is firm size, which is often small due to residual regulations left over from the autarchic phase of the Indian economy in the sixties and seventies. In 2017/18, 56.5% of all workers in industry and services were employed in firms with five or fewer workers; 15.9% were employed in enterprises with 20 or more workers.[49] Due to strict labor laws, larger firms tend to be capital intensive or employ mainly skilled laborers.[50]

The services sector, which employs about one third of the working population, is the most productive sector of the economy—with a value added of 49.4% of GDP in 2019.[51] The manufacturing sector contributed 13.6% of GDP in 2019—a significant drop from its peak of 17.86% in 1995. Using the broader category of industry (which includes value added in manufacturing, construction, mining, electricity, and gas), then about a quarter (24.8%) of GDP can be explained. However, even industry has experienced a significant decrease since 2008 when it contributed 31.1% to GDP.[52]

Activity in all sectors remains mainly in the untaxed, informal economy. Thus, the dual challenge for India remains to move its population from the less productive agricultural sector to the more productive service and manufacturing sectors, and to move from the informal to formal economy.

The Smile Curve

Given the inversion and deepening of the "smile curve" in the global production chains in recent decades (see Figure 1 below), which implies greater value added in pre-manufacturing (e.g., design, branding, marketing, finance) and post-production (e.g., sales, distribution, technical support) services, there is little reason to fetishize the manufacturing sector in the current global economy. In addition, countries with large industrial sectors

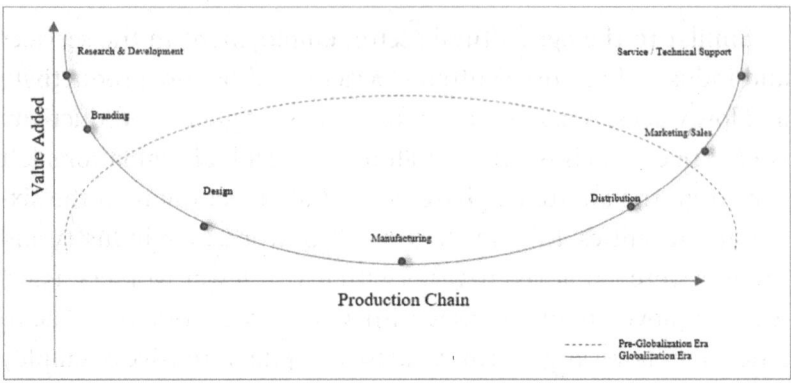

Figure 1. The Smile Curve
Source: Based on Baldwin (2019)

are increasingly shifting toward capital-intensive, flexible-labor manufacturing practices that rely on very low-cost inputs (e.g., energy in North America). In other words, the need to outsource manufacturing is diminishing as it becomes cost effective to manufacture items that were previously sent to offshore facilities. Moreover, a weak recovery from the 2008 financial crisis as well as the pandemic limits demand and thus makes the prospect for another China-sized export-led growth economy unrealistic. The East Asian pathway to economic development via industrialization appears to be closing; although global trade will remain vital, India will need to forge a different path than the East Asian economies.[53]

Formal and Informal Employment

The movement of workers from unregistered, informal employment to the formal sector is associated with improving conditions of employment, the provision of social security, enhancement of the rule of law, and the widening of the state's tax revenue base. While India continues to be characterized by a large informal sector, there are debates about the size of the sector and the barriers that prevent workers from entering the formal economy. The size of the formal sector also matters in a democracy because it indicates the extent to which the main sources of livelihood for the masses are linked to the main sources of economic growth.

According to the International Labor Organization (ILO), almost 80.9% of Indian workers were employed in the informal sector in 2012.[54] By the ILO's measure, the formal sector employed only 6.5% of workers and the remaining 0.8% were in the household sector.[55] However, this data includes farm employment and thus gives a somewhat skewed picture of the economy, particularly in urban areas. If one only looks at non-agricultural informal employment, the ILO found 64.3% of the labor force was employed in the informal sector in 2012.[56] Further restricting the data to non-agricultural employment in urban areas yields 56% employed in the informal sector.

Of course, the size of the formal and informal sectors of the economy hinge on the definition of "formal." If a firm's registration to pay the Goods and Services Tax (GST) is considered a sufficient marker of formal status, then 53% of non-farm employment (127 million out of 240 million) was in the formal sector in 2018.[57] If a private firm must be registered under the three markers of formality (i.e., GST, the Employees' Provident Fund Organisation (EPFO), Employees' State Insurance Corporation (ESIC)), then only 18% of non-farm employment (or 45 million out of 240 million) jobs were in the formal sector (see Figure 3 below). To this category of "purely formal" sector employment, one could also add the 6.3% share of non-farm employment (or 15 million workers) supplied by the government.

In terms of India's 71 million firms, 8.8 million firms (12% of all firms) are registered under the GST but not the social security net of the EPFO or the ESIC. These firms account for 41% of turnover in the economy and 13% of exports. Only 400,000 (or 0.6% of) firms are "purely formal" in the sense of being registered

Table 3. Informal and Formal Employment of Non-Farm Labor in India (2018)

Level of Formality			Share of Non-Farm Jobs	Number of Non-Farm Jobs	Share of Firms	Number of Firms
Purely Informal			38%	92 million	87%	62 million
Not Informal*	GST Registered		53%	127 million		
		GST Only	28%	67 million	12%	8.8 million
	EPFO/ESIC Registered		25%	60 million		
		EPFO/ESIC Only	0.6%	1 million	0.1%	90,000
	Government		6.3%	15 million	n/a	n/a
Purely Formal		GST+EPFO/ESIC	18%	45 million	0.6%	400,000
	Total			240 million		71 million

* Includes the "purely formal" category.

GST—Goods and Services Tax; EFPO—Employees' Provident Fund Organisation; ESIC—Employees' State Insurance Corporation. Firms registered with EPFO/ESIC but not paying GST are either in GST-exempt sectors (e.g., health, education, electricity) or are below the threshold required to pay the GST.

Source: Based on *Times of India*, 30 January 2018.

under all three markers of formality: the GST, EPFO, and ESIC. Nevertheless, these 400,000 firms account for 38% of total turnover and 87% of India's exports.[58]

Firms have limited incentive to enter the formal economy or provide workers with social security in a competitive market with a large labor pool. During India's autarchic phase, when limited competition meant large oligopolistic firms could pass on the costs of social security provision and regulatory compliance to consumers, firms in the formal sector could offer more generous terms of employment.[59] As competition has increased with deregulation and liberalization, the incentive structures have changed.

As India's labor laws only apply to large employers, there is an incentive for firms to remain small. For example, firms employing ten or more workers are governed by the Factories Act (1948), which bans the employment of women for more than nine hours per day and forbids women working between 7 pm and 6 am. For firms employing 50 or more workers, the Industrial Disputes Act (1947) makes reassignment of workers from one task to another excessively difficult. For firms with one hundred or more workers, the Industrial Disputes Act makes it practically impossible to terminate an employee—even if they are repeatedly caught sleeping on the job.[60] Employers seeking to terminate or lay off workers must obtain permission from the government, which naturally does not have an interest in increasing unemployment regardless of the needs of the private firm. Meanwhile, efforts to reform India's overweening and paternalistic labor laws have been met with strong resistance from labor unions.[61] Thus, it is not surprising that larger firms have opted for strategies that are capital intensive and/or reliant on more flexible, low wage, contracted, and self-employed labor from the informal sector. The "pro-business" Indian state has accepted the latter practice by devolving regulatory authority to federal states and reducing resources of labor ministries that are infamous for rent-seeking rule enforcement.[62] The inflexibility of labor unions has meant that the dominant labor pool remains unorganized for collective bargaining in the informal economy while union members watch their effective power steadily erode. Politicians benefit by championing the mass of informal workers, who often resent labor union leaders in the formal sector. Indian political parties also continue to support party-affiliated union federations (e.g., the ruling BJP is linked to the Bharatiya Mazdoor Sangh).[63]

Another reason why firms are reluctant to move contract and casual workers into their formal structure is the level of education of workers. Approximately 30% of the labor force was illiterate in 2012 and half (52%) had a secondary-level education. Barely 3% had a technical education at the tertiary level and an additional 7.2% had a general education at the tertiary level. In 2017–18, only 2.4% of the workforce had acquired any vocational education or training.[64] Hardly any illiterate workers have salaried positions; most illiterate workers are engaged in low productivity tasks.

INCOME

India has witnessed a significant increase in average national income per adult. At Independence in 1947, the average national income per adult per year was $1,506 (in 2019 USD), in 2019 it had risen to $9,970 in terms of purchasing power parity (PPP). If measured at market exchange, the average national income per adult rose from $404 in 1947 to $2675 in 2019.[65] By either measure, average national income has increased six-fold in seven decades. The sharpest increase came after 1991 when income rose three-fold from $3,349 to $9,970 in three decades in terms of PPP (or from $881 to $2,675 at market exchange rate). Rural areas in particular witnessed a significant increase in wages after 2005.[66] As noted earlier, the rise in wages is attributable to the public works employment scheme (MGNREGA) as well as other government programs (e.g., Minimum Support Price) that allow farmers to pay agricultural workers higher wages. The rise of non-farm jobs, particularly in construction, has made farm wages more competitive.[67]

TRADE FLOWS

On a per capita basis, India is resource poor.[68] Moreover, given the weakness of the national currency, the Indian rupee (₹), India needs to acquire international reserve currencies (i.e., the US dollar, the Euro, the British pound) to purchase goods on international markets (e.g., petroleum, weaponry). This implies that despite its massive population, India must trade with the world to thrive. However, India's interface with the global economy was relatively handicapped for the first four and a half decades after independence from the United Kingdom in 1947 due to policies that became increasingly autarchic, or inward-facing. This posture meant that India's export infrastructure and technological sophistication was quite inadequate when it shifted its stance in 1991. Moreover, India's autarchy resulted in slow growth and stagnant poverty alleviation. As economist Arvind Panagariya writes,

> at the aggregate level, there is a compelling case that autarkic policies are at the heart of any explanation of slow growth and stagnant poverty ratios in the first three decades. Symmetrically, a switch to sustained liberalization was essential to sustaining rapid growth and poverty alleviation in the subsequent decades.[69]

Today, India is a major trading economy. In 2019, before the onset of the COVID-19 pandemic impacted India, trade as a percentage of India's GDP was around 40%, a remarkable development considering that it was 7.6% in 1970. Moreover, the 2019 figure actually represented a sharp decline from 2012 when trade constituted a peak of 55.8% of GDP. Notably, China's trade as a percentage of GDP is around 36% in 2019 and America's was 26.3%.[70] In fact, for the last decade (since 2011), trade has formed a greater share of India's GDP than for China even though the popular perception is that China is more oriented toward international trade. Similarly, trade has been a larger share of India's GDP relative to the US for over two decades. In recent years, India has become America's ninth largest goods trading partner and it is near the top ten trade partners for China. The US and China are India's top two trade partners.

Despite India's strong trade posture, it is remarkably unintegrated with its own geographic region, much of which was economically integrated under the British Empire. Although India shares a border with most of the countries of its region and even has free trade agreements with most of its neighbors, these countries have not integrated well with one another. The lack of integration is despite the fact that the combined population of South Asia constitutes a quarter of the world population and hence a massive potential market. In fact, South Asia remains the least integrated region in the world.[71] Domestic industrial and agricultural lobbies have generally discouraged politicians from engaging in bilateral trade and regional free trade agreements, out of a concern that Indian firms are not competitive in most areas of manufacturing and agriculture. The key exceptions are areas in which India has a decided competitive advantage, e.g., the pharmaceutical industry.[72] Moreover, India's longstanding fraternal tension with Pakistan and India's unfortunate reputation as a domineering regional hegemon complicate prospects for peace and economic cooperation. Thus, India continues to look beyond its own geo-region for trade. In fact, it is almost 20% cheaper for India to trade with Brazil than Pakistan.[73]

In 2019, India exported a total of $330 billion worth of goods, making it the 15th largest exporter in the world; it imported $474 billion worth of goods, making it the 11th largest importer in the world.[74] India's largest export markets for goods in 2019 were the United States of America (16.8%), the United Arab Emirates (8.68%),[75] and China (5.27%). China was India's largest source of goods imports (15.3%) in 2019, followed by the US (7.11%) and the UAE (5.66%).[76] It should be noted that if the EU-27 were included as a single country, it would be the second largest market for goods exports (14%) and India's third largest trade partner overall.[77] China may decline as a major trade partner in the near future. Due to a border conflict with China in the summer of 2020, India has been attempting to cut imports from China by half.[78] It will not achieve that symbolic target, but the effects of the boycott for bilateral trade could be significant nonetheless.

In terms of trade in services, India was the sixth largest exporter in the world in 2018 with $119 billion; and it was the seventh largest importer of services at $120 billion.[79] Services also contribute a quarter (25.2%) of the value of India's gross manufactured exports, particularly for basic metals and motor vehicles.[80]

India ranks 45th out of 157 countries for the complexity of its exported products. India's largest exports are refined petroleum products, diamonds and jewelry, and pharmaceutical products. Its largest imports are crude petroleum, gold and diamonds, and electrical machinery and equipment. By way of comparison, China ranks 29th in terms of economic complexity. This difference is manifest in bilateral trade, where India exports raw materials to China (e.g., refined petroleum, iron ore, cyclic hydrocarbons—styrene) and China sells telephones, computers, integrated circuits, semiconductors, and broadcast equipment to India.[81] This asymmetry is a key reason why India cannot simply find domestic substitutes as it seeks to partially extricate itself from trade with China. Nor can it simply cobble together trading relationships overnight with other partners in place of the vast Chinese market, especially amid the general disruption in global supply chains brought on by the COVID-19 pandemic.

A paradox of the Indian economy is that even though it is heavily oriented toward international trade, it remains a heavily protected economy. India continues to have relatively very high average tariffs, particularly in agriculture where the average tariff rate for imports in 2018 was 38.8% for most favored nation (MFN) status trade partners.[82] India's average tariff rate with MFN partners for non-agricultural product imports was 13.6% in 2018. India's overall average MFN tariff was 17.1%—the highest of any major economy in the world.[83]

Despite India's need for market access and its relatively weaker bargaining position, its trade relationship with its major partners is still subject to periodic squabbles over trade barriers at the World Trade Organization (WTO). The large disparity between India's MFN tariff rate and its permitted "bound rate" at the WTO, which hovers at 50.8% on average, permits India to increase tariffs dramatically to limit international competition, much to the chagrin of its trade partners.

Global Value Chains

As one of the only major emerging economies that is not located near a region populated by high-income countries, India's integration with global value chains (GVCs) was bound to be exceptional relative to the trajectory of other emerging economies.[84] As India displayed remarkable economic growth in the first three decades after liberalizing its economy in 1991, it forged its own path in an already crowded and competitive economic climate. India became a leader in information technology services, relying initially on a narrow, English-educated, elite and upper middle-class base. The ILO estimated in 2013 that about 19% of employment in India involves jobs in global supply chains.[85] The OECD[86] stated that by 2015, 16.4% of India's domestic value added was driven by consumption abroad.[87]

In recent years, as global economic integration has stalled, India's role in GVCs has adjusted. The foreign value-added content of India's exports has declined significantly since a peak of 25.1% in 2011–12. By 2016, the foreign value-added content of exports, a measure of "backward linkages" in value chain analysis, had fallen to 16.1%, likely indicating a shift to domestic suppliers for intermediate inputs, particularly in business services in the information and communications sector. The decline may also indicate a shift in India's approach to free trade since countries with open and liberal trade regimes and high levels of foreign investment generally have higher foreign content in their exports. Other factors that may account for India's declining foreign value-added content in its exports include commodity price volatility and changes in specialization.[88]

Foreign "final demand" for Indian services, a measure of an industry's export orientation, has also decreased. The decrease may indicate that there is a growing domestic demand for Indian business services. For most of India's manufactured goods, however, the share of imported intermediate goods intended for products that are exported has increased. Nevertheless, as services constitute almost half of India's gross exports, a decrease in service exports is significant.[89] Moreover, it is worth noting that less than a quarter of India's total goods and services imports (23.2%) was embodied in its exports. This compares poorly to the OECD average of 45.5% of imports used in subsequent exports.[90]

To summarize, despite the rhetoric of liberalization, India remains a predominately mercantilist economy that generally seeks its own prosperity at the expense of its trade partners. India attempts to spur domestic production and innovation, especially in labor-intensive products as well as electronics and communications devices, through the erection of very high tariff walls.[91] India has yet to shed fully its distrust of international trade and to embrace global integration and competition confidently. In fact, India is shifting away from its integration into GVCs.

INVESTMENT FLOWS

Domestic Financial Sector

In any economy, a stable, liquid, and efficient financial system is vital to channel accumulated capital toward profitable investments that spur sustainable economic growth. India's financial sector has veered from laissez-faire policies in the context of a shallow banking sector (1947–60s) inherited by the post-colonial regime; to bank and insurance company nationalization, monetary erosion,[92] and financial repression[93] (1970s–80s); and, finally, financial liberalization and calibrated financial deepening (1991–present).[94]

Reforms in the equity market (e.g., India's four stock markets) preceded reforms in the debt market (e.g., bond market) by nearly a decade, but the debt market is beginning to outpace the equity market in terms of new issues.[95] However, despite growing and increasingly vibrant equity and debt markets, private placements dominate rather than public trading. Publicly traded bond markets are thin and dominated by central and state government issuers as well as public sector entities.[96] Even in the equities market, private placements dominate.[97] As equity and bond markets help banks to assess performance and credit worthiness of firms, publicly traded equities and debt are vital to the financial system as a whole.

Liberalization of the banking sector was accomplished by reducing the cash reserve ratio (CRR)[98] and the statutory liquidity ratio (SLR)[99] and by eliminating the direct state control of interest rates. These reforms allowed commercial banks to have greater investible resources and permitted accurate price discovery in the market. The government developed indirect instruments to influence interest rates and inflation (e.g., a call money market or an overnight inter-bank money market).[100] The state also strengthened the financial sector by ending its dubious practice of automatically funding (i.e., monetizing) the government's debt using Treasury bills (T-bills).[101] Finally, the government began licensing additional private banks and permitting foreign banks to compete with domestic banks. In 2021, public sector banks constitute 59% of market share in loans, private sector banks constitute 36%, and foreign banks the remainder.[102]

Although banking is still dominated by public sector banks, their market share has dropped dramatically in the last decade, mainly due to increased privatization.

The impact of financial sector reforms has been a dramatic increase in aggregate deposits and credit as a percentage of GDP.[103] On the surface, the financial health of India's banking sector has improved as its balance sheets have grown, but there are still a large number of non-performing assets (NPAs, i.e., a loan with unpaid interest or principal for 90 days or longer) on the books. Since 1991, the government has twice (in 1993 and 2017) infused liquidity to recapitalize the banking sector using taxpayer funds because of a large accumulation of NPAs.[104] In the wake of the COVID-19 pandemic, and despite central bank measures to protect banks, gross NPAs (GNPAs) were expected to rise above 11% in fiscal year 2021.[105] Moreover, restructured loans, which should be downgraded as per international standards, are not downgraded in India.[106] The effect is to mask the actual weaknesses in the financial system, particularly in public sector banks. In essence, India's banking sector remains vulnerable.

Economist Arvind Panagariya argues that

> the government and RBI [Reserve Bank of India, i.e. India's central bank] failed to implement international best practice in regulation in one important respect: treatment of restructured loans as substandard. For a long time, RBI chose to treat them as standard. The regime regulating NPAs was thus effectively subverted.[107]

Moreover, it was a working group set up by the RBI that recommended against downgrading restructured loans in 2012. Initially, the RBI only slightly raised the provisioning requirement for restructured loans. It was not until 2015 that the RBI adopted international standards and downgraded restructured loans. But even then, the RBI offered firms several loopholes to escape the reclassification of their loans as NPAs.[108] To some extent, non-deposit taking non-bank financial corporations (NBFCs; e.g., mutual funds, pension funds, insurance funds) and real estate companies that raise money directly from the market helped to offset the slow growth in bank credit due to the large number of NPAs.[109] As a result, very little progress was made in tackling the growing problem of NPAs until it became self-evident that credit growth was being seriously impacted by the problem in 2017. Since then, the government has acted to create early detection protocols for NPAs and to compel defaulters to implement resolution plans or file for insolvency within specified periods.

Of course, the underlying reason for the large accumulation of NPAs is the crony-capitalist nature of India's economy and its congested judicial system. So long as politicians can pressure state-owned banks and even private banks to lend to favored entrepreneurs, there is little likelihood for reducing NPAs. In this regard, it is noteworthy that in 2017, there were 12 borrowers whose loans had a cumulative value of ₹3.45 trillion ($46.5 billion), representing a quarter of all NPAs.[110] Clearly the state is reluctant to police and protect the financial sector until aggregate economic growth is seriously threatened.

Foreign Direct Investment

Foreign direct investment (FDI) is long-term investment by a home country firm or individual in a host country enterprise above a certain minimal threshold (e.g., >10% of ordinary shares in a firm). FDI is sought after by emerging economies not only to supplement domestic capital investment but also as a mechanism for technology transfer and managerial insights.[111] In the 20 years from (April) 2000 to (March) 2020, India received $680 billion in foreign direct investment, which includes foreign equity investment

($469 billion), reinvested earnings, and other capital. In 2019, India attracted a record high $50.6 billion in net inflows.[112]

FDI particularly increased from 2014 to 2019 with the "Make in India" policy, which permitted full foreign ownership of firms in certain sectors without prior government or central bank authorization (e.g., coal, iron, steel, cement, energy) as long as end products were for domestic consumption. It should be noted, though, that the top two sources of investment in this period were from Mauritius ($143 billion or 30% of total FDI) and Singapore ($98 billion or 20% of total FDI), potentially indicating that a significant portion of the investment was "round-tripping" capital that originated in India and was part of an effort to launder money. Notably, Cyprus ($11 billion or 2%) and the Cayman Islands ($8 billion or 2%) were also in the top ten list of sites for FDI to India. Other major sites for capital investment into India were the Netherlands ($34 billion or 7%); Japan ($33 billion or 7%); the US ($30 billion or 6%); and the UK ($28 billion or 6%).[113]

Foreign direct investment flocked to the services sector, which includes finance, banking, and insurance ($82 billion or 17% of total FDI); computers ($45 billion or 10% of total FDI); and telecommunications ($37 billion or 8% of total FDI).[114] In the manufacturing sector, FDI has been a statistically significant factor in determinants of profit, employment, and wages across production sectors in the manufacturing economy.[115]

Foreign Portfolio Investment

Indian capital market deregulation (for non-resident Indians) nominally began in the 1980s under PM Indira Gandhi's "Operation Forward." In fact, significant liberalization of the market did not begin until after the 1991 balance-of-payments crisis. Foreign institutional investors (FIIs; e.g., banks, asset management firms, trusts, foundations, insurance companies, pension funds, and hedge funds) have gained increasing access to financial markets since liberalization. Today, there are no restrictions or taxes on foreign portfolio investment (except for the qualifying condition of who can participate and the requirement to register with the Securities and Exchange Board of India and the Reserve Bank of India). India has witnessed one of the fastest expansions in its stock market of any emerging economy.[116] Yaha et al. and Patnaik et al. contend that despite its openness to FIIs, India did not witness a significant transmission of economic shocks from high-income economies, including during the 2008 US financial crisis.[117] Garg and Dua disagree, but do note that in 2009, India had the "largest bounce back" from the 2008 crisis, and by 2010 portfolio investment increased by almost 90% compared to the previous year.[118]

ECONOMIC GROWTH

Despite its lingering protectionism and occasional tariff disputes, from 1980 to 2020, India averaged an enviable 6.11% growth in real gross domestic product. If one counts from 1992, a year after economic liberalization, India grew at almost 6.47% annually in real terms. India's spectacular performance appeared to start fizzling after 2017. Thus, even before the pandemic, India's economy was in trouble. The impact of the pandemic was −7.3% growth rate (i.e., a contraction) of the economy. Current projections indicate that India will bounce back in 2021 as the fastest growing major economy in the world and it will retain that rank at least into 2022.

CORRUPTION

India remains a very corrupt economic environment. In a World Bank survey (stratified random sample) of 9281 firms in India in June 2013 to December 2014, over a third of business owners and top managers surveyed (35.8%) stated that corruption was a major constraint and 19.9% of firms listed corruption as "the biggest obstacle" to the firm's success. Over a fifth (22.7%) of businesses

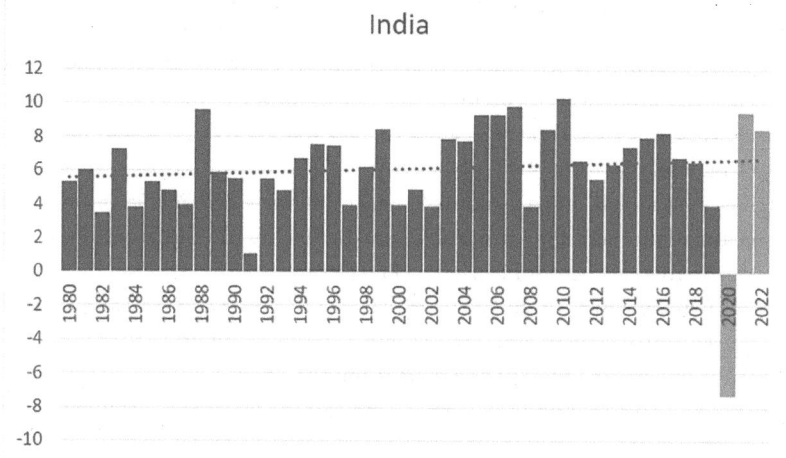

Figure 2. Real GDP Growth in India (Annual Percent Change)
Source: IMF Data Mapper (2021)[120]

reported at least one bribe request. And almost a fifth (19.6%) of all public transactions are characterized by requests of gifts or bribes. Fifteen percent of firms reported an expectation that they would give "gifts" in meetings with tax collectors. Over half of firms reported having to give gifts to get an electricity (51.5%) or water (52.5%) connection.[119]

In summary, India's economic foundations are weak, despite its strong economic growth in recent decades. Wise government policies could go a long way to redressing many of these issues. Unfortunately, as we will see in the next chapter, the Modi government has not engaged in the difficult task of buttressing a fundamentally weak economy.

NOTES

1. Pratap Bhanu Mehta, "The Story of Indian Democracy Written in Blood and Betrayal."
2. A rent-seeking firm is one that attempts to obtain competitive advantages through political arrangements (e.g., subsidies, monopoly licenses, regulations, tariff protection, etc.) rather than innovation and productivity.

3 A capitalist economy is defined as one in which the means of production is predominantly privately owned, legally free labor is hired on the basis of contractual arrangements, and the coordination of resources, inputs, and finished products is predominantly decentralized.
4 Crabtree, *The Billionaire Raj*, 46–47.
5 Crabtree, 36.
6 Aseema Sinha, "India's Porous State," in *Business and Politics in India*, ed. Christophe Jaffrelot, Atul Kohli, and Kanta Murali, Modern South Asia (New York, NY: Oxford University Press, 2019).
7 GDP is a measure of the monetary value of all goods and services produced in a country (or economic area) within a given year (or other time frame).
8 Calculated using the Atlas method in current US$.
9 World Bank, "World Development Indicators," Database, DataBank, 2021, https://databank.worldbank.org/.
10 IMF, "IMF DataMapper," Database, IMF DataMapper, 2021, https://www.imf.org/external/datamapper/.
11 IMF.
12 Ella Hurworth, "India to Overtake China as the World's Most Populous Country: UN," *CNN*, June 19, 2019, https://www.cnn.com/2019/06/19/health/india-china-world-population-intl-hnk/index.html.
13 World Bank, "World Development Indicators."
14 McKinsey & Company, "India's Tuning Point: An Agenda for India's Economic Growth" (McKinsey Global Institute, August 2020), vi.
15 McKinsey & Company, 2.
16 World Bank, "Poverty & Equity Brief: South Asia" (World Bank, April 2021), 1, https://databank.worldbank.org/data/download/poverty/987B9C90-CB9F-4D93-AE8C-750588BF00QA/SM2021/Global_POVEQ_IND.pdf.
17 World Bank, "Poverty & Equity Brief: South Asia," Poverty & Equity Brief (World Bank, April 2021), 1.
18 Based on the purchasing power of a US dollar in 2011.
19 Based on the purchasing power of a US dollar in 2011.
20 World Bank, "Poverty & Equity Brief," 1.
21 World Bank, "Poverty & Equity Brief," 1.
22 World Bank, "Poverty & Equity Brief," 2.
23 Arvind Panagariya, *Free Trade and Prosperity: How Openness Helps Developing Countries Grow Richer and Combat Poverty* (New York: Oxford University Press, 2019), 240.
24 Panagariya, 241.

25 World Bank, "Poverty & Equity Brief," 2.
26 World Bank, "Poverty & Equity Brief," 2.
27 UN, *World Social Report 2020: Inequality in a Rapidly Changing World* (United Nations, 2020), 29, https://doi.org/10.18356/7f5d0efc-en; World Inequality Database, "World Inequality Database," Database, World Inequality Database, accessed August 14, 2020, https://wid.world/country/india/.
28 WID, "World Inequality Database." Note: The data is based on tax tabulations and surveys and is therefore not highly reliable, but it is useful in getting an approximation of the income and wealth distribution.
29 Note: India's Gini relies on consumption data (rather than income) and an aggregation of rural and urban households. This method of compiling data makes India appear less unequal in comparison to other countries. Data Source: World Bank. It is not clear why the Indian government has not released updated data on inequality to the World Bank in over a decade.
30 Panagariya, *Free Trade and Prosperity*, 146–49.
31 UN, *World Social Report 2020*, 44.
32 UNDP, *Human Development Report 2019: Beyond Income, beyond Averages, beyond Today: Inequalities in Human Development in the 21st Century.* (United Nations Development Programme, 2019), 120. Notably, the top 1% of the population witnessed a 213% increase in income over the same period.
33 UNDP, 56. The multidimensional poverty index is the non-monetary measure of deprivation published in the UNDP's *Human Development Report* since 2010.
34 Panagariya, *Free Trade and Prosperity*, 149.
35 Panagariya, 152.
36 Panagariya, 150.
37 McKinsey & Company, "India's Turning Point," 6.
38 Kanta Murali, "Economic Liberalization and the Structural Power of Business," in *Business and Politics in India*, ed. Christophe Jaffrelot, Atul Kohli, and Kanta Murali, Modern South Asia (New York, NY: Oxford University Press, 2019), 34.
39 Times of India, "Formal Sector Much Bigger Than What You Thought All This While," *Times of India*, January 30, 2018, https://timesofindia.indiatimes.com/business/india-business/formal-sector-much-bigger-than-what-you-thought-all-this-while/articleshow/62706273.cms.
40 World Bank, "World Development Indicators."
41 World Bank, "World Development Indicators."

42 Arvind Panagariya, *New India: Reclaiming the Lost Glory* (New York: Oxford University Press, 2020), 43.
43 Santosh Mehrotra, "Informal Employment Trends in the Indian Economy: Persistent Informality, but Growing Positive Development," Working Paper, Employment Policy Department (Geneva, CH: International Labor Organization, 2019), 7, https://ilo.userservices.exlibrisgroup.com.
44 World Bank, "World Development Indicators."
45 World Bank, "World Development Indicators."
46 UN, *World Social Report 2020*, 112.
47 Panagariya, *New India*, 33.
48 UN, *World Social Report 2020*, 121.
49 Panagariya, *New India*, 56.
50 World Bank, "Enterprise Surveys: What Businesses Experience," Text/HTML, World Bank, accessed June 8, 2021, https://www.enterprisesurveys.org/en/data/exploreeconomies.
51 World Bank, "World Development Indicators."
52 World Bank, "World Development Indicators."
53 Richard E. Baldwin, *The Great Convergence: Information Technology and the New Globalization* (Cambridge, Massachusetts: The Belknap Press of Harvard University Press, 2016); Raghuram Rajan, "Make in India, Largely for India," *Indian Journal of Industrial Relations* 50, no. 3 (2015): 361–72.
54 The results were published in 2018, but the dataset for India was based on the 2012 Employment and Unemployment Survey and the 2012 India Human Development Survey.
55 ILO, "Women and Men in the Informal Economy, 3rd Edition" (ILO, 2018), 100, https://www.ilo.org/wcmsp5/groups/public/---dgreports/---dcomm/documents/publication/wcms_626831.pdf.
56 ILO, 88.
57 Times of India, "Formal Sector."
58 Times of India.
59 Rina Agarwala, "The Politics of India's Reformed Labor Model," in *Business and Politics in India*, ed. Christophe Jaffrelot, Atul Kohli, and Kanta Murali, Modern South Asia (New York: Oxford University Press, 2019), 96.
60 Panagariya, *New India*, 98.
61 Agarwala, "The Politics of India's Reformed Labor Model," 97.
62 Agarwala, 99.
63 Agarwala, 101.
64 Mehrotra, "Informal Employment Trends," 4.

65 WID, "World Inequality Database."
66 Mehrotra, "Informal Employment Trends," 1.
67 Mehrotra, 10–11.
68 Sandy Gordon, "Widening Horizon's: Australia's New Relationship with India," Widening Horizons (Australian Strategic Policy Institute, 2007), 32, JSTOR, https://www.jstor.org/stable/resrep04164.8.
69 Panagariya, *Free Trade and Prosperity*, 237.
70 World Bank, "World Development Indicators."
71 USTR, "2020 National Trade Estimate on Foreign Trade Barriers" (United States Trade Representative, March 2020), 47, https://ustr.gov/sites/default/files/2020_National_Trade_Estimate_Report.pdf.
72 Amitendu Palit, "Will India's Disengaging Trade Policy Restrict It from Playing a Greater Global Role?," *World Trade Review* 20, no. 2 (May 2021): 206, https://doi.org/10.1017/S1474745620000518.
73 Margot Schüller and Jan Peter Wogart, "The Emergence of Post-Crisis Regional Financial Institutions in Asia—With a Little Help from Europe," ed. Matthias Helble and Margot Schüller, *Asia Europe Journal* 15, no. 4 (2017): 486, https://doi.org/10.1007/s10308-017-0491-4.
74 OEC, "Economic Complexity Rankings (ECI)," Database, The Observatory of Economic Complexity, 2021, https://oec.world/en/rankings/eci/hs6/hs07.
75 Trade with the UAE is often a form of triangular trade with Pakistan.
76 CRS, Shayerah Ilias Akhtar, and K. Alan Kronstadt, "US–India Trade Relations," *In Focus* (Congressional Research Service, February 14, 2020), 1, https://fas.org/sgp/crs/row/IF10384.pdf; WITS, "India Trade," Database, World Integrated Trade Solution (WITS) Data, 2021, https://wits.worldbank.org/countrysnapshot/en/IND.
77 European Commission, "India—Trade—European Commission," Countries and Regions—India, 2021, https://ec.europa.eu/trade/policy/countries-and-regions/countries/india/.
78 Prachi Gupta, "India Cuts China Imports by Half in a Year; Needs Measured Approach to Further Lower Dependence: SBI," *Financial Express*, July 8, 2020, http://search.proquest.com/docview/2421102086?pq-origsite=summon.
79 OEC, "Economic Complexity Rankings (ECI)."
80 OECD, "Trade in Value Added: India," Trade in Value Added—Country Notes (OECD, December 2018), https://www.oecd.org/industry/ind/TIVA-2018-India.pdf.
81 OEC, "Economic Complexity Rankings (ECI)."

82 CRS, Akhtar, and Kronstadt, "US-India Trade Relations," 1; USTR, "2020 National Trade Estimate on Foreign Trade Barriers," 238. India's "bound rate" or upper limit for non-MFN countries averaged 113% for agricultural products (the top Indian tariff rate was 300%) in 2018.
83 USTR, "2020 National Trade Estimate on Foreign Trade Barriers," 238.
84 Baldwin, *The Great Convergence*.
85 UN, *World Social Report 2020*, 64.
86 The Organization for Economic Cooperation and Development (OECD) is a club of 38 high-income countries.
87 OECD, "Trade in Value Added: India," 2.
88 OECD, "Trade in Value Added (TIVA) Indicators: Guide to Country Notes," Guide (OECD, December 2018), 2, https://www.oecd.org/sti/ind/tiva-2018-guide-to-country-notes.pdf.
89 OECD, "Trade in Value Added: India," 1.
90 OECD, 3.
91 USTR, "2020 National Trade Estimate on Foreign Trade Barriers," 238.
92 Monetary erosion implies the failure of a currency to constitute itself relative to competing currencies and (particularly in the Indian case) relative to other tangible assets (e.g., gold or real estate). See: Waltraud Schelkle, *Constitution and Erosion of a Monetary Economy: Problems of India's Development since Independence*, GDI Book Series, no. 3 (London, UK: Frank Cass, 1994).
93 Financial repression includes activities in which state spending "crowds out" private investment; interest rates are regulated by the state; and the state establishes quantitative limits on sectoral credit.
94 Rakesh Mohan and Mohan Ray, "Indian Financial Sector: Structure, Trends and Turns" (Washington, DC: IMF, January 2017), 5.
95 Panagariya, *New India*, 139.
96 Panagariya, *Free Trade and Prosperity*, 132–33.
97 Panagariya, *New India*, 139.
98 The CRR is the minimum level of cash deposits kept with the central bank. The CRR fell from 15% in 1991 to a low of 3% in 2021.
99 The SLR is the minimum level of cash and other nearly liquid assets kept at the bank. The SLR dropped from 38.5% in 1991 to 18% in 2021.
100 The government influences the interest rate by setting the "repo rate" (repurchase rate), which is the rate at which the central bank lends money to commercial banks and the "reverse repo rate," which is the rate at which the central bank agrees to repurchase a security from commercial banks.
101 Mohan and Ray, "Indian Financial Sector," 8.

102 K. Ram Kumar, "Public Sector Banks Losing Market Share in Loans to Private Sector Rivals," *The Hindu Business Line*, May 7, 2021, https://www.thehindubusinessline.com/money-and-banking/public-sector-banks-losing-market-share-in-loans-to-private-sector-rivals/article34504920.ece.

103 Mohan and Ray, "Indian Financial Sector," 11.

104 Panagariya, *New India*, 146.

105 Business Today, "Budget 2021: Banks Set for NPA Shock; What'll Govt Do?," February 1, 2021, https://www.businesstoday.in/union-budget-2021/expectations/budget-2021-banks-set-for-npa-shock-what-ll-govt-do/story/429746.html.

106 Panagariya, *New India*, 153–54.

107 Panagariya, 151.

108 Panagariya, 156–57.

109 Panagariya, 138.

110 Panagariya, 158–59.

111 Keshab Bhattarai and Vipin Negi, "FDI and Economic Performance of Firms in India," *Studies in Microeconomics* 8, no. 1 (June 1, 2020): 46–47, https://doi.org/10.1177/2321022220918684.

112 World Bank, "World Development Indicators."

113 Department for the Promotion of Industry and International Trade, "Quarterly Factsheet on FDI from April 2000 to March 2020," Factsheet (Government of India, n.d.), 1–6, https://dipp.gov.in/sites/default/files/FDI_Factsheet_March20_28May_2020.pdf.

114 Department for the Promotion of Industry and International Trade, 10.

115 Bhattarai and Negi, "FDI and Economic Performance of Firms in India."

116 Anick Yaha, Nirvikar Singh, and Jean Paul Rabanal, "How Do Extreme Global Shocks Affect Foreign Portfolio Investment? An Event Study for India," *Emerging Markets Finance & Trade* 53, no. 8 (2017): 1923, https://doi.org/10.1080/1540496X.2016.1204599.

117 Yaha, Singh, and Rabanal, 1935; Ila Patnaik, Ajay Shah, and Nirvikar Singh, "Foreign Investors under Stress: Evidence from India," *International Finance* 16, no. 2 (2013): 213–44, https://doi.org/10.1111/j.1468-2362.2013.12032.x.

118 Reetika Garg and Pami Dua, "Foreign Portfolio Investment Flows to India: Determinants and Analysis," *World Development* 59 (July 2014): 16, https://doi.org/10.1016/j.worlddev.2014.01.030.

119 World Bank, "Enterprise Surveys."

120 India's real GDP is calculated based on national accounts. Up to 2011 the base year is set at 2004/05; thereafter the base year is 2011/12. Note: Data estimates for 2020–2022 is based on the IMF's World Economic Outlook Update of 27 July 2021. The WEO Update does not account for inflation.

SUGGESTED FURTHER READING

Das, Gurcharan, *India Grows at Night: A Liberal Case for a Strong State* (Penguin, 2012). ISBN: 978-0670084708.

Drèze, Jean, and Amartya Sen, *An Uncertain Glory: India and Its Contradictions* (Princeton University Press, 2015). ISBN: 978-0691165523.

Joshi, Vijay, *India's Long Road* (Oxford University Press, 2017). ISBN: 978-0190610135.

Kohli, Atul, *Poverty Amid Plenty in the New India* (Cambridge University Press, 2012). ISBN: 978-0521735179.

CHAPTER FOUR

INDIA'S ECONOMIC POLICY UNDER MODI

The Modi government's economic policy has been characterized by opportunism and economic nationalism, rebranding of the policy initiatives of previous administrations, and misguided interventions in the market. The nominal goal of economic policy clearly has been to spur a growth acceleration and propel India to the status of a great power; however, the actual outcomes coupled with exogenous shocks have unnecessarily weakened India. Nevertheless, as an old saying goes, India continues to "grow at night" while the government slumbers, despite the Modi administration's mediocre management of the economy.

Ideologically, the reforms often seem to be nominally pro-market or even technocratic and "neo-liberal." However, we argue that scholars who view the Modi administration as pro-market or "neo-liberal" are mistaken.[1] The Modi government's economic policy is mainly "pro-business" with a strong hint of mercantilism and even autarchic ambitions in certain sectors (e.g., defense). Thus, the Modi government is not in any serious respect either liberal or neo-liberal, as both of those ideologies are oriented toward promoting interdependence and the centrality of decentralized market allocation of goods and services. In line with a pro-business tilt, the administration has used its domestic economic policies to weaken the power of labor unions, environmental protections, social welfare, and civil society organizations. At the international scale, the Modi administration's mercantilism comes more sharply into focus. Thus, deeper reforms and greater liberalization should only be expected in response to significant economic slowdowns or crisis. This section highlights some of the major economic policy initiatives undertaken by the government from 2014 to 2021.

DOMESTIC ECONOMIC POLICIES

Modi's domestic economic policies are more appearance than substance. While the administration has made concerted efforts to increase financial inclusion, there have not been substantial changes in behavior. Similarly, top-down development schemes have often been diluted and downgraded. Finally, Modi's personal penchant to act decisively has led to significant policy blunders. The end result is that little of India's economic resilience can be traced to wise policy implementation.

Seeming Inclusive

Financial Inclusion (2014), Life Insurance (2015), Pension (2015), Loans (2015)

The Modi administration unleashed a slate of financial policy schemes in 2014 and 2015 to promote "financial inclusion," particularly for the poor and illiterate. Of course, the aim of these initiatives was not completely novel. India has been attempting to increase financial inclusion for six decades. In 2006, the Reserve Bank of India (RBI), India's central bank, defined financial inclusion as a business objective for all banks under its supervision. There was a renewed push for banks to open branches in unbanked villages from 2010–13. Unfortunately, branch expansion efforts were generally ineffective in getting more citizens to open an account.[2] In the same period, there was also a shift to using "bank correspondents" working at "customer service points" within 15 km of unbanked villages to help the poor open very basic savings accounts.[3]

India's financial inclusion policies were also in line with the World Bank's "Universal Financial Access 2020" goal adopted in 2015, which in turn was based on reports funded by the Bill and Melinda Gates Foundation and Gallup Inc.'s Global Findex Database launched in 2011.[4]

The Pradhan Mantri Jan-Dhan Yojana (PMJDY or National Mission for Financial Inclusion, August 2014) aims to provide basic banking services for every household in India using their biometric national ID card. Building on the expansion of bank accounts, the Pradhan Mantri Jeevan Jyoti Bima Yojana (PMJJBY, May 2015) is a state-supported life insurance policy whose annual premium ($4.60) is automatically debited from participating citizens' bank accounts and pays out ($2600) for death due to any cause. Similarly, the Atal Pension Yojana (APY, May 2015) provides a minimum monthly pension to subscribers. Finally, the Pradhan Mantri Mudra Yojana (PMMY, April 2015) provides loans to non-corporate, non-farm, small enterprises up to $13,581 (₹1 million).

From a statistical perspective, there has been demonstrable progress along the most basic metrics of financial inclusion, although much work remains to create an inclusive "cashless" economy. From 2011 to 2017, the share of Indian adults with an account doubled to 80% of the population, as 690 million citizens opened bank accounts for the first time.[5] The gender gap in financial inclusion declined from 20% in 2011 to 6% in 2017.[6] From 2014 to 2017, bank accounts for adults rose by 40%.[7] Rural account ownership increased from 33% in 2011 to 79% by 2017.[8] Leakage of pension fund payments decreased by 47% (2.8 percentage points) when payments were made using biometric smart cards.[9] In large part, financial inclusion efforts have been assisted by the government's push to link account ownership with national biometric identification smart cards (which began to be used widely in 2010) as well as the fact that almost half of the "unbanked" own a mobile phone, which can be used to open a bank account. Nevertheless, India still has 190 million citizens without a bank account, the second highest after China (225 million).[10] And India is still far from becoming a digital economy, as most individuals still receive wages or remittances in cash, and make payments or save for the future in cash.

For now, however, almost half of the accounts opened remain inactive.[11] One could infer that from the disparity between the enrollment drive and actual utilization of the accounts that the Modi administration is more focused on achieving targets that improve India's global ranking than in actually addressing structural-societal challenges to genuine inclusivity.

It is also striking that these schemes are state funded, although the World Bank works in partnership with the microfinance institutions and mobile phone companies. A reliance on the state's coffers to provide services available from the market—although realistically out of reach for the poor—belies the notion that the Modi administration is "neo-liberal" in its economic ideology merely because it is encouraging greater financial inclusion, security, and autonomy of its citizens. From a market perspective, a great deal of government resources has been spent to encourage citizens to open accounts, but actual banking activity from the new accounts is sparse,[12] indicating one of the limits of state-led, top-down efforts at development.

Promising Techno-Modern Utopias

Smart Cities Mission (2014)

The aim of the Smart Cities Mission under the Modi administration was to create cities with "smart" physical, social, and economic infrastructure. These completely new, comprehensively planned cities would rely on clean technology for energy, information and communication technology (ICT) for integration, and on public–private partnerships (PPPs) for financing.[13] The goal was to supply territorially bounded Indian elites with their fantasy: a world-class urban oasis consisting of reliable electricity, dependable security, high speed internet, quality education, efficient health care, affordable housing, and so on—all within an Indian socio-cultural milieu that upholds their own status and renders superfluous the economic and lifestyle opportunities historically associated with emigration. Of course, the components of the smart city were always shifting and amorphous sound bites; it was never quite clear how the land would be acquired, much less how the social, physical, and digital infrastructures would be individually assembled and combined to generate economic innovation, social cohesion, and efficient municipal management.

The specific notion of a "smart city" (either as a retrofit/brownfield or a new greenfield site) developed in America, Europe, and East Asia at the dawn of the twenty-first century. The European variants tended to emphasize incremental retrofitting of new technologies in already highly networked societies to improve e-governance services for residents.[14]

In the Indian context, the idea of smart cities was not an invention of the Modi administration. If one strips down the idea of a smart city to its core symbolic purpose, then the colonial cities of the British Raj (e.g., Lutyens' Delhi) or Mayer and Le Corbusier's plan for Chandigarh, as commissioned by India's first prime minister in the 1950s, would also fit the tradition of building an ultramodern, comprehensively planned city in India to showcase elite ambitions and state power. More recent predecessors of the smart city project date to the early liberalization period with Bangalore's "Mega City Scheme" (1993) and the Jawaharlal Nehru National Urban Renewal Mission (JNNURM Phase I—2005; JNNURM Phase II—2012). These earlier projects were marred with difficulties in land acquisition, funding delays, and incompetent devolution of power to state and local governments.[15]

The Modi administration eventually settled on a set of smart city projects that had the distinct advantage of allowing them to appropriate and rebrand the work done by the previous administration. The $100 billion state-funded, Delhi–Mumbai Industrial Corridor (DMIC) was not initially intended to seed a series of new smart cities, but it gradually became associated with those buzzwords. Launched in 2007, DMIC came to envision initially creating seven new smart cities, adding up to a total of 24 cities to be phased in over time along the route between India's political capital (New Delhi) and financial capital (Mumbai). Specifically, the DMIC envisioned a 1,500 km dedicated freight corridor linking six of India's northern and western states: Uttar Pradesh, Haryana, Rajasthan, Gujarat, Madhya Pradesh, and Maharashtra, and the national capital territory of Delhi. Two of the cities in this project, Dholera and GIFT (Gujarat International Finance Tec-) City, were established as special economic zones (SEZs) and special investment zones (SIZs) in the state of Gujarat when Modi was chief minister. By 2012, the Manmohan Singh government announced it would create two smart cities in every Indian state under JNNURM Phase II. Campaigning in 2014, Modi announced he would create 100 completely new smart cities.[16]

As Modi's vision came into predictable conflict with issues related to forcible land acquisition, financing, and inclusiveness, the grand vision was modified to a humbler project of upgrading the infrastructure of existing cities. Almost any urban renewal project that had at least some technology component, however small, was now considered under the smart city umbrella. The government also began at least paying lip service to the notion of increasing citizen participation in shaping urban design decisions even though the emphasis remained on incorporating ICT. Finally, the smart city concept was heavily diluted by associating it with the Atal Mission for Rejuvenation and Urban

Transformation, the Swachh Bharat Yojana (Clean India Mission), and the Heritage City Development & Augmentation Yojana (HRIDAY)—which was essentially an offshoot of the previous administration's JNNURM.[17] In the meantime, the southern state of Andhra Pradesh chose to go ahead with building a smart city without federal funding after the state's plans for a new capital, "Amaravati," was not selected to be part of the SCM.[18] Thus, the SCM, which predates the Modi administration, has been diluted after facing pushback, and the state's control over the concept has begun to splinter.

Blundering Market Intervention and Reform

Demonetization Policy (2016)

On November 8, 2016, Prime Minister Modi abruptly announced in a televised address to the nation that all ₹500 (~$7.50) and ₹1000 (~$15.02) notes then in circulation needed to be returned to a bank or post office branch (initially) by November 24 and exchanged for new ₹500 and ₹2000 notes. The announcement impacted 86.4% of banknotes in circulation, worth about 11% of India's GDP.[19] The stated aim of the policy was to mitigate the use of cash for illicit activities. The policy failed to make any noticeable dent in corruption and instead led to a major, short-term contraction in India's economic growth.

A cover story for *India Today*, a generally supportive magazine, offered this withering assessment in May 2017:

> Demonetisation, which sucked out Rs 15.4 lakh crore [$210.7 billion] of currency from the system in November 2016, severely set back the manufacturing sector. The automobiles sector was a case in point, with monthly sales dipping 19 per cent the next month, in December, the biggest monthly fall in 16 years, as buyers delayed purchases. Sales of FMCG [Fast Moving Consumer Goods, e.g. milk, soft drinks, candy] products too fell 40–50 per cent on

the cash squeeze. The informal sector, which comprises over 80 per cent of the economy, was the worst hit. Hundreds of small units downed their shutters, leaving thousands jobless.[20]

Demonetization is usually a policy of last resort in an economy fighting hyperinflation or massive counterfeiting. India itself had demonetized in January 1946 (a year prior to Independence) and 1978, both times to fight the counterfeiting of high value notes. Those efforts had negligible impacts on the currency in circulation (affecting 1.7% of notes in circulation in January 1978) or on the country's GDP (impacting 0.1% of GDP in 1978). The 2016 demonetization was far more ambitious but much less thought through, given that India is one of the most cash dependent societies in the world and 600 million citizens still lacked a bank account in 2016.[21] The state mints had not been alerted to the secretive policy announcement and hence were unable to supply new notes. This led to a severe cash shortage, limits on cash withdrawals, delayed payment of wages for most workers, and the consequent business closures noted above.

Initially, the policy had aimed to devalue "black money," i.e., cash supposedly hoarded by criminals, terrorists, counterfeiters, tax cheats, and other corrupt individuals, who presumably would be reluctant to approach (apparently incorruptible) bank officials with their "dirty money" and would be unable to find proxies to exchange funds on their behalf. However, the Central Bank noted that 99.3% of invalidated currency was eventually returned, rendering the entire exercise a pointless waste of time for over a billion people, with severe short-run damage to the economy.[22] The obvious reason for the policy's failure to curb corruption is that criminals and corrupt individuals store their wealth in a wide range of assets but rarely in large piles of cash—a fact that was well known to government officials since at least the 1978 demonetization.

At best, demonetization may have given a bump to the effort to move toward a cashless economy with digital transactions, and increased mobile phone purchases as a mechanism to use a digital wallet.[23] The policy may also have temporarily hamstrung opposition politicians who were reliant on cash contributions for distributing patronage before the upcoming election, advantaging the BJP (if one assumes that news of the policy announcement was leaked within the ruling party leadership).[24]

The Farm Bills

In the midst of the COVID-19 pandemic and without significant parliamentary debate, the Modi administration introduced and passed three separate, highly controversial farm bills in September 2020. According to the government, the broad objective of the three bills was:

1. Farmers Produce Trade and Commerce Ordinance—to liberate farmers from limits on when, where, and how they could trade their produce;
2. Farmers Agreement on Price Assurance and Farm Services Ordinance—to provide a framework for private contracts between farmers and traders and for a dispute settlement mechanism (starting at the sub-divisional magistrate level); and
3. The Essential Commodities Ordinance—to lift restrictions on food stockpiling by private firms and require the government to use prices to compensate farmers for any limits on farm production imposed by the state.

The bills led to one of the largest strikes in human history and sensational images of protracted protests from farmers at the outskirts of Delhi that eventually forced the BJP government to concede to protesters' demands and repeal all three bills in late November 2021. The protesting farmers preferred to retain the right to sell their produce in government-regulated markets at a minimum fixed price. They expressed widespread distrust to the media that "large corporates" would exploit farmers and then hoard commodities to raise prices and profits. The general public, fearful that the new bills might create food insecurity, was generally sympathetic to the farmers. In essence, if media reports were to be believed, the protests seemed to be a reaction to the imposition of market relations in an area previously regulated by the state.

As discussed earlier, India's agricultural sector is highly inefficient and the majority of farmers have tiny plots of land; thus, their sensitivity to risk is high. The government claim that the bills only sought to empower farmers was certainly disingenuous, since many small farmers would likely have to liquidate their assets in cases of drought or disease. Moreover, the lack of unskilled, labor-intensive factory employment in urban areas made the prospect of transitioning out of agriculture daunting for most marginal farmers. When the farmer protests were linked to previous spates of farmer suicides in the public imagination by the press, the situation appeared dire.

Some state governments, particularly ones that are not ruled by the BJP, sided with the farmers. They viewed the legislation as a constitutional issue, since agriculture is in their purview and not that of the federal government. Eventually, the Supreme Court suspended the new laws indefinitely and asked for the creation of a committee to determine if the laws were in the national interest.

Of course, the issue is more complex than it seems from the headlines. Contract farming is actually a well-established informal practice in India. In fact, only about a fifth of marginal farmers in Punjab, one of the main states from which the protests originated, sold their products at government-regulated (i.e., Agricultural Produce Marketing Committee or APMC) marketplaces.[25] Direct contract farming in independent India dates to at least the 1990s, when PepsiCo began purchasing tomatoes directly in the state of Punjab. Formal liberalization of the government monopsony on agricultural marketplaces began in

2003 by permitting private actors to set up their own alternative agricultural market yards, engage in contract farming, directly purchase products from farmers at their farm, establish electronic trading of agricultural commodities, simplify taxes, and so on. These reforms were expanded in 2017 to include livestock.[26] Thus, the real fear among opponents of the new legislation was that it would eliminate the fixed minimum price as a safety net or alternative marketing channel.[27]

It is worth noting that providing a minimum fixed price implies a significant cost for a government keen on reducing its fiscal deficit. There are costs in terms of (open-ended) procurement, transportation, storage, and re-sale of stock at below the cost of acquisition. It is estimated that the food subsidy costs almost 1% of India's GDP.[28] In any case, government granaries infamously lose a significant share of their procured agricultural products to rather obese rodents.

Finally, the idyllic image of an orderly government agricultural market that protects highly precarious small farmers is mainly a myth. From a historical perspective, even a quasi-socialist state like India was not benevolent toward small farmers in its procurement practices. Developing countries use minimum price supports and export restraints to tax farmers implicitly in order to supply cheap food to urban areas and thus control urban wage demands and limit consumer price inflation. Although the farmers have the assurance of a fixed price for their products and therefore a stabilized income, the price set by the government is not necessarily in their best interest. The farmers who bring their products to government marketplaces also have limited bargaining power, incur substantial transportation costs, face harassment by laborers, and must manage a range of rent-seeking intermediaries.[29]

For small land holders, farming is a highly precarious occupation. On average, 16,000 agrarian workers commit suicide every year in India, but that phenomenon needs to be understood in context.³⁰ First, government statistics on suicide combine self-employed farmers and agricultural laborers. Second, while the rate of suicide among farmers (13.47%) was significant as a proportion of all suicides in the country from 1995 to 2015, it was less than the rate for housewives (19.61%) or persons engaged in other professions (15.74%) or self-employed (17.94%). Moreover, the growth rate in the rate of suicides for farmers (as well as government workers) was negative over the 20 years (for which data was available).³¹ The intense media attention focused on farmer suicides and the almost complete neglect of suicides by housewives indicates some of the parameters along which this issue has been politicized. Third, the phenomenon of agrarian worker suicides is heavily concentrated geographically in southern and central India.³² Notably, the farm bill protesters in 2020–21 mainly originated from the prosperous northwestern states of Punjab, Rajasthan, and Haryana.

In sum, even though the situation for the majority of agricultural workers who protested the farm bills was not quite as dire as portrayed in the press, and despite piecemeal liberalization of the sector over two decades, the existing arrangements were still highly inefficient and needed reform. However, the Modi government failed to garner support for stakeholders before passing its legislation and then failed to manage the backlash from farmers, state governments, the general public, and the Supreme Court once the bills were passed.

INTERNATIONAL ECONOMIC POLICIES

Despite rhetoric to the contrary, the Modi administration's economic policies have exhibited a reluctance to move beyond a mercantilist outlook on international trade, efforts to supplement liberal intergovernmental institutions in order to gain access to additional financing, and finally a desire for self-sufficiency when relative economic gains cannot be achieved.

Enduring Mercantilism

Disputes and Disengagement at the WTO

India's relations at World Trade Organization (WTO) can be best understood as a triadic contest, pitting India alternately against China and the US. Like China, India is a fundamentally mercantilist economy that relies heavily on protectionist policies to limit imports and subsidies to expand exports. For years, India has been able to use exemptions (e.g., on tariff barriers) meant for poorer developing economies to excuse its illiberal trade posture, essentially wrapping self-serving positions in the rhetoric of broader advocacy on behalf of developing countries. Due to exemptions stemming from its status as a developing country, India used to provide hesitant support for the liberal trade regime at the WTO. However, as India has become one the fastest growing middle-income emerging markets, the forbearance of India's trade partners has ended—as has India's tepid support for liberal trade.

Unsurprisingly, India has had to learn that it cannot have it both ways in its international identity as an economy and as a trading state: the more boastful the official rhetoric about India's economic achievements and potential, the more skeptical its trading partners have become of its desire for developing country exemptions. Yet India's defensive posture on trade reflects an underlying insecurity on the part of its policy elites about the country's prospects in a highly competitive global economy, along with its relative exclusion from global value chains in manufacturing (compared to East Asian economies) and lower level of foreign investment relative to India's key competitors.[33]

Like the US with its $308.8 billion trade deficit with China in 2019, India runs a large trade deficit with China ($48.6 billion in FY 2019–20).[34] And although the Sino-Indian trade deficit has been declining for several years, border tensions and geopolitical rivalry have made the trade balance a sensitive issue. India runs a trade surplus with the United States ($28.8 billion in 2019).[35]

One of the first acts of the Modi administration was to threaten to renege on India's commitments to the WTO worked out at Bali in 2013, which was part of the deadlocked Doha trade round first launched in 2001. At Bali, India had argued on grounds of food security that developing countries should be permitted to stockpile food to assist low-income producers or poor consumers. The argument implied that price supports for agricultural production and subsidies for consumers should be permitted over and above what had already been agreed (i.e., stockpiling permitted up to 10% of the value of production). The greater than 10% stockpiling exception was concerning to major food exporters such as the US, Brazil, and Argentina, which viewed excessive stockpiling as a mechanism to limit competition from imported food products. India argued for an "indefinite peace clause," which would mean that trade partners could not refer stockpiling countries to the WTO dispute settlement mechanism. India initially had the support of poorer countries in its hardline position, but eventually found itself isolated as the entire agreement appeared to be heading toward yet another deadlock. A compromise was finally hammered out permitting a "interim mechanism" until a permanent solution to India's concerns could be negotiated.[36] Having agreed to the compromise in December 2013, India then refused to sign the agreement by the deadline of July 31, 2014. India argued that the high-income countries were only interested in the "trade facilitation" (i.e., the simplification, modernization, and harmonization of export and import processes) portion of the agreement and would fail to negotiate a permanent solution to the food stockpiling issue if India signed on. Beyond scuttling the 2013 Bali agreement, India's about-face behavior threatened to set a precedent that would undermine future negotiated agreements. The standoff was eventually resolved through intense bilateral negotiations between President Obama and PM Modi. The agreement provides India with a firm commitment that WTO members would not file complaints against countries stockpiling food in the short-term and there would be intensified negotiations to work out a permanent solution.[37] While the Modi administration counted the concession from the Obama administration as a victory, the longer arc of India's posture on Bali negotiations demonstrates that India's fundamental outlook on the agreement did not change much from 2013 to 2014.

In 2017, India withdrew from the ongoing WTO negotiations to expand the coverage and scope of the 1997 International Technology Agreement (ITA). The Indian government stated that the agreement had nearly wiped out India's IT industry and that China had seen a gain in global market share from 2% in 2000 to 14% in 2011.[38] By 2018, India had already begun imposing tariffs on items that were covered under the original ITA, upsetting India's trade partners.

The Trump administration imposed two rounds of protectionist tariffs in January and March 2018. Trump's primary target was China, with which the US had a massive trade deficit, and initially India was exempted from the trade war since it was classified as a developing country. However, the second round of tariffs did impact Indian exports to the US as the Trump administration removed India's protected status as a developing nation under the Generalized System of Preferences (GSP). Therefore, India announced retaliatory tariffs worth $1.4 billion on US imports. Indian tariffs were still within the very high "bound rate" that India had agreed to at the WTO, so these new tariffs were not a violation of WTO agreements. The tariffs were mainly symbolic since they only amounted to 6.3% of India's total imports from the US—and the impact was felt most acutely in the US almond export business, which accounted for 42% of listed products.[39] India hoped that its growing strategic partnership with the US in security affairs would limit the parameters of the trade dispute.

However, the US persisted in targeting India. The US requested to use the WTO dispute settlement mechanism and accused India of subsidizing its manufactured exports through the Modi administration's "Make in India" policy (discussed below). The conflict over the "Make in India" program had been simmering since its inception, but now the US formally pressed its case at the WTO. The US also announced new restrictions on H1-B visas, which impacted Indian nationals seeking to work in the US. India responded by announcing additional retaliatory tariffs. The trade spat eventually cooled after direct meetings between Trump and Modi at the G20 Summit in Osaka (June 2019) and Modi's visit to the US (September 2019).[40]

In October, the WTO dispute resolution body ruled in favor of the US and demanded that India withdraw its $7 billion in export subsidies from the "Make in India" policy within 90 to 180 days. India appealed the verdict.

With regard to China, India has made ample use of the WTO's "anti-dumping" provisions to retaliate against Chinese exports to the Indian market. In fact, India was the most frequent issuer of complaints (accounting for 16% of all cases) from 1996 to 2016. In almost two-thirds of India's cases, China was the sole or one of the main targets of the complaint. In 2018, as the US ramped up its trade war with China over steel and aluminum, India imposed tariffs on Chinese (and Vietnamese) stainless steel pipes and tubes—possibly indicating a fear that China would divert exports intended for the US market to India's market.[41]

"Make in India" Policy (2014)

The Modi administration announced "Make in India," the centerpiece of its economic policy, in September 2014. The broad goal of the policy package was to make India into a manufacturing hub by improving the production efficiency of 25 key manufacturing and service sub-sectors.[42] Capital for efficiency enhancements would come by clearing access for foreign direct investors and lowering the cost of basic inputs. The policy specifically aimed to simplify the tax system and end "retrospective" taxation of cross-border investments; deregulate prices for diesel, gas, kerosene; eliminate minimum price supports for agricultural goods; permit 49% or greater foreign investment in insurance, defense, and railways; reduce restrictions on foreign investment in multi-brand and single-brand retail; integrate development of infrastructure; improve waste management; provide long-term federal subsidies to manufacturers; and so on.[43] The project did attract investment announcements from Apple, Xiaomi, Kia Motors, and Samsung. However, the policy did not increase the productive output of Indian manufacturing as envisioned,[44] nor did it propel India into significantly more sophisticated manufacturing.

The policy seemed rational at the time given the dramatic increase in India's manufactured exports and service exports as a share of GDP and as a share of world trade since India's liberalization in 1991.[45] Exports of goods and services rose from 8.5% of GDP in 1991 to 25.4% in 2013.[46] Of course, the actual scope for improving India's low-tech and low-skilled manufacturing was limited by China's (and other emerging market manufacturers') incumbency advantage.[47] Moreover, the notion that India could simply replicate the export-led industrial strategy of the Asian Tiger economies and China ignored significant changes in the international political economy, away from national production of final commodities and toward global value chains (GVC) that encouraged the dispersed production of manufacturing inputs.[48] Hence, the policy's potential for generating employment for India's large unskilled population was always questionable. India's exportable services are more competitive in the global marketplace than its manufacturing, particularly in research and development. However, India imports nearly as much in services as it exports. In 2018, for example, it imported $111 billion in services and exported $113 billion.[49] Hence, there was no clear pathway for India to improve rapidly its exportable goods and services.

By 2019, India's export of goods and services actually fell to 18.4% of GDP.[50] The "Make in India" policy was unable to match

India's peak performance in 2013. Given that the Indian rupee has continued to weaken relative to the US dollar (moving from ₹61.0 in 2014 to ₹74.1 in 2019), exports should have performed better. India's export prospects are not helped by its growing insularity. India's decision to opt out of the RCEP (Regional Comprehensive Economic Partnership) in November 2019 (as discussed below) will limit its access to markets in the largest trading bloc on Earth.

More positively, India has seen an improvement in its Economic Complexity Index (ECI) ranking, which is a measure of the relative knowledge intensity of an economy, from 52nd place (ECI 0.39) in 2013 to 44th place (ECI 0.59) out of 146 in 2019.[51] India has always performed better than countries with similar GDP per capita (e.g., Tunisia, Vietnam, Egypt, Kenya). However, it is worth noting that China's ECI ranking also improved from 31st place (ECI 0.83) in 2013 to 27th place (ECI 1.03) in 2019. In other words, India improved its sophistication ranking, but so did its most important major competitor. Today, India's most sophisticated exports are chemical compounds (phosphides, inorganic acids, and salts), rods of stainless steel, and hand tools (wrenches, sockets, etc.); its most specialized products are spice seeds, organic compounds, processed hair, and granite.

Foreign direct investment (FDI) did increase in absolute terms, but only marginally as a percent of GDP. Net inflows of FDI moved from 1.7% of GDP (or $34.6 billion in current US$) in 2014 to a high of 2.1% of GDP in 2015 (or $44 billion), but declined thereafter. In 2019, FDI stood at 1.8% of GDP (or $50.6 billion). These numbers pale in comparison to the height of FDI in 2008, which reached 3.6% of GDP (or $43.4 billion) just before the US sub-prime financial crisis.

The Modi administration also introduced the category of "Indigenously Designed, Developed and Manufactured (IDDM)" to promote indigenous manufacturing and reduce "import dependence" in the defense industry.[52]

The government did relax investment rules in 15 sectors, including civil aviation, banking, defense, retail, and news broadcasting.[53] India also seemed to improve its "Ease of Doing Business" score with the World Bank, moving from a 54.0 in 2015 to 71.0 in 2019 on a scale of 0 to 100.[54] India jumped in the World Bank's Ease of Doing Business ranking from 142nd place in 2015 to 63rd in 2019 for the cities of Mumbai and Delhi. It is worth noting, though, that the World Bank detected irregularities in its data from 2016 to 2020 that were inconsistent with its methodology. Thus, the suspiciously high jump in rankings should be taken with a heavy dose of skepticism. The World Bank is currently undertaking an internal audit and review of the data.[55]

Foreign Trade Policy (2015)

India announced a new foreign trade policy (FTP) in April 2015 with the objective of increasing India's share of world trade from 2% to 3.5%.[56] The policy aimed to consolidate India's export subsidies and drawbacks[57] in goods and services to boost exports that had begun to decline due to falling demand and currency appreciation.[58] The FTP scheme envisioned drawbacks of 2% to 5% for selected manufactured items and a reduction from 10% to 3% – 5% for service providers located in India.[59]

Only two years later, however, India became subject to Annex VII of the Subsidies and Countervailing Measures (SCM) Agreement at the WTO. This meant that India needed to disassemble all its subsidies in all sectors by 2018, since by India's own admission it had reached "export competitiveness" in 2010. However, India argued that duty remissions were not subsidies and so the SCM was not relevant.[60] In October 2019, a WTO dispute settlement body found that five of India's export subsidy programs were inconsistent with its obligations as a member country.[61] India appealed the ruling the following month.

In the meantime, India announced a new scheme, the Remission of Duties or Taxes on Export Products (RoDTEP). PM Modi's government approved the scheme in March 2020. The difference between the FTP and RoDTEP is that the latter reimburses "embedded taxes" (e.g., taxes on petroleum, electricity, etc.) and duties already incurred by exporters in their supply chain. The RoDTEP is more likely to comply with global trade norms as all countries are permitted to "zero-rate" exports to eliminate taxes incurred in the cost of production.[62] In essence, while India remains fundamentally mercantilist, it is becoming more adept at playing the game.

Exploring Alternatives

In a bid to build resilience, increase funding for development projects, and demonstrate the potential of emerging powers, India joined with other emerging markets to build several alternative multilateral financial arrangements. However, these initiatives have generally remained supplementary to the US-led liberal institutions.

Contingent Reserve Arrangement (CRA, 2014)

The BRICS (Brazil, Russia, India, China, and South Africa) group of "emerging market" economies established the Contingent Reserve Arrangement in 2014 to provide mutual financial assistance during a short-term balance-of-payments crisis. China contributed $41 billion, while Brazil, Russia, and India contributed $18 billion each, and South Africa gave $5 billion. These "contributions" mainly involve rendering existing foreign exchange reserves callable in case of a crisis. An added motivation to set up the CRA was to dilute the leverage of the International Monetary Fund (IMF) during an economic crisis.[63] Although Brazil, Russia, India, and China are among the top ten largest shareholders in the IMF, these states have been frustrated by the slow pace with which the US has acceded to adjusting voting power in the institution and the ideologically inflected technical advice doled out to member countries seeking financial aid during a crisis. However, since BRICS members needing access to more than 30% of their CRA quota must first arrange a structural adjustment loan from the IMF, the CRA paradoxically is still nested within the architecture of the IMF.[64]

New Development Bank (NDB, 2014)

In order for an emerging economy to maintain its pace of economic growth, it needs to invest in infrastructure (including water, power, renewable energy, transportation, and telecommunications) that progressively eliminates bottlenecks between producers and consumers.[65] The idea of the New Development Bank was first introduced in 2012 at the fourth BRICS summit in New Delhi, and the bank was created at the BRICS Summit in Fortaleza in 2014.[66] The bank was conceptualized to have equal subscription shares and voting power for each of the five BRICS countries. In contrast to the CRA, the funds of the NDB are available to other middle- and low-income countries.

The NDB is oriented toward the China model of speedier project preparation and approval. Moreover, unlike the US-led liberal institutions, the focus is on physical infrastructure rather than social capabilities. Finally, there is no "conditionality" (e.g., environmental stipulations on project proposals) and the loans are based on "non-cash financing" (e.g., payment of debts by issuing shares) to attempt to avoid wholesale corruption.[67]

To date, ten projects in India worth a total of $3.5 billion have been approved by the NDB. Five of these projects are targeted to develop transportation, two are in water resource management, two are in urban redevelopment (including the Mumbai Metro Rail), and one is in clean energy.

It is worth noting that both the CRA and NDB are US dollar denominated institutions (as opposed to using a basket of currencies from the BRICS member countries). This implicitly reinforces the hegemony of the US as the manager of an international reserve currency and limits the development of alternative financial centers of power.[68] Moreover, these new institutions continue to rely on US-based credit ratings agencies and have yet to challenge a host of other standard-setting bodies in international finance (e.g., the Basel Committee on Banking Supervision at the Bank for International Settlements, or the International Organization of Securities Commissions, etc.), or the sovereign debt restructuring regime (i.e., "The Paris Club").[69]

Asian Infrastructure Investment Bank (AIIB, 2015)

India became a founding member and the second largest shareholder in the China-led Asian Infrastructure Investment Bank (AIIB) under PM Modi. In fact, Modi was asked in person by China's President Xi Jinping to join the AIIB at the BRICS summit in Brazil in 2014.[70] India contributed just over $8 billion to capitalize the bank, which paled in comparison to China's nearly $30 billion initial funding. Nevertheless, India's contribution provided it with access to nearly $100 billion in loans to fund its infrastructure development. Unsurprisingly, India has become the AIIB's single largest borrower.

Aside from prestige and influence in this budding multilateral institution, India will be able to fast-track mega-infrastructure projects and powerplants that had been hamstrung by the regulations of the World Bank and the Asian Development Bank (ADB). The role of the World Bank and the ADB will be relegated to irrigation projects and arterial roads as well as social capacity and capability enhancement.[71]

Since 2017, 27 projects have been approved in India by the AIIB for a total value of $6.2 billion. The projects, some of which are sponsored by the government of India and others proposed by private corporations operating in India, include funding for solid waste management, gas distribution, solar power plants, metro rail, etc. Several of the loans are also co-financed by the World Bank, the ADB, and regional banks.[72]

It is worth noting that while the subscribed capital of the NDB ($50 billion in 2021; plus an additional $40 billion callable) and the AIIB ($96.7 billion in 2021) is substantial and larger than the ADB ($36.6 billion in 2020), it is still considerably less than the total subscribed capital of the World Bank ($275 billion in 2021).[73] Similarly, while the BRICS' CRA has a substantial pool of resources ($100 billion in capital contributions), it pales next to the IMF ($687 billion in 2021 from member quotas, plus $526 billion in credit arrangements, and $183 billion in bilateral borrowing arrangements in 2021—for a total of $1.4 trillion). Given the size of the global economy ($93.86 trillion in 2021), even these massive resources would likely not be sufficient in the case of another major global financial crisis.

Going It Alone

Rejecting RCEP (2019)

Given India's general reluctance to engage vigorously in competitive trade, it is not surprising that India backed out of the Regional Comprehensive Economic Partnership (RCEP), after seven years of negotiations, in November 2019.[74] The RCEP, which consists of all ten ASEAN member countries plus China, South Korea, Japan, Australia, and New Zealand, is the largest free trade bloc in the world, even without India's participation. Although the members of RCEP remain open to India rejoining at any time, it is unlikely that India will return to the group. India has pre-existing free trade agreements with ASEAN, Japan, and South Korea.

Indian firms would have gained expanded export markets in commodities like textiles and clothing, consumer goods, vegetables, and leather as RCEP partners lowered their tariff barriers, but India feared opening its domestic market to imports of the same items. In other areas (e.g., chemicals), India would not have gained significantly as most RCEP partners already had modest tariffs. In general, India did not view itself as dynamically competitive relative to the other members of RCEP. While India had a trade deficit with 11 of the 15 RCEP countries, it was particularly concerned about its trade deficit with China.[75] Specifically, India had wanted protection against "import surges," a tariff differential with China, improved rules of origin criteria, a change in the base year for tariff reductions from 2014, and safeguards on services and labor markets where India has a competitive advantage.[76]

From the perspective of domestic politics, the Swadeshi Jagran Manch (SJM), a nationalist anti-free trade group with direct ties to the hard-right RSS, began a national agitation against RCEP in mid-October 2019. Given the Modi government's strong ties to the RSS, it would have been costly to move forward with the RCEP despite the sunk cost of years of negotiations and reputational effects.[77]

Atma Nirbhar Bharat Abhiyan / Self-Reliance Mission (2020)

Prime Minister Modi announced a new plan to make India "self-reliant" in May 2020, after the outbreak of the COVID-19 pandemic. Facing a sharp drop in domestic and global demand due to the pandemic as well as increasing border tension with China, the notion of creating a self-reliant India was rhetorically seductive. However, the scheme was primarily a thinly disguised economic stimulus package. In subsequent months, there have been two further iterations (October 2020, November 2020) of the scheme; in total, approximately $420 billion has been allocated to the program to date.

The stimulus package did add a production linked incentive (PLI) scheme to attract foreign and domestic investment in the manufacture of electronics, pharmaceutical ingredients, and medical devices.[78] The aim was to reduce India's non-petroleum import bill by producing inputs and intermediate goods locally and to spur exports while creating a manufacturing ecosystem. After reportedly locking in $178 million in investments and potentially generating 22,000 new jobs in the large-scale electronics manufacturing scheme, the self-reliance mission was quickly extended to ten other sectors, including defense, chemical fertilizer, and space research. The PLI scheme now covers a wide range of manufactured products, including air-conditioners, laptops, tablets, personal computers, food processing equipment, printed circuit boards, solar photovoltaic cells, and LED lights.[79] Seventy firms, most notably including Apple Inc., have shown an interest or announced plans to invest in India—but no firm has actually filed an incentive disbursement claim to date. The scheme represents a massive $26.6 billion taxpayer funded subsidy to manufacturers over the next five years. The Indian government is essentially agreeing to "top-up" the profits of firms (at a rate of around 5 to 6%) during a fixed period in exchange for the firm fulfilling prearranged annual, incremental investment, and production criteria.[80] In other words, India is paying private (foreign and domestic) firms to manufacture goods and create jobs domestically. The arrangement is valid under the rules of the WTO.

It should be noted that the notion of "self-reliance," a throwback to India's anti-colonial struggle and its autarchic period in the sixties and seventies, was also—in part—a rhetorical mask for the erection of trade barriers targeting Chinese products. The plan gained urgency after a bloody border clash with China in June 2020 in the disputed Aksai Chin region of the Himalayas (discussed in the chapter on foreign policy). The Indian government cancelled a slew of Chinese investments, including in 4G and

5G telecommunications, smart electricity meters, railway signaling devices, and a monorail project in Mumbai. Import restrictions were also added to several hundred Chinese products. Finally, FDI rules were changed for countries sharing a border with India.[81]

More broadly, the PLI scheme itself was designed to shift manufacturing from China to India—a fact that was not lost on the Chinese, who quickly lobbied to disincentivize firms from shifting their production facilities.[82]

EXPLAINING THE BOOM

Given the mixed economic environment inherited by the Modi administration, with its characteristic cronyism, corruption, accumulated debt, entrenched poverty, and labor issues, not to mention the incompetent management and mercantilist outlook of the Modi administration, why is India's stock market booming? And why is India's overall economy projected to be the fastest growing major economy in the world for the next several years?

Part of the answer to India's economic trajectory is external. As global investors sour on China's increasingly repressive political system—particularly toward its own IT sector—and slowing economic growth due to demographic shifts, India begins to look more attractive. Another part of the answer is that India's RBI has engaged in a bond buying program that is similar to the Quantitative Easing used by central banks in high-income countries to restore consumer confidence.[83] Increased government spending on infrastructure to relieve supply bottlenecks and pent-up consumer demand from the pandemic may also be fueling market optimism. Finally, speculative turnover is reaching heights not seen since 2009. In February 2021, the Bombay Stock Exchange's Sensex Index was valued at 24 times next year's earning—the highest this century and more than the American S&P 500.[84] With new public listings on Indian IT firms (e.g., the digital payment and e-commerce firm Paytm), institutional investors and sovereign wealth funds see the potential for major profits in India. Of course, as laid out in the economic overview and this chapter, India's economic fundamentals remain weak and its economy vulnerable; thus, the performance of the stock market should not be taken as an indicator of underlying health or sustainability of the economy or its potential to create an equitable recovery from the COVID-19 pandemic.

NOTES

1 See for example, Sanjay Ruparelia, "'Minimum Government, Maximum Governance': The Restructuring of Power in Modi's India," *South Asia: Journal of South Asian Studies* 38, no. 4 (October 2, 2015): 775, https://doi.org/10.1080/00856401.2015.1089974.
2 Vinay Kumar Singh and Rohit Prasad, "Diffusion of Banking Products in Financial Inclusion Linked Savings Accounts: A Case Study Based on Pradhan Mantri Jan Dhan Yojana in India," *Global Business Review* (2021): 3–4, https://doi.org/10.1177/09721509211006866.
3 Saibal Ghosh, "Financial Inclusion in India: Does Distance Matter?," *South Asia Economic Journal* 21, no. 2 (2020): 219, https://doi.org/10.1177/1391561420961649.
4 World Bank, "Enterprise Surveys"; World Bank, "Global Findex Database," Database, World Bank Global Findex, 2017, https://globalfindex.worldbank.org/.
5 Asli Demirgüç-Kunt et al., "The Global Findex Database, 2017: Measuring Financial Inclusion and the Fintech Revolution" (Washington, DC: World Bank, 2018), 19.
6 Demirgüç-Kunt et al., xii.
7 Demirgüç-Kunt et al., 19.
8 Demirgüç-Kunt et al., 32.
9 Demirgüç-Kunt et al., 2.
10 Demirgüç-Kunt et al., 35.
11 Demirgüç-Kunt et al., 48–65.
12 Singh and Prasad, "Diffusion of Banking Products in Financial Inclusion Linked Savings Accounts," 2–3.

13. Kristian Hoelscher, "The Evolution of the Smart Cities Agenda in India," *International Area Studies Review* 19, no. 1 (2016): 29, https://doi.org/10.1177/2233865916632089.
14. Hoelscher, 31–32.
15. Hoelscher, 29–30.
16. Hoelscher, 33.
17. Hoelscher, 36.
18. Hoelscher, 37–38.
19. Cyril Fouillet, Isabelle Guérin, and Jean-Michel Servet, "Demonetization and Digitalization: The Indian Government's Hidden Agenda," *Telecommunications Policy* 45, no. 2 (March 2021): 1–2, https://doi.org/10.1016/j.telpol.2020.102079.
20. M. G. Arun, "3 Years Later, Narendra Modi's Dream Make in India Plans Yet to Take Off," *India Today*, May 29, 2017.
21. Fouillet, Guérin, and Servet, "Demonetization and Digitalization," 2; Masudul Hasan Adil and Neeraj R. Hatekar, "Demonetisation, Banking and Trust in 'Bricks' Or 'Clicks,'" *South Asia Research* 40, no. 2 (2020): 183, https://doi.org/10.1177/0262728020915566.
22. Adil and Hatekar, "Demonetisation, Banking and Trust in 'Bricks' Or 'Clicks,'" 185.
23. Adil and Hatekar, 190–93; Fouillet, Guérin, and Servet, "Demonetization and Digitalization," 2.
24. Fouillet, Guérin, and Servet, "Demonetization and Digitalization," 3.
25. Aashish Argade, Arnab Kumar Laha, and Anand Kumar Jaiswal, "Connecting Smallholders' Marketplace Decisions to Agricultural Market Reform Policy in India—An Empirical Exploration," *Journal of Macromarketing* 41, no. 3 (2021): 472, https://doi.org/10.1177/0276146721997885.
26. Argade, Laha, and Jaiswal, 473.
27. Anonymous, "India: Behind the Farmers' Strike," *Against the Current* 35, no. 6 (2021): 10–10.
28. Marc A. Rosenbohm, "The Impact on Domestic Prices and Government Costs of Limiting Wheat Procurement in India," *ProQuest Dissertations and Theses* (M.S., Ann Arbor, University of Missouri—Columbia, 2016), 2, (2164291931).
29. Argade, Laha, and Jaiswal, "Connecting Smallholders' Marketplace Decisions to Agricultural Market Reform Policy in India," 472.
30. Sthanu R. Nair, "Agrarian Suicides in India: Myth and Reality," *Development Policy Review* 39, no. 1 (2019): 4, https://doi.org/10.1111/dpr.12482.
31. Nair, 6.

32 Nair, 12.
33 Palit, "Will India's Disengaging Trade Policy Restrict It from Playing a Greater Global Role?," 203-4.
34 Ministry of Commerce & Industry Government of India, "Trade Deficit Between India and China," Press Release, Press Information Bureau, February 3, 2021, https://pib.gov.in/Pressreleaseshare.aspx?PRID=1575818.
35 USTR, "2020 National Trade Estimate on Foreign Trade Barriers."
36 Amrita Narlikar and Diana Tussie, "Breakthrough at Bali? Explanations, Aftermath, Implications," *International Negotiation* 21, no. 2 (2016): 217-18, https://doi.org/10.1163/15718069-12341331.
37 Narlikar and Tussie, 226-27.
38 Prema-chandra Athukorala, "Trump's Trade War: An Indian Perspective," *Asian Economic Papers* 19, no. 1 (2020): 97, https://doi.org/10.1162/asep_a_00749.
39 Athukorala, 99.
40 Athukorala, 100-101.
41 Athukorala, 102.
42 The sectors were: automobiles, food processing, renewable energy, automobile components, information technology, roads and highways, aviation, leather, space, biotechnology, media and entertainment, textiles and garments, chemicals, mining, thermal power, construction, oil and gas, tourism and hospitality, defense manufacturing, pharmaceuticals, wellness, electrical machinery, ports, electronic systems, and railways.
43 Chang Woon Nam and Peter Steinhoff, "The 'Make in India' Initiative," *CESifo Forum; München* 19, no. 3 (Autumn 2018): 44-45.
44 Benjamin Parkin, "Has the 'Make in India' Campaign Run out of Steam?," *Financial Times*, December 18, 2019, https://www-ft-com.ezproxy.babson.edu/content/3fbe1c46-0c7f-11ea-8fb7-8fcec0c3b0f9.
45 Rahul Anand, Kalpana Kochhar, and Saurabh Mishra, *Make in India*, IMF Working Papers, WP/15/119 (Washington, DC: International Monetary Fund, 2015), 6.
46 World Bank, "World Development Indicators."
47 Anand, Kochhar, and Mishra, *Make in India*, 43.
48 Baldwin, *The Great Convergence*.
49 OEC, "Economic Complexity Rankings (ECI)."
50 World Bank, "World Development Indicators."
51 OEC, "Economic Complexity Rankings (ECI)." Calculations were conducted using the Harmonized System (HS07) with a depth of 6 digits. The dataset

includes countries with a population of at least 1 million and exports of at least $1 billion, and products with world trade over $500 million.

52 Sandeep Unnithan, "Policy Paralysis, Bureaucratic Lethargy Undoing Modi's Make in India Plan to Indigenise Weapons Production: With Strategic Partnerships Paving the Way for Joint Ventures between Indian and Foreign Firms, the Weak Link Is Slow Decision-Making in the Defence Ministry, Which Hands out the Contracts," *India Today* (New Delhi: Living Media India, Limited, March 6, 2017).

53 Arun, "3 Years Later, Narendra Modi's Dream Make in India Plans yet to Take Off."

54 World Bank, "World Development Indicators."

55 World Bank, "Doing Business—Data Irregularities Statement," World Bank, August 27, 2020, https://www.worldbank.org/en/news/statement/2020/08/27/doing-business---data-irregularities-statement; World Bank, "World Bank Group Statement on Doing Business Data Corrections and Findings of Internal Audit," World Bank, December 16, 2020, https://www.worldbank.org/en/news/statement/2020/12/16/world-bank-group-statement-on-doing-business-data-corrections-and-findings-of-internal-audit.

56 USTR, "2020 National Trade Estimate on Foreign Trade Barriers," 247.

57 A drawback is essentially an import duty that is refunded if the imported product or input is exported.

58 Dinesh Kanabar and Ritesh Kanodia, "Column: FTP Boost for Brand India," *Financial Express*, April 3, 2015.

59 Kanabar and Kanodia.

60 WTO, "Concerns Grow about Slippage in Subsidy Notifications," April 25, 2017, https://www.wto.org/english/news_e/news17_e/scm_25apr17_e.htm. The WTO calculated that India had achieved export competitiveness by 2007.

61 USTR, "2020 National Trade Estimate on Foreign Trade Barriers," 247.

62 Mondaq Business Briefing, "Tax Street—June 2020," *Mondaq Business Briefing*, July 14, 2020, Business Insights: Essentials, https://bi-gale-com.ezproxy.hws.edu/essentials/article/GALE%7CA629427346?u=nysl_ro_hobart&sid=summon.

63 Schüller and Wogart, "The Emergence of Post-Crisis Regional Financial Institutions in Asia—With a Little Help from Europe," 490.

64 Daniel McDowell, "Emergent International Liquidity Agreements: Central Bank Cooperation After the Global Financial Crisis," *Journal of International Relations and Development* 22, no. 2 (2019): 460, https://doi.org/10.1057/s41268-017-0106-0; Patrick Bond, "BRICS Banking and the Debate over

Sub-Imperialism," *Third World Quarterly* 37, no. 4 (2016): 613, https://doi.org/10.1080/01436597.2015.1128816.

65 Bas Hooijmaaijers, "Understanding Success and Failure in Establishing New Multilateral Development Banks: The SCO Development Bank, the NDB, and the AIIB," *Asian Perspective* 45, no. 2 (2021): 448–49.

66 Deepa M. Ollapally, "India and the International Order: Accommodation and Adjustment," *Ethics & International Affairs* 32, no. 1 (2018): 67–68, https://doi.org/10.1017/S0892679418000102.

67 Renu Rana, "Asian Infrastructure Investment Bank, New Development Bank and the Reshaping of Global Economic Order: Unfolding Trends and Perceptions in Sino-Indian Economic Relations," *International Journal of China Studies* 10, no. 2 (2019): 277–78.

68 Bond, "BRICS Banking and the Debate over Sub-Imperialism," 614.

69 Eric Helleiner and Hongying Wang, "Limits to the BRICS' Challenge: Credit Rating Reform and Institutional Innovation in Global Finance," *Review of International Political Economy* 25, no. 5 (September 3, 2018): 573–95, https://doi.org/10.1080/09692290.2018.1490330.

70 Schüller and Wogart, "The Emergence of Post-Crisis Regional Financial Institutions in Asia—With a Little Help from Europe," 493.

71 Gregory T. Chin, "Asian Infrastructure Investment Bank: Governance Innovation and Prospects," *Global Governance* 22, no. 1 (2016): 18–19, https://doi.org/10.1163/19426720-02201002.

72 Rana, "Asian Infrastructure Investment Bank, New Development Bank and the Reshaping of Global Economic Order," 279.

73 AIIB, "AIIB Q1-2021 Financial-Statements" (AIIB, March 2021); NDB, "Annual Report 2020: Meeting Ever Evolving Development Challenges" (New Development Bank, 2020), https://www.ndb.int/wp-content/uploads/2021/06/NDB-AR-2020_complete_616.pdf; World Bank, "Debt Products FAQs," Text/HTML, World Bank, accessed July 21, 2021, https://treasury.worldbank.org/en/about/unit/treasury/ibrd/debt-products-faqs; ADB, "ADB Annual Report 2020" (ADB, December 2020).

74 Palit, "Will India's Disengaging Trade Policy Restrict It from Playing a Greater Global Role?," 206.

75 Amlan Ray, M. G. Deepika, and G. Badri Narayanan, "Analysis of India's Competitive Position in RCEP," *Vision (New Delhi, India)* 25, no. 3 (2021): 339, https://doi.org/10.1177/09722629211003699.

76 Ray, Deepika, and Narayanan, 337.

77 Palit, "Will India's Disengaging Trade Policy Restrict It from Playing a Greater Global Role?," 211–12.

78 Joe C. Mathew and Nidhi Singal, "Factory to the World?: The Production Linked Incentive Scheme Aims to Build an Indian Manufacturing Base across 13 Key Sectors. What Works. What Doesn't," *Business Today*, May 2, 2021.
79 Mathew and Singal.
80 Mathew and Singal.
81 Shankar Kumar, "How India Is Quietly Resetting Its Economic Engagement with China," *Governance Now*, June 29, 2020.
82 Mathew and Singal, "Factory to the World?"
83 Matt Phillips and Emily Schmall, "Stocks Soar in India, Luring Investors at Home and Abroad," *New York Times*, November 11, 2021.
84 Mike Bird, "India's Stock Market Mania Defies Economic Reality; India's Stocks Are Outperforming Those in Similar Markets, Even as the Pandemic May Have Exacerbated Its Longer-Term Economic Challenges," *Wall Street Journal*, February 19, 2021, Eastern edition.

SUGGESTED FURTHER READING

Baru, Sanjaya, *The Accidental Prime Minister: The Making and Unmaking of Manmohan Singh* (Penguin, 2015). ISBN: 978-0143424062.

Jaffrelot, Christophe, Atul Kohli, and Kanta Murali, eds., *Business and Politics in India* (Oxford University Press, 2019). ISBN: 978-0190912475.

Panagariya, Arvind, *New India: Reclaiming the Lost Glory* (Oxford University Press, 2020). ISBN: 978-0197531556.

Soz, Salman Anees, *The Great Disappointment: How Narendra Modi Squandered a Unique Opportunity to Transform the Indian Economy* (Penguin Random House, 2019). ISBN: 978-0670091799.

CHAPTER FIVE

INDIA'S FOREIGN POLICY UNDER MODI

On March 12, 2021 (March 13 in Australia), Indian Prime Minister Narendra Modi, his Australian and Japanese counterparts Scott Morrison and Yoshihide Suga, and new US President Joe Biden came together via videoconference for a historic meeting: the first-ever leader-level summit of a diplomatic club known as "the Quad." The optics reflected the ongoing global COVID-19 pandemic, as Biden, US Secretary of State Antony Blinken, and other US officials spread out across "socially distanced" tables in the State Dining Room of the White House in Washington, DC. They were flanked by large flat-screen monitors linking them to the leaders in Canberra, New Delhi, and Tokyo, whose countries' names and flags were displayed above their larger-than-life images.[1] With the exception of Biden while he spoke, the Americans in the room all wore face coverings to protect against the coronavirus. While the new US administration sought to distance itself from the Donald Trump White House in this and almost every other conceivable way, the Quad summit signified strategic continuity (even if Trump's outgoing secretary of state, Mike Pompeo, somewhat oversold the initiative by calling it an "Asian NATO"[2] to contain China).

Formally the Quadrilateral Security Dialogue, the Quad was launched in 2007 by Japan's then-Prime Minister Shinzo Abe, building on cooperation among the countries after the cataclysmic 2004 Indian Ocean earthquake and tsunami. After making initial commitments, Australia had cooled on the Quad concept. A new Labor Party government pulled back from the forum in 2008, even as the other countries' relationships—and particularly, the US–India "strategic partnership"—drew closer in response to China's rise. Without Canberra's participation, the Quad was dormant from 2009 to 2017. Meanwhile, in China, Xi Jinping took hold of the key levers of power—as general secretary of the Chinese Communist Party and Chairman of the Central Military Commission from 2012, and as president from 2013—and returned China to a more authoritarian leadership model. Xi then launched an aggressive nationalist project to "rejuvenate" China and mark its arrival as a great power.

To a significant degree, Modi's India held the key to the Quad's own rejuvenation.[3] In the summer of 2017, a sudden flare-up in long-simmering border tensions with China sparked India's renewed interest in cultivating broader strategic partnerships. At Japan's suggestion, the Quad countries' foreign ministers came together on the sidelines of the November 2017 meeting of the Association of Southeast Asian Nations (ASEAN) in the Philippines. The Quad met, in various capacities, a total of five times over 2017–19. With the outbreak of the COVID-19 global pandemic in early 2020, the group invited New Zealand, South Korea, and Vietnam for a wider "Quad Plus" dialogue (held remotely) on the unfolding public health and economic crisis.

The four leaders now marked their March 2021 summit with a joint statement on a vision for the Indo-Pacific:

> We strive for a region that is free, open, inclusive, healthy, anchored by democratic values, and unconstrained by coercion. We recall that our joint efforts toward this positive vision arose out of an

international tragedy, the tsunami of 2004. Today, the global devastation wrought by COVID-19, the threat of climate change, and security challenges facing the region summon us with renewed purpose.

The statement continued,

Together, we commit to promoting a free, open, rules-based order, rooted in international law to advance security and prosperity and counter threats to both in the Indo-Pacific and beyond. We support the rule of law, freedom of navigation and overflight, peaceful resolution of disputes, democratic values, and territorial integrity.... Full of potential, the Quad looks forward to the future; it seeks to uphold peace and prosperity and strengthen democratic resilience, based on universal values.[4]

Biden, Modi, Morrison, and Suga also contributed a joint op-ed published by the *Washington Post*, adding references to "new technologies [that] have revolutionized our lives" and "geopolitics [that] have become ever more complex."[5]

The Quad statements amounted to an indirect but unmistakable criticism of China, which had been recently aggressive in its territorial claims in the South China Sea and hostile to Hong Kong's pro-democracy movement. Presently, China was engaged in a relentless public diplomacy campaign to reshape global perceptions of its role in the COVID-19 pandemic—sending personal protective equipment and other supplies around the world—even as the regime tightly controlled the flow of information about COVID-19's origins in Wuhan province and about its own initial response, which had allowed the virus to spread rapidly in China and beyond.

But for all the apparent solidarity behind the statements, the Quad leaders left out certain inconvenient facts that made the pandemic and broader geopolitical realities confronting them even more complicated than they acknowledged. The Quad's self-congratulatory reference to "the progress our countries have achieved on health security" offered no acknowledgment of the severity of the public health crises stemming from COVID-19 deaths in the US and India, particularly for their most vulnerable citizens. While the US was the clear global leader in vaccine development, it had also accounted for the world's largest share of COVID-19 in 2020 after the pandemic's initial outbreak in China and spread in Europe. Two months after the Quad's March meeting, the WHO would identify in India a new, more transmissible "Delta variant" of the coronavirus that causes COVID-19. A calamitous new wave of COVID-19 infections and deaths engulfed India, threatening the country's economic progress and the fragile livelihoods of millions of Indians only recently lifted above the poverty line, and leading the Indian government to claw back vaccine stocks it had promised to Asian and African countries. By early summer, Delta would be the dominant strain worldwide.[6]

Likewise, despite much lofty rhetoric about shared democratic values, the Quad statement evinced no introspection about the recent challenges to democracy in the US and India. It would have been unusual for a joint diplomatic statement to do so, but these were unusual times. Just weeks earlier, on January 6, 2021, there had been the infamous assault on the US Capitol in Washington by a mob of Trump supporters seeking to disrupt Congress' constitutionally mandated counting of electoral college votes from the previous November's US presidential election. Just over a year prior to the Quad summit, India had been wracked by violence in Delhi that killed 53 and injured hundreds—mostly Muslims attacked by Hindu mobs—following continuing protests and counterprotests over the controversial exclusionary Citizenship (Amendment) Act of 2019. The leaders' statement seemed hardly to acknowledge the broader continuing crisis in democracy worldwide,[7] other than to proclaim "the urgent need to restore democracy" in Myanmar following its military's latest power grab in February.

The Quad's joint statement bore the names of four elected leaders, but in its mix of outward bravado and seeming lack of self-awareness, it fit particularly well with Modi's leadership style: always project strength, and deflect attention when vulnerabilities are exposed.

By contrast, the Quad statement was notably specific about regional security matters, with an eye on China. Analyst Abhijnan Rej observed, "The joint statement was unexpectedly blunt" in its call for "collaboration, including in maritime security, to meet challenges to the rules-based maritime order in the East and South China Seas"—suggesting "significant future potential for common action" and "a surprising degree of formal buy-in for such action from India," given its traditional preference for "more oblique language."

While Rej praised the joint statement as "ambitious, concrete, and direct,"[8] Kishore Mahbubani was more skeptical. In a piece for *Foreign Policy* titled "The New Anti-China Alliance Will Fail," the Singaporean diplomat and scholar agreed that the Quad member countries all "have perfectly legitimate concerns about China." But he argued,

> Unfortunately, the Quad will not alter the course of Asian history for two simple reasons: First, the four countries have different geopolitical interests and vulnerabilities. Second, and more fundamentally, they are in the wrong game. The big strategic game in Asia isn't military but economic.[9]

Australia, he said, was "most vulnerable" due to its high and asymmetric economic dependence on China. India, too, faces a serious challenge from China, Mahbubani observed: "In 1980, the economies of China and India were the same size. By 2020, China's had grown five times larger. The longer-term relationship between two powers always depends, in the long run, the relative sizes of the two economies."

In late September 2021, the Quad leaders met in person for the first time, with Biden again hosting at the White House. The *Wall Street Journal* columnist Sadanand Dhume observed, "A few years ago, when tiptoeing around Chinese sensibilities was more of a global norm, such a gathering would have been almost unimaginable."[10] But if the summit symbolized how much had changed in global politics in the space of just a few years—in perceptions and in actual conditions—it also showed the importance of prior relationships and arrangements for the foreign policy responses of India and its international partners.

THE MODI FACTOR IN INDIA'S FOREIGN POLICY: CONTINUITY AND CHANGE

Previous chapters have detailed strengths and weaknesses of India's economy and political system. This chapter turns to India's foreign policy under Narendra Modi. As the Quad diplomacy demonstrates, India seeks the recognition and status of association with other leading democracies in the greater "Indo-Pacific" region. Even Modi, with his Hindu nationalist and exclusivist politics, claims the mantle of democratic mandates behind the BJP's formidable electoral victories in 2014 and 2019, and he appears to value demonstrations of respect from elected peers such as the Quad partners.

Modi's efforts to position India as a major world power have been no less ambitious than his transformational domestic goals. And just as Modi has faced political and institutional constraints on domestic action, the external regional and global environment places limits on Modi's foreign policy action. But in contrast to the domestic sphere—where Modi, for better or worse, often seems to be setting the agenda and pace of change—in international relations, Modi's India often appears to be reacting to moves by others. In responding to external challenges and pressures, Modi exhibits some of the same hardline and hasty tendencies we have seen in his domestic governance, albeit with less clarity about his intentions—and less certainty about his strategic acumen.

Prominent Indian strategist C. Raja Mohan made the bold declaration in a 2015 book that Modi, only a year into his tenure, had already ushered in a "Third Republic" in India's foreign policy (the first being the Nehru era of non-alignment during the Cold War, and the second the partial embrace of globalization and economic liberalization in the 1990s).[11] Writing in 2017, midway through Modi's first government, scholar Sumit Ganguly asked the question, "Has Modi truly changed India's foreign policy?" Ganguly answered with a qualified "not fundamentally." Modi's frequent foreign travel and "heightened emphasis on foreign affairs" may have set a different tone, Ganguly acknowledged, and initially surprised analysts "since during the election campaign he had evinced little interest in foreign policy issues" aside from talking tough about China and Pakistan.

For Ganguly, Modi's most significant departure from tradition was his "deafening silence on the subject of nonalignment," traditionally a central tenet of India's foreign policy. But this may have been simply to drop the "pretense" that it retained any "utility as a guiding principle" so long after the Cold War.[12] Modi appeared to have "few, if any, ideological reservations about a closer relationship with the United States."

In other words, Modi's foreign policy is not so much transformational as cognizant of realities already set by his predecessors' policies and broader forces in international relations. Other scholars basically shared this assessment. Rajesh Basrur, also writing in 2017, argued, "foreign policy under Modi picks up from where his predecessors left off and is characterized by essential continuity."[13] Manjari Chatterjee Miller and Kate Sullivan de Estrada even doubted that Modi was really more "pragmatic" than his predecessors in the foreign policy domain. They argued that "Modi is not unique or uniquely pragmatic" and that, "like many Indian leaders before him, his pragmatism is of the procedural kind" rather than reflecting a substantially different set of ideas about India's national interest or how to exercise power.[14]

Modi's effect on Indian foreign policy thus has been mainly to bring a new attitude and style. Substantively, with some qualifications (such as on Kashmir and the India–Pakistan conflict; see below), another Indian prime minister presented with the same circumstances he has faced likely would have made broadly similar choices.

INDIA–CHINA RELATIONS UNDER MODI: ECONOMIC COOPERATION AND TERRITORIAL CONFRONTATION

India's foreign policy under Modi can be seen as a kind of "grand straddle" as much as grand strategy. Essentially, India seeks the status, security cooperation, and other benefits of an increasingly close association with the US-led democratic club, even as it needs trade with China to continue growing its economy and access to Chinese-led multilateral lending to support its vast infrastructure investment requirements.

China, above all, has forced India's hand in an increasingly bitter conflict over territory and regional influence, even as India has sought China's favor in multilateral economic relations. Even as their border conflict has drawn Indian interest back to the Quad as a strategic forum, India and China have been partners in economic diplomacy, as fellow members of the BRICS group (Brazil, Russia, India, China, and South Africa), now in its second decade, with India hosting its 13th annual summit in 2021 (having previously hosted in 2012 and 2016). The BRICS group formed the New Development Bank in 2014 as a Shanghai-based alternative to the Washington, DC-based, US-led World Bank; an Indian banker, K. V. Kamath, served as the first NDB president.

India is also a founding member of the Chinese-led Asian Infrastructure Investment Bank (AIIB), established in 2015 and having 87 member states as of 2021, and has quickly become the

AIIB's single largest borrower: at US$6 billion in total lending (as of September 2020), it accounted for almost a third of AIIB lending across Asia and the world.[15] Whereas the NDB emerged out of shared frustration at constraints the countries experienced with the World Bank—as both borrowers and voting members—the AIIB was a Chinese-proposed initiative that initially seemed of a piece with its ambitious Belt and Road Initiative linking Asia and the world through massive infrastructure investment (an initiative that India does not support). But both Indian officials and the Chinese-appointed AIIB president, Jin Liqun, have pointed to uninterrupted and even expanding AIIB lending to India amid the border hostilities between China and India as evidence that the AIIB is a genuinely international multilateral institution that does not get caught up in bilateral disputes between member countries.[16]

It is jarring to see the deterioration in the China–India security relationship that has recently unfolded alongside this pattern of economic diplomacy. From mid-June to late August 2017, Indian and Chinese armed forces faced off over China's move to extend a road into Doklam, an area disputed by China and Bhutan. Doklam abuts the two countries' trijunction with India, in a geographic area defined by a major plateau and valley; it is considered strategically important by all three countries, but its terrain makes it difficult to defend. India, an ally of tiny Bhutan under 1949 and 2007 treaties, said officially it was acting out of defense obligations to the kingdom, and that China's "significant change of the status quo" would have "serious security implications for India."[17] Curiously, though Bhutan officially protested the Chinese action, the kingdom did not confirm India's claim of having coordinated with it prior to sending 270 armed troops and two bulldozers into its territory to oppose the Chinese activity.

Though India and China had engaged in standoffs at their disputed border in Ladakh in 2013 and 2014, this was, as India's former foreign secretary Shyam Saran noted, the "first time that

Indian forces [had] engaged China from the soil of a third country."[18] As analyst Ankit Panda explains, from India's perspective, China's road building came too close to the Siliguri corridor to the south, a 17-mile-wide "chicken's neck" connecting India's mainland to its northeastern hill states, and regarded by Indian strategists as a "core vulnerability." For China, on the other hand, "this was a case of India creating a bilateral standoff where no reason for one should exist."[19] Ultimately, after weeks of tense diplomacy, both China and India announced on August 28 that they had withdrawn all their forces from the site of the standoff. China halted its road construction, and both sides claimed diplomatic victory.

Doklam was "the most serious military standoff between the two countries" since a 1986–87 episode in the Sumdorong Chu Valley, following India's granting of statehood to Arunachal Pradesh, a major part of which is claimed by China. That mid-1980s standoff was the first since India and China fought a war in October–November 1962 along their disputed border (temporally overlapping, by Cold War coincidence, the Cuban Missile Crisis between the United States and the Soviet Union). In the wake of the Doklam episode, Jonah Blank, an analyst for the Rand Corporation, an American think tank, offered the following essential primer on China–India conflict:

> China and India share a border over 2,500 miles long, with almost all of it based on colonial-era agreements and surveys, and much of it still disputed. China claims pieces of territory held by India, mostly in the states of Arunachal Pradesh and Jammu and Kashmir, with smaller pieces claimed in Uttarakhand and Himachal Pradesh. India claims land held by China, most notably a piece of land called Aksai Chin through which Beijing built a road in the 1950s connecting Xinjiang to Tibet. Reflecting its unsettled nature, the portions of the border separating disputed territories are referred to as the Line of Actual Control. There are periodic skirmishes along

the LAC, but both nations have carefully choreographed them to avoid escalation; as a result, there have been no casualties stemming from land disputes in half a century.[20]

While there were no reported casualties in the Doklam episode (despite a mass rock-fight, captured on video and posted to YouTube), it marked a new and dangerous phase in the long-running conflict between India and China over territory and status. This comes at a time when both countries are led by assertive nationalists, in Narendra Modi and Xi Jinping, who seem willing to gamble that a confrontation will raise their side's regional standing and strategic position. As Blank points out, the Doklam episode may have started as a "field level initiative" by China, but "after the first week or so," it became "a policy choice undertaken at the highest echelon of the Chinese government."[21]

India's response also reflected the policy of its top leadership, though scholars disagree on how much of a role Modi played in creating conditions for the confrontation in the first place. In a pair of *Pacific Affairs* articles published a year after the standoff began, Sumit Ganguly and Kanti Bajpai offer different assessments of Chinese actions and Modi's China policy leading up to Doklam. China's military moves may have started the Doklam standoff, but China had been making territorial probes for years, within a larger context of military and diplomatic moves that seemed calibrated to test India's tolerance for provocations and slights. (For example, in 2007, China denied a visa to a single Indian official from Arunachal Pradesh seeking to visit China as part of an Indian delegation, on the grounds that to do so would be to accept India's claim of the territory). Both Ganguly and Bajpai agree that the conditions for a confrontation had been building for years; even the latter, who sees Modi as significantly responsible for the episode, says "its roots go back at least to 2007."[22] Both Ganguly and Bajpai observe that Modi's campaign rhetoric in 2014 was hawkish with respect to China (warning Beijing to abandon its "expansionist mindset," for example), but both also note how he initially struck a more conciliatory tone after taking office.

Ganguly places significant emphasis on China's "limited probes along the Himalayan border" and its continued efforts to make "diplomatic, commercial, and strategic inroads into India's neighbors, trying to reduce India's influence in those countries."[23] He essentially sees India's development of closer ties with the US, and the sputtering back to life of the Quad mechanism, as eliciting China's "pique" and "umbrage," leading the People's Republic "to adopt a more aggressive stance" and "to periodically test India's preparedness and resolve" along the border.[24]

Bajpai argues that "while Chinese policies certainly challenged Delhi's conceptions of its status and security, India under Modi contributed to the unprecedented spoiling of relations" with Beijing.[25] In particular, he stresses Modi's break with a longstanding policy framework, in place since 1988, under which "Delhi accepted Beijing's contention that the two countries needed to normalize [relations] in preparation for a final settlement of the border." Under this "normalization" rubric, India and China would work toward a resolution of territorial disputes through "four pillars of interaction: border negotiations; confidence-building measures; summits and other high-level meetings; and enhanced trade and people-to-people (P2P) links."[26] Over time, Bajpai observes, "hawkish opinion in India has lost patience with the orthodoxy" of normalization, and Modi's views "seemed to mirror" hardliner sentiments.[27] In his first summit with Xi, in September 2014, Modi called for "clarifying" the Line of Actual Control and seeking "early settlement of the boundary question" before further normalization.[28] While such positions "may seem innocuous," Bajpai explains, they represented a break from diplomatic agreements reached by previous Indian and Chinese governments and "challenged China's long-standing assertion that the border question should be left to future generations."[29]

Bajpai argues that Modi's "contrarian diplomacy" constituted a "revisionist stance on normalization and the border"[30] and turned decades of India's China policy "upside down"—in the view, "rightly or wrongly," that normalization and steady border negotiation had "run its course, with little to show" for India. In sum,

> India had been averse to combining with other powers against China; a concerted effort [through the Quad and "Act East"] would now be made to do exactly that. Delhi had hoped for years that normalization would deliver a border settlement; progress towards a settlement would now be the condition of further normalization.[31]

Simply put, the different levels of responsibility Ganguly and Bajpai assign to China and India for the standoff come down to different perspectives on what constitutes a break with established understandings between the countries—which in any case are fragile and ever subject to revision, even on seemingly accepted matters (as with China's recent contestation of part of Ladakh, for example, and in the Doklam dispute with Bhutan). The two scholars' differing perspectives on causes also lead them to contrasting predictions about consequences. In Ganguly's view, "A policy of firmness and resolve in its dealings with the PRC may at least help protect India's vital security interests."[32] Bajpai sees Modi's policy as making India *less* secure, as

> China continues to hold to long-held stances on bilateral issues, to expand its influence in South Asia, and to disrupt India's larger diplomatic efforts such as in the UN. Nor is there any sign that Beijing has changed its mind on the nature of border negotiations…. Modi's China policy therefore finds itself in a state of limbo and faced with the possibility of more Doklams around the corner.[33]

Did China back down in Doklam? Perhaps, but its official statement that "China will continue fulfilling its sovereign rights to safeguard territorial sovereignty in compliance with the stipulations of the border-related historical treaty" indicated that its position on the border tri-junction remained unchanged.[34]

The de-escalation of Doklam created diplomatic space for several meetings between Modi and Xi during the interim that followed, though their progress was ephemeral. Modi traveled to China for the BRICS summit in September 2017, where India "informed China that it would not intervene in the Maldives and expected China to reciprocate this measure by not crossing certain 'lines of legitimacy.'"[35] Then, in April 2018, Modi and Xi held an "informal summit" in Wuhan, China, at which no joint statement was signed, but Xi reportedly did express interest in expanding cultural exchange around Indian and Chinese films, and India's Ministry of External Affairs released a press statement saying the leaders had "agreed that proper management of the bilateral relationship will be conducive for the development and prosperity of the region, and will create conditions for the Asian Century."[36] India even participated in a joint military exercise of the Shanghai Cooperation Organization, involving Chinese and Pakistani troops, in August 2018.

In early 2019, amid heightened tensions between India and Pakistan following the Pulwama terrorist attack against Indian forces and India's retaliatory air strikes on Balakot in Pakistan (see below), China initially opposed India's proposal that the UN Security Council designate Jaish-e-Mohammed's Masood Azhar as a global terrorist, though it later conceded to remove its hold on the designation by the UN Sanctions Committee. Following India's August abrogation of Article 370 and Article 35A of the Constitution, which had given Jammu and Kashmir special status in the Indian union and its new designation of Ladakh as a separate Union Territory, a Chinese spokesperson criticized the Indian move on Ladakh, saying it challenged China's sovereign interests.

China also maintained its traditional support of Pakistani efforts to internationalize its Kashmir dispute with India, now seeking a UN Security Council challenge to India's moves on the constitutional status of Jammu and Kashmir. (The other 14 Security Council members did not take up China's call for a discussion.)

In October, Modi and Xi held a second informal summit at Mamallapuram, near Chennai in India's Tamil Nadu state, announcing a "Chennai Connect" initiative to build on the "Wuhan Spirit" and pledging to make 2020 the "Year of India–China Cultural and People-to-People Exchanges." Modi himself would not speak publicly of Doklam until December 2019, when he suggested that India had shown strength in the 73-day standoff.[37]

In June 2020, India and China would engage in alarming clashes high in the Himalayas, along the disputed border and Line of Actual Control, resulting in the deaths of 20 Indian soldiers, at least 76 injured, and unknown numbers of Chinese casualties—the first combat deaths along the border in at least 45 years, and the highest level of violence since the 1962 war. Though there were reports of gunfire (which both sides officially denied), the fighting mainly involved clubs, rocks, and hand-to-hand combat, with at least some of the Indian soldiers falling (or being pushed) to their deaths from high precipices. Others, an Indian Army statement said, had been "exposed to sub-zero temperatures in the high-altitude terrain" and "succumbed to their injuries."[38]

The confrontation followed India's construction of a new road in a sensitive area along the LAC in Ladakh, which angered China. India then accused China of sending thousands of troops into Ladakh's Galwan River Valley and occupying nearly 15,000 square miles of its territory.[39] Only days before the June 15–16 fighting, which the Indian Army described as a "violent face-off," the two sides had begun a "de-escalation process" in the Galwan Valley. This timing only underscored the acrimony and distrust in bilateral relations.

Popular protests began as soon as the Indian casualties were reported, and within days a "boycott China" campaign had "quickly gathered momentum on both local and government levels across India."[40] Government officials announced plans to impose higher trade barriers and to raise import duties on around 300 Chinese products. The Telecom Ministry ordered government providers and private companies to ban future deals and equipment upgrades with Chinese companies, which would also be ineligible to submit tenders for projects (such as upgraded 4G wireless services). The Confederation of All-India Traders, an association with 60 million members, announced boycotts covering "over 3,000 Chinese products ranging from cosmetics to handbags and furniture."[41] India banned 59 Chinese apps (smartphone/computer tablet applications), including the massively popular TikTok platform, without naming China but saying in a government statement that the apps were "engaged in activities which is [sic.] prejudicial to sovereignty and integrity of India, defence of India, security of state and public order" and that the broad ban was a "targeted move to ensure safety and sovereignty of Indian cyberspace."[42]

Modi was much quicker to speak about the Galwan episode than on Doklam. His remarks, however, elicited some confusion and were criticized by Congress Party leaders in the opposition. Speaking at an "all-party meeting" on the Galwan clash on June 19, Modi (speaking in Hindi, translated for English news media) said that "this time, Chinese forces have come in much larger strength to the Line of Actual Control" and "the Indian response is commensurate," but somehow also managed to say that "no one entered Indian territory." Given the strongly nationalist tone of Modi's remarks overall ("not an inch of land lost"), the prime minister could not possibly have intended to imply that the hostilities had occurred on Chinese territory. But on its face, his statement seemed to support the Chinese Foreign Ministry's claim that "Galwan Valley is located on the Chinese side of the Line of Actual Control." Opposition leaders were quick to point out the discrepancy, implying that the prime minister had failed to honor India's fallen soldiers, and prompting the Prime Minister's Office to issue a defensive clarification, saying Modi's "no intrusion" claim had clearly referred to the situation *after* the June 15–16 violence.[43]

The situation between China and India remained tense for months, against the backdrop of the COVID-19 pandemic. While the two militaries disengaged in July from the location in Galwan where the fighting took place, both sides poured additional forces and infrastructure into the wider area in preparation for colder temperatures, even as the foreign ministries attempted to reach agreement on disengagement. In September, the defense ministers for both countries met on the sidelines of the SCO meeting in Moscow, agreeing after 14 hours to "stop sending more troops to the frontline."[44] The countries took further disengagement steps in February at the transborder Pangong Lake, amid frigid field conditions, but several other potential hot spots remained militarized and poised for a potential resumption of hostilities. Amid the partial disengagement, China officially acknowledged the loss of four of its soldiers in the Galwan clash eight months earlier.

One year on from Galwan, India and China appeared to have entered a new bilateral era. Around 50,000 Indian troops remained deployed across Ladakh (Chinese force numbers are less clear) and both sides still had much of their new infrastructure and military equipment in place. India's defense priorities had shifted perceptibly: both in the allocation of resources from its navy to its active land forces, and within the army, from the India–Pakistan front to the northern border with China.[45]

INDIA AND THE UNITED STATES IN THE MODI ERA

For almost a decade before he ascended to national stature and became India's prime minister, Narendra Modi was barred from even visiting the United States. In 2005, the US State Department refused to issue a visa to Modi, then chief minister of Gujarat, to speak to large Indian American audiences at events organized by a hotel owners association and business leaders in Florida and New York. The State Department's announcement of the ban invoked a 1998 US law, the International Religious Freedom Act, which makes foreign officials who are responsible for "particularly severe violations of religious freedom" ineligible for US visas.

The State Department's decision reflected a view—held in India at the time in elite circles, and held especially by international news media, human rights groups, and India-watching academics in the West—that Modi was at least tacitly responsible for the vicious anti-Muslim violence that took place in Gujarat in 2002. A series of pogrom-like attacks on Muslims had followed the burning of a passenger train at Godhra station, in which 59 Hindus were killed. Details of the Godhra incident and its aftermath remain a source of contention even now, as estimates of perhaps more than 2,000 people killed in statewide violence—most of them Muslim—far exceed the official counts of 790 Muslim and 254 Hindu dead. Though a commission appointed by the central government (later nullified as unconstitutional) found that the train fire that sparked the wider killings had been an accident, a competing investigation commissioned by the state government blamed a conspiracy by a Muslim mob.

The 2005 US decision followed intensive lobbying by human rights groups and American Muslims, directed at members of Congress from both parties and at the US Commission on International Religious Freedom (a bipartisan appointed panel created by the 1998 Act). The US State Department agreed with the commission's position that Modi should not be eligible for a US visa, declaring that "he was responsible for the performance of state institutions" during the 2002 riots. (Among other concerns was the failure of police to protect Muslim victims from organized attacks, at least some of which appeared to have been planned using official records to locate Muslim residences and businesses).

In 2012 India's Supreme Court concluded an inquiry by declaring that Modi "had no case to answer,"[46] even as individual prosecutions continued for some of the most heinous murders. In 2013 Modi maneuvered to eclipse L. K. Advani as the Bharatiya Janata Party's clear national leader and presumed prime ministerial candidate and in 2014, as multiple polls began to forecast a BJP victory in India's general elections, US officials were confronted with the possibility that the next elected prime minister of the world's largest democracy would be the only person ever denied a US visa under the provision.[47]

Twelve years and multiple official inquiries in India may have given President Barack Obama's administration sufficient distance and political cover to move on from the events of 2002. But, more fundamentally, the administration simply held India's importance to US interests to outweigh the value of maintaining Modi's visa ban. Critics of the prime minister seemed to grasp this political reality, even if they rejected the reputational rehabilitation that a change in the US position might seem to confer. Shaik Ubaid, an Indian American, Long Island physician, and co-founder of the Coalition Against Genocide, told the *Los Angeles Times*, "It is our view that the stigma and accusations still lie around his neck. At the same time, many members of the coalition said that if he wants to visit the US as a head of government, we should not oppose him."[48]

In September 2014,

> Modi made his first triumphant visit to the United States, where he had a private dinner with Obama, toured the Martin Luther King Jr. Memorial with the president and headlined a program at Madison Square Garden attended by more than 18,000 cheering members of the Indian diaspora.[49]

The prime minister visited a second time one year later, meeting with Silicon Valley leaders, including Apple's Tim Cook, Facebook's

Mark Zuckerberg, and Google's Sundar Pichai to promote his Digital India campaign for expanding internet access and digital government services. In June 2016, President Obama hosted Modi at the White House, a day ahead of the prime minister's address to a joint session of the Republican Party-led US Congress—both capping an extraordinary turnaround from the 2005 ban.

Relations between India and the United States reached peak personalization in the era of Donald Trump, as well as peak organization on the part of politically active Indian Americans. Just weeks before the 2016 US presidential election, candidate Trump appeared at an Indian American charity benefit in Edison, New Jersey, organized by the Republican Hindu Coalition. "I am a big fan of Hindu [sic.], and I am a big fan of India," Trump told an enthusiastic audience. "Big, big fan." Maggie Haberman of the *New York Times* observed that the remark seemed "to entangle the faith with the nation," a point not likely to have been lost on Modi's BJP government. Haberman also noted that Trump's "anti-bureaucracy and country-first language closely tracks that of Mr. Modi."[50] While Trump's Democratic rival Hillary Clinton polled far ahead of him among Indian Americans overall, that a presidential candidate would make a mid-October campaign stop in a non-battleground state to profess affection for Indian Americans and India sent a clear signal. Indeed, the Trump administration would continue to advance the strategic partnership between the two countries, even if its hardline anti-immigration policies would also create friction. (Trump officials opposed H1-B visas for high-skilled foreign nationals including computer scientists and engineers, three-quarters of which go to Indian-born workers—alienating both US tech companies and India on this issue.[51])

In September 2019, 50,000 Indian Americans gathered for a Modi rally in Houston, where the prime minister was joined by President Trump. The rally, billed "Howdy Modi" and organized by the Texas India Forum (a non-profit created specifically for the $2.5 million event), was "the largest-ever gathering with a foreign political leader in the United States."[52] In late February 2020, exactly one month before Modi would place India under "lockdown" in the grip of the COVID-19 pandemic, the prime minister hosted the American president in his inaugural visit to India at a reciprocal "Namaste Trump" event, held in an Ahmedabad, Gujarat stadium in front of more than 100,000 people. Trump's 36-hour visit to India included a requisite visit to the Taj Mahal in Agra: the former real estate developer had once operated a billion-dollar Atlantic City, New Jersey, casino named for the famous mausoleum, before filing for bankruptcy.

But away from the pageantry of Namaste Trump, Delhi was gripped by riots for six days beginning on February 23, the eve of the American president's arrival in India, which began after a local BJP leader called on Delhi Police to break up a road-blocking sit-in by a group of women protesting the Citizenship (Amendment) Act of 2019—and threatening to "hit the streets" if police did not heed his ultimatum. Explicitly acknowledging the US president's visit, the BJP's Kapil Mishra (a former cabinet minister and legislator for Delhi who switched his affiliation from the Aam Aadmi Party to the BJP), put out a tweet and video in which he warned Delhi Police in Hindi, "We will be peaceful until Trump leaves. After that, we won't listen to even you if the roads are not cleared. We will have to hit the streets."[53] Stone-throwing and gun-wielding counter-protestors and vigilantes, some shouting the Hindutva slogan "Jai Shri Ram" ("Victory to Lord Ram"), terrorized majority-Muslim and mixed neighborhoods in northeast Delhi, killing 53. Two-thirds of the victims were Muslim. When asked about the outbreak of violence, Trump praised Modi's commitment to "religious freedom" and declined to discuss the citizenship law, saying the issue "was really up to India."[54]

Bookended by contrasting reactions to Hindu–Muslim violence in 2002 and 2020, the deepening American embrace of India across very different US presidencies reflects an evolving realism in US–India relations, which have traditionally touted a shared commitment to democratic ideals. From the US perspective, while Modi's rise and the BJP's decisive electoral victory in 2014 reflected legitimate political and institutional processes, there are still troubling questions about the Modi government's commitment to minority protections and rights under law, a key pillar of India's secular democracy. Even so, India's strategic significance has led the United States to largely subordinate these concerns to a shared interest in countering China's rise. Another security concern, counterterrorism, also remains a key priority of the partnership, though not as prominently as in the years immediately after 2001, when the US confronted the September 11 terrorist attacks and India experienced a deadly security breach of its Parliament grounds in New Delhi on December 13.

China's influence on Indo-American relations has origins in twentieth-century history, reflecting the global Cold War's regional dynamics in Asia and the subcontinent. Tanvi Madan analyzes China's generally underappreciated impact on the development of US–India ties from 1949 to 1979 to draw potential lessons for the twenty-first-century relationship, arguing that "a US–India partnership to tackle a China challenge is neither inevitable nor impossible." The two countries "*have* come together against China," she finds, but only under certain conditions: when they could agree on the nature and urgency of the threat posed by China, *and* on how to deal with it. During the Cold War, India and the US also diverged in their understandings of how Pakistan and the Soviet Union factored into relations with China.[55] After a period of relative convergence in views of the threats posed by China and by international communism (1956–62), Madan traces a deepening disillusionment and disengagement in US–India relations, culminating in the 1970s as the Nixon administration utilized Pakistan's alliance with China to pursue a rapprochement with Mao Zedong's government, while India "continued to see China as a challenge, alone and in collusion with Pakistan."[56] India moved closer to the Soviet Union; the two countries signed a Treaty of Friendship and Cooperation in August 1971. Later that year, India and Pakistan fought their third war with India's intervention in Pakistan's civil war, which ended with East Pakistan becoming independent Bangladesh. India's threat perception was crystalized by US efforts to isolate it during the war, even as China supported Pakistan. The Soviet invasion of Afghanistan at the end of the decade drew the US and Pakistan closer yet again, and the Soviet Union's eventual defeat in that conflict (and disintegration soon after) left India strategically adrift until the Indian and Pakistani nuclear weapons tests of May 1998 drew American interest back to the subcontinent.

Originally, the new dawn in US–India relations was born out of the May 1998 nuclear tests between India and Pakistan. Strobe Talbott, the US Deputy Secretary of State, and Jaswant Singh, India's Minister of External Affairs, engaged through a series of 14 meetings in a wide-ranging "dialogue" that began over nonproliferation, disarmament, and other security issues—at first, the US sought to limit India's nuclear weapons program—but later expanded to encompass democracy, economic globalization, and the wider spectrum of issues that now define the partnership. India's economic liberalization, meanwhile, opened new economic opportunities for American businesses, creating conditions for the broader and deeper Indo-American engagement of the twenty-first century. After 2001, counterterrorism became the catalyst to the formalization of the partnership, which has been sustained through multiple rounds of political leadership and amid changing ideological currents in both countries.

China's emergence as the key driver of US–India ties in recent years reflects both its own geopolitical and economic ascent as well as the relative abatement of other factors—nuclearization, terrorism, the headiest hopes for India's economy—that drove the relationship in the late 1990s and early 2000s. As we will explore later in this chapter, Pakistan still figures prominently in the China–India–US strategic triangle, though the nuclearization of the

India–Pakistan conflict, the shift of the India–Pakistan rivalry from full-scale wars to grinding "low-intensity" conflict, and the role of terrorism in catalyzing crisis episodes between India and Pakistan have both attenuated and complicated Pakistan's role. Russia also remains a factor, though with far less regional influence than the Soviet Union held during the Cold War.

Affirmations of shared democratic values remain a central ritual of US–India diplomacy. Nevertheless, there has been a subtle but perceptible shift toward other dimensions of the relationship—particularly military cooperation—as China's increasingly aggressive posture has provided an external motivation for the deepening of ties. This latest phase in the US–India relationship comes at a time when liberal democracy faces global challenges, including in the United States itself, and as democracy promotion has faded as an organizing principle of American foreign policy. As Arjit Mazumdar and Erin Statz observed in 2015, "Democracy promotion has never been an integral element of India's foreign policy," and what efforts it has made—through bilateral development aid and technical assistance "to develop the building blocks of democracy" in countries like Afghanistan, Bhutan, and Nepal—reflect realist concern for stability and economic interests "rather than any idealistic commitment to democracy."[57]

REDEFINING STRATEGIC AUTONOMY AND NON-ALIGNMENT

It is essential to understand that India and the United States formally have a "strategic partnership," not an alliance. This nomenclature emerged among policy specialists around 2001 and was officially embraced in 2004 by the UPA government (led by Manmohan Singh) and by the George W. Bush administration.[58] To understand why India and the United States have not cemented a full alliance, we must appreciate the legacy of "nonalignment" in India's foreign policy. India's non-aligned stance originated in the

Cold War. It was more than a policy: under Jawaharlal Nehru, India along with Egypt, Ghana, Indonesia, and Yugoslavia sought to lead a movement of mostly post-colonial states that, as the Non-Aligned Countries, would maintain strategic autonomy from both superpowers and their respective blocs of allies and client states. Chief among the group's founding principles were mutual respect for sovereignty and territorial integrity, non-interference in one another's domestic affairs, non-aggression, peaceful coexistence, and equality. (After 1976, the group called itself the Non-Aligned Movement; it remains a forum for 120 mostly Global South countries, comprising some two-thirds of the United Nations' membership.)

In practice, non-alignment became an increasingly diffuse concept. For India, Harsh Pant and Julie Super observe, non-alignment

> forms a part of its national identity. Yet this has never entirely precluded alignments in practice, as was apparent in the 1962 war [between China and India, in which India sought American help], during the remainder of the Cold War, and even into the post-Cold War era.[59]

In 2012, scholar Sunil Khilnani and seven prominent co-authors produced a strategy document, *NonAlignment 2.0: A Foreign and Strategic Policy for India in the Twenty First Century*,[60] for the Centre for Policy Research, a leading Indian think tank in New Delhi. Explaining the report's title, the authors observed:

> Strategic autonomy has been the defining value and continuous goal of India's international policy ever since the inception of the Republic. Defined initially in the terminology of NonAlignment, that value we believe continues to remain at the core of India's global engagements even today, in a world that has changed drastically since the mid-twentieth century. The challenge is to renovate that value and goal for the twenty-first century...[61]

The authors characterized the twenty-first-century global system as US-led, but also as a "polycentric field" offering greater opportunities for rising powers than the Cold War-era bipolar order permitted. The "relative decline of the American alliance system," they suggested, "is already evident," and "America's ability to 'call the shots' in finance and energy...too now appear less steady and reliable."[62] The authors characterized China as "America's principal competitor in economic and also military terms," though they maintained, "the military gap will remain enormous for years to come."

"In this context," they observed, "India holds a special attraction for the US because it is the biggest of the new powers (apart from China itself) and also has a complicated relationship with Beijing." India, they conceded, "has more interests in 'direct" competition with China" than with the US, so "it may be tempting to conclude that the US is a likely alliance partner. But this conclusion would be premature."

Summarizing the case against an Indo-American alliance, the authors argued:

> While there may appear to be attractions for India to exploit its derivative value, the risk is that its relations with the US could become a casualty of any tactical upswing in Sino-American ties. Nor is it entirely clear how the US might actually respond if China posed a threat to India's interests. The other potential downside is that India could prematurely antagonize China.
>
> It is often said that India is well placed to improve its relations with all powers simultaneously....But such an approach also poses real challenges, given that at least two of these powers have angularities. The US can be too demanding in its friendship and resentful of other attachments India might pursue. The historical record of the United States bears out that powers that form formal alliances with it have tended to see an erosion of their strategic autonomy. Both India and the US may be better served by being friends rather than allies.[63]

Since this report was published, Chinese and American economic and security competition has intensified, and as we have already seen, so too have the border dispute and general tensions between China and India. Pant and Super, writing in 2015, characterized non-alignment as outdated—a "twentieth-century policy in a changing world"—and saw the early Modi government as signaling "a move away from even the rhetoric of non-alignment, with significant implications for the future of Indian foreign policy."[64]

More recent developments call into question whether Modi's rhetorical and symbolic gestures really signal a significant distancing of his government's foreign policy from the ideational legacy of non-alignment. Pant and Super catalog various ways in which Modi seemed to be initiating "a departure from India's past manner of balancing relations": demonstrating increased assertiveness toward China even as appealed for Sino-Indian cooperation and resolution of the border dispute, pursuing deeper partnerships in Southeast Asia, asserting India's (mainly Hinduism's) traditions during his September 2014 visit to the US (gifting Obama a copy of the Bhagavad Gita, sipping water at the White House dinner in observance of a fast), and generally engaging "confidently with the outside world."[65] It is not clear how all of this marked a break with non-alignment thinking; in fact, Modi's self-confident stylings could just as readily be interpreted as consistent with non-alignment's traditional emphasis on strategic autonomy and defense of India's sovereignty. The authors see significance in Modi's use of the phrase "natural allies" to describe India and the United States in a March 2015 interview with *Time* magazine,[66] but in fact, the BJP's previous prime minister, Atal Bihari Vajpayee, had used the same words in 2000 at the dawn of sustained diplomatic engagement between the two countries. When Modi again invoked the phrase in his speech to the US Congress in June 2016, he credited Vajpayee by name. (Manmohan Singh, too, had invoked the phrase in his 2005 speech to the US Congress, though he did not cite Vajpayee's coinage.[67]) At none of these earlier junctures had the enthusiastic words indicated that India and the United States were on the cusp of a formal alliance.

But as Harsh and Super also observe, "The Modi government is redefining strategic autonomy as an objective that is attainable through strengthened partnerships rather than the avoidance of partnerships."[68] This assessment generally holds across the Modi era so far and captures both the continuity and change in non-alignment as a framework for India's foreign policy. The Indian diplomat P. S. Raghavan, a former ambassador to Russia and secretary in the Ministry of External Affairs, has something like this in mind in suggesting "multi-alignment" as an alternative framing,[69] though the term has not entered broader or official use.

At the January 2019 meeting of the Raisina Dialogue, an annual policy conference organized by the Observer Research Foundation in New Delhi, Foreign Secretary Vijay Gokhale said, "India has moved on from its non-aligned past. India today is an aligned state—but based on issues." Rather than endorsing an Indo-American alliance per se, Gokhale suggested that India should deepen its participation "in the rules-based order" and "have a stronger position in multilateral institutions" led by the US and its allies.[70]

In 2020, Modi surprised many observers by participating in the Non-Aligned Movement's Contact Group summit, held virtually amid the COVID-19 pandemic, after skipping the prior two NAM summits of his tenure in 2016 and 2019 (India's vice president attended instead). Analyzing Modi's sudden interest in the 120-member NAM group, *The Diplomat*'s Ashutosh Nagda saw a "tactical shift" in Modi's foreign policy, timed to exploit frustration with China's role in the pandemic and to assert India's autonomy amid growing talk of a "new Cold War" between China and the United States. Reclaiming India's leadership position in the NAM, Nagda suggested, had the additional advantage of differentiating Modi from the more isolationist tendencies of nationalist contemporaries like Trump and Brazil's Jair Bolsonaro.[71]

DEFENSE COOPERATION, DEFENSE SPENDING, AND MILITARY MODERNIZATION

Barring a more fundamental shift in the regional security environment and in India's foreign policy discourse, it remains unlikely that India will become a formal US ally, in the sense of a mutual defense agreement or treaty. Nevertheless, security cooperation between India and the United States has advanced significantly in the Modi era. In November 2019, the two countries conducted the first land, sea, and air exercise—dubbed Tiger Triumph—in their history of military exchanges. Over a nine-day period, around 1,200 Indian soldiers, sailors, and air force personnel trained side-by-side in India and the Bay of Bengal with 500 American Marines and sailors, focusing on training for rescue operations and disaster response but also on search-and-seizure and live-fire drills. This elaborate exercise built on previous, smaller joint trainings between branches of the two militaries held outside of India, and on a 15-year history of annual peacekeeping and counterterrorism trainings known as the Yudh Abhyas (War Exercise), held alternately in both countries. (The 2019 edition, involving almost 700 troops, was held at Joint Base Lewis-McChord in Washington State; the 2020 exercise was delayed by the COVID-19 pandemic, but was held at the Mahajan Field Firing Ranges in western Rajasthan in February 2021.)

Alyssa Ayres, a senior fellow at the Council on Foreign Relations, told the *New York Times*, "You hear officials say now that the US exercises more with India than any other non-NATO partner. You would never have imagined that 20 years ago."[72] Indeed, as the newspaper reported,

> The only other country with which India [ever] has held similar exercises involving its armed forces is Russia. During the Cold War, India was closer to the Soviet Union than to the United States, and much of the Indian arsenal still harkens back to that era.

India continues to hold joint military trainings with Russia. At the same time, befitting the Quad framework, India has joined the US in conducing military exercises with Japan, beginning in 2018.

The US–India joint training exercises enacted one of the goals of a security agreement the two countries signed in September 2018, which also facilitates India's purchase of advanced American weaponry and the sharing of sensitive military technology, including high-tech communications platforms. A US delegation including the Trump administration's Secretary of State Mike Pompeo and Defense Secretary James Mattis met with their Indian counterparts, Minister of External Affairs Sushma Swaraj and Minister of Defence Nirmala Sitharaman, to finalize the agreement under a new configuration called the 2+2 Ministerial Dialogue, which has since met yearly. At a joint news conference with the US delegation, Sitharaman told reporters, "The defense cooperation has emerged as the most significant dimension of our strategic partnership and as a key driver of our overall bilateral relationship."[73]

The deepening of Indo-American security ties has come at a time of increased defense spending by the Indian government under Modi, driven primarily by concerns about China. As a legacy of the Cold War's Indo-Soviet "friendship," India continues to buy Russian equipment such as fighter aircraft, missile systems, a nuclear submarine, and antiaircraft missiles—the latter a 2018 transaction that defied US congressional sanctions on Russia during the Trump presidency. But US–India defense trade has become a centerpiece of the two countries' security cooperation, and in some recent years, the US has eclipsed Russia as India's leading defense supplier. Starting "virtually from scratch," US–India defense trade totaled $20 billion over the 13 years prior to 2020—for aircraft, helicopters, artillery, and other equipment—with billions more in the pipeline.[74] A Defense Technology and Trade Initiative (DTTI) between the two countries, launched in 2012, sputtered for several years amid the very same bureaucratic obstacles it was designed to overcome before seemingly springing to life in 2020. It includes near-, medium-, and long-term projects ranging from air-launched small unmanned systems and lightweight small arms technology to Terrain Shaping Obstacle and Counter-UAS (unmanned aircraft systems) Rocket, Artillery, and Mortar systems.[75] Though a planned Raven mini-UAV (unmanned aerial vehicle, or drone) was rejected by the Indian Army for being too low-tech,[76] in 2021 the two countries signed an agreement for cooperation in developing an air-launched UAV.[77] All this portends significant expansion and much-needed modernization of India's military capabilities.

In 2018, India's annual budget put defense spending at $62 billion, a "quiet milestone" surpassing that of Britain and ranking behind only the United States, China, Saudi Arabia, and Russia. India was the world's leading importer of arms. Even so, the *Economist* opined, India's "fortune" spent on defense "gets poor value," especially since "some three quarters" of the overall defense budget would be "consumed by salaries and benefits, leaving scant funding for procurement, let alone such luxuries as research and development."[78] That year, India's service chiefs set off a public debate about India's defense capabilities when they testified before Parliament that "some 68% of the army's equipment, much of which was first supplied by the Soviet Union [...], may be described as 'vintage'"; only 8% could be considered "state-of-the art," leaving India unprepared for an eventuality such as a two-front war.[79] Indian fighter jets were still "antiquated" MiG-21 types dating from Soviet times. Naval capabilities were also lacking: India had 18 submarines in service, while China had 78.[80]

India's defense spending and capabilities remain far behind those of China, which spent over $250 billion on defense in 2020—around 1.75% of its GDP, which is between four and five times the size of India's. The recent border hostilities have been an impetus to India's prioritization of somewhat higher (and smarter) defense spending. The economic crisis brought on by the COVID-19 pandemic in 2020 has created new constraints, but India still managed to spend almost $73 billion on defense in 2020, an increase over 2019, making it third among world powers.[81] (The US and China also saw increased military spending during the pandemic year.) Perhaps more importantly, the non-pensions share of the defense budget has increased to $48 billion in 2021–22, an increase of more than 3% from the previous year, while new capital expenditure of $18.5 billion for arms procurement represented a 16% increase. Defense Minister Rajnath Singh boasted that this would be the highest increase in capital spending for defense in 15 years.[82] Relative to GDP, however, India lately has been spending an historically low amount on defense. According to the World Bank, India budgeted just 2.1% of estimated GDP on defense in 2019, the lowest figure since 1960.[83] When GDP for 2019 turned out to be below initial estimates, the actual ratio was around 2.5%, crossing a threshold recommended by defense analysts. Subsequent budgets have increased the ratio, to an estimated 2.88 in 2020, reflecting India's prioritization of its military amid tensions with China even as the COVID-19 pandemic struck a blow to GDP.

Alongside efforts to modernize its military through increased spending and new trade agreements with the US, India under Modi has undertaken a significant reorganization of its military's top command structure. After Independence in 1947, the new government led by Jawaharlal Nehru abolished the commander-in-chief office established by Britain for India's military. Over the subsequent decades, India's chiefs of army, navy, and air force held coequal positions, although the army accounted for the largest share of defense spending and the service branches competed with one another for resources. On January 1, 2020, the second-term Modi government appointed General Bipin Rawat to a newly created position, Chief of Defence Staff (CDS). While the move symbolically delivered on a Hindu nationalist aspiration to place the military under a unified command, the reality of the position would be less than meets the eye. According to the *Economist*,

Unlike his British counterpart, General Rawat will not in fact exercise any military command at all. He instead chairs a committee of the three service chiefs, who will still be able to go over his head to the defence minister. But he will have an office of over 60 people and influence over promotions and postings, giving him powerful levers to force the services to work together on everything from logistics to training.[84]

In effect, General Rawat's brief was to the lead the effort to modernize India's armed forces. Some in India worried that bringing the military under a single powerful office established by the Modi government might make it susceptible to political influence. General Rawat, seen as close to Modi, made public statements that did little to dispel such concerns. In December 2019, the *Economist* reported, "Just days before becoming CDS, General Rawat provoked anger by criticizing students protesting against a controversial citizenship bill," passed as the Citizenship (Amendment) Act.[85] As army chief, he had "awarded a commendation letter to an officer who had tied a civilian to the front of his car in the disputed Kashmir region as a human shield to get through stone pelting."[86]

In the event, General Rawat would not serve long in the role: he died in a helicopter crash in southern Tamil Nadu state in December 2021, along with his wife and 11 others. The tragedy occurred midday along a 50-mile flightpath that was a routine route to a local defense academy, but the crash took place amid forested slopes in an area known for sudden weather changes. The Indian Air Force announced a standard official inquiry; according to the *New York Times*, "Experts said nothing about the incident raised immediate red flags."[87] This did not dissuade social media accounts based in Pakistan from spreading conspiracy theories about General Rawat's death in a disinformation campaign that blamed "[Indian] Tamil insurgents, Nagaland militia groups and even China" for a conspiracy of some kind.[88]

RELATIONS WITH PAKISTAN AND AFGHANISTAN

India's asymmetric rivalry with Pakistan historically has been not only its most vexing bilateral relationship, but also nested in both countries' complex relations with China and the United States. The dispute over Kashmir, a portion of which is also claimed by China, can be traced back to Partition in 1947 (see previous Inset: "Jammu and Kashmir and the Limits of Asymmetric Federalism"). Kashmir was central to the wars between India and Pakistan in 1947–48 and 1965, and played a peripheral role in a third war in 1971 that spiraled out of Pakistan's civil war in East Pakistan and ended with the beleaguered province's independent statehood as Bangladesh. Just over a year after India and Pakistan both tested nuclear weapons in a series of blasts in May 1998,[89] their forces fought a limited war in the remote Kargil district of India's Jammu and Kashmir state. This mid-1999 conflict elicited a diplomatic intervention by Bill Clinton's administration in the US, which helped to facilitate a de-escalation of tensions but left Pakistan's Nawaz Sharif vulnerable to a military coup in October, led by Kargil architect and army chief Pervez Musharraf.

The September 11, 2001, terrorist attacks by Al Qaeda and the subsequent US war in Afghanistan pushed Pakistan into an uneasy alliance with the US, resuming a Cold War-era relationship that had become increasingly strained during the 1990s after the end of the Soviet Union's war in Afghanistan and the subsequent collapse of the Soviet Union itself. To a significant degree, terrorism for India also became the defining issue for India in its conflict with Pakistan. In December 2001, the Pakistan-based Islamist group Jaish-e-Mohammed (JeM) organized an attack on the Indian Parliament building in New Delhi, sparking a tense months-long mobilization of both countries' militaries along the international border and Line of Control in Kashmir, and drawing another diplomatic intervention by the US. In November 2008, a gruesome spectacle of terrorism across multiple sites in

Mumbai, conducted by another Pakistan-based group, Lashkar-e-Taiba (LeT) with alleged support from within Pakistan's Inter-Services Intelligence (ISI), brought the two countries to the brink of conflict again. But ultimately, India's UPA government favored a diplomatic approach centered on law enforcement cooperation.

The Modi government has sought to advance a two-pronged approach in India's relations with Pakistan, combining a diplomatic dialogue with the projection of military power to challenge Pakistan's "red lines" and to bolster its nationalist image at home, particularly with the right-wing constituencies eager to see Pakistan punished for supporting terrorism.[90] Over a series of terrorist attacks from 2016 to 2019, the scale slid toward confrontation, setting up a new phase of strategic uncertainty and diplomatic impasse even as India's conflict with China, an ally of Pakistan, has heated up.

Modi initially led with a diplomatic approach, inviting Pakistan's Prime Minister Nawaz Sharif and other South Asian leaders to his swearing-in ceremony in 2014. Later that year the two leaders shook hands at the annual summit of the South Asian Association for Regional Cooperation (SAARC) in Kathmandu. Modi also paid an "unscheduled" visit to Pakistan on his way back from a tour of Afghanistan in December 2015. These overtures did not yield tangible results, but they did demonstrate an apparent commitment to the peace process and normalization of relations.

On January 2, 2016, Pakistan-based terrorists breached the Indian Air Force's base at Pathankot. India cited intelligence that JeM was responsible, and while Modi asked Sharif to take action, "he did not directly blame the Pakistani state." In an unprecedented arrangement, the Modi government "even allowed a team of Pakistani investigators to visit the site of the terror attack to conduct joint investigations with their Indian counterparts." But the Indian side had doubts about "the lack of seriousness in Pakistan's security establishment to improve relations with India,"[91] leading Modi to adopt a harder response to the next terrorist attack.

On September 18, 2016, armed fighters attacked an Indian Army camp at Uri, near Srinagar, killing 19 Indian soldiers. Ten days later, the Modi government announced that India had carried out raids, which it called "surgical strikes," on camps in Pakistan-controlled Kashmir, where it said terrorists were being trained to carry out attacks in India. But notably, Modi directed his ministers to "avoid chest-thumping" and the Ministry of External Affairs issued a statement saying that Indian "operations aimed at neutralizing terrorists" had ceased, and there were no plans for "further continuation." Indian opposition parties led by the INC demanded proof of the government's claims about the surgical strikes, but the Modi government did not release video footage until mid-2018, possibly "to help the Pakistan government avoid calls for revenge against India."[92] The release of footage did little to settle debate within India over what exactly the "surgical strikes" had entailed and accomplished.

Later in 2016, India boycotted the SAARC summit in Pakistan, leading Bangladesh, Bhutan, and Afghanistan to follow suit. India instead focused its regional diplomacy on the Bay of Bengal Initiative for Multi-Sectoral, Technical, and Economic Cooperation (BIMSTEC), which does not include Pakistan, and hosted the organization's summit in Goa. Speaking from the conference, Modi referred obliquely but unmistakably to Pakistan as "this country in India's neighborhood" that "embraces and radiates the darkness of terrorism."[93] Further terrorist attacks on Indian Army bases in Nagrota and Sunjawan in late 2016 and early 2018 killed 10 and 11 (including one civilian) respectively. Bilateral relations deteriorated further in September 2018 when India abruptly cancelled an announced meeting of the two countries' foreign ministers on the sidelines of the UN General Assembly in New York.

On February 14, 2019, a home-grown Kashmiri suicide bomber identifying with JeM crashed his vehicle into an Indian convoy on the national highway in Kashmir's Pulwama district, killing 40 Indian security personnel. With elections looming in India, news channels and social media erupted in nationalist fervor. Immediately, the Modi government mounted a diplomatic campaign "aimed at securing tacit support from some major Western countries" and was met with sympathetic comments from US President Donald Trump and National Security Adviser John Bolton, who supported India's "self-defense" against terrorism.[94]

Less than two weeks after the Pulwama attack, India announced that it had carried out airstrikes at a JeM camp in Balakot, in Pakistan's Khyber Pakhtunkhwa district. Pakistan confirmed that India had struck its territory but denied that there had been any loss of life or damage to any installations. Even so, the next day Pakistan's air forces retaliated and shot down an Indian MiG-21 fighter plane, capturing its pilot. After a tense 60 hours, Pakistan released the pilot in what it called a "gesture of goodwill and peace." India claimed to have also shot down a Pakistani F-16 in the aerial combat—the first ever between two nuclear powers. Pakistan denied India's claim, with its foreign ministry calling it "a classic case of Indian fabrications and pure fantasy." Debates involving professional scholars[95] and amateur social media sleuths, using satellite imagery and supposed video evidence, went on for months without definitive resolution, but April articles in *Foreign Policy* and the *Washington Post* cast serious doubt on India's claims about both the training camp destruction and the downed F-16.[96]

The *Indian Express* reported in June 2019 that Pakistan shared intelligence with both India and the US about the possibility of another "impending attack" in Pulwama by a vehicle carrying an improvised explosive device (IED).[97] India put its security forces in Jammu and Kashmir on high alert; the attack did not materialize.

But apart from critical intelligence sharing, the diplomatic aftermath of the Pulwama attack and India's Balakot airstrikes was acrimonious—even by the bitter standards of India–Pakistan relations. In September 2019, Pakistan's prime minister, Imran

Khan, spoke at the UN General Assembly and said that India had used the crisis for domestic electoral gains; he repeated the charge in January 2021, citing published transcripts of chats on the WhatsApp social media chapter suggesting that a prominent right-wing Indian TV anchor, Arnab Goswami, may have had advance knowledge of India's air strikes.

Whatever their motives and achievements, India's cross-border air strikes at Balakot carried high stakes. Vinay Kaura, reflecting a widely shared view, suggests that India was "trying to upset the fragile equilibrium that had kept the two countries at an uneasy peace for years," as "Pakistan has often used its nuclear weapons as a shield for spreading terrorism against India and as a deterrent against any Indian conventional retaliation that might follow."[98]

Until the next incident threatens to unravel the uneasy peace, analysts will debate whether India has really reset that fragile equilibrium. Kaura's formulation that "India crossed a huge psychological barrier but stopped short of crossing Pakistan's nuclear red lines" seems both apt and obvious, though it is less clear just what threshold of Indian punitive action would trigger a nuclear response. Rakesh Sood, writing for the *Hindu*, suggested that it could be any one of these: India's "capture of a large part of Pakistan's territory"; Pakistan's military "facing unacceptable loss"; India "attempting economic strangulation"; and Pakistan facing "large-scale political destabilization."[99] Since each of these scenarios entails subjective perceptions on Pakistan's side, the implications for India's future brinkmanship and escalation control, should it remain committed to a policy of punitive response, are ambiguous. Red lines may turn out to come in different hues. That Balakot easily could have escalated further—particularly around Pakistan's capture of India's pilot, amid a pre-election surge of Indian nationalism and anti-Pakistan jingoism—may or may not lead India to be more restrained after the next attack, which seems all but inevitable.

The more general risk to India may be to give "a disproportionately high share of attention to Pakistan" in its own "strategic mind space," which Kaura cautions "may be electorally rewarding for the government, but may be risky in the long run since it takes the focus away from the challenge posed by China."[100] A two-front crisis involving simultaneous conflicts along the Line of Control with Pakistan and the Line of Actual Control with China would be an unprecedented challenge for India, but it is now a real possibility. China and Pakistan can also create diplomatic challenges for India, independently and in coordination. While India seeks to frame Kashmir as a domestic issue, Pakistan has a longstanding interest in internationalizing the conflict. India's 2019 abrogation of Article 370 on Jammu and Kashmir's special status, and simultaneous bifurcation of the state into two Union Territories, drew criticism from both countries. China, which holds a permanent seat on the UN Security Council, raised the Kashmir issue before the body for the first time since the 1972 Simla Agreement between India and Pakistan, which had cast the conflict in India's preferred bilateral frame. China did not receive (and may not have expected) wider Security Council support for revisiting the Kashmir issue, but even as symbolism such a move challenges India's narrative and limits its diplomatic options.

In February 2021, India and Pakistan recommitted to a ceasefire, said to be shaped by both countries' intelligence agencies in a process that began after Imran Khan took office in Pakistan in 2018.[101] Both countries' forces have since participated in counterterrorism joint military exercises through the Shanghai Cooperation Organization (SCO), which includes China and Russia and which India and Pakistan both joined in 2017.

Finally, India's relations with Pakistan and the risks of further instability in Kashmir may be shaped by developments in Afghanistan following the Taliban's return to power in August 2021. In the 20 years following the September 11, 2001, terrorist attacks, India spent $3 billion supporting the US-backed government in Kabul, with investments in roads, dams, electricity, schools, hospitals, trade promotion, democracy assistance, and other areas. Bilateral trade between India and Afghanistan—despite the two countries not sharing a border, and having a hostile Pakistan between them—had reached $1 billion.[102] After Afghan President Ashraf Ghani fled the country and the Taliban reclaimed Kabul, India evacuated its citizens from Afghanistan and closed its embassy and consulates there. It issued a six-month "emergency e-visa for Afghan nationals who want to come to India," but awkwardly, this appeared "to prioritize Sikh and Hindu refugees over Muslims, in an echo of the Islamophobic 2019 Citizenship Amendment Act."[103]

Speaking just over two weeks before the fall of Kabul in a joint appearance with US Secretary of State Antony Blinken, India's external affairs minister Subrahmanyam Jaishankar said, "Afghanistan must neither be home to terrorism nor a source of refugees."[104] Either scenario—or both—may have become more likely with the Taliban's return to power. But generationally if not ideologically, this is a different Taliban than the dispensation that claimed power from 1996 to 2001, and it remains to be seen how they will govern a changed country in a changed region and changed world.

Moreover, the Taliban are not the only actors whose vision and capabilities matter in the new regional context after regime change in Afghanistan. JeM, LeT, and more obscure Islamist groups focused on Kashmir could be emboldened by the Taliban victory over a US-backed government. In October 2021, a "little-known militant outfit," the Resistance Front, claimed responsibility for killing two Hindu schoolteachers and a pharmacist in Srinagar, "saying the victims were espousing a Hindu right-wing agenda." This came amid an alarming uptick of similar incidents targeting Hindus in the region.[105]

In an encouraging sign, after India and Pakistan recommitted to a ceasefire in February 2021, ceasefire violations (cross-LoC firing and raids) declined to their lowest level in a decade, after "the year 2020 saw over 5,100 incidents of ceasefire violations" (the highest since 2003, when an earlier ceasefire was enacted). This offers at least some indication of what can be achieved if both countries' security establishments remain committed to keeping the peace. In September, "the [Indian] General Officer Commanding of 15 Corps in Srinagar confidently pointed out that the guns on the LoC between India and Pakistan had remained silent since the reiteration of the ceasefire agreement," telling Indian media:

> The ceasefire violations have not increased. This year there has been none. At least in the Kashmir Valley, there has been zero...

But within a week of this statement, there were reports of "brief gunfire" between the two armies along the LoC for the first time in seven months. India also claimed recovery of multiple AK-47 rifles, pistols, and hand grenades in search operations responding to new infiltrations from the Pakistan side of the LoC, with India's same Lt Gen D.P. Pandey now telling media,

> It is just not possible that such number of activities can take place without the complicity and connivance of local Pak army commanders.... The intent of sending the small weapons in terms of pistols and grenades is to ensure that you are arming the so-called hybrid terrorist, the youth who are studying in the day and in the evening they are given a task to hit.[106]

If past is precedent, another Pulwama-type incident could quickly unravel the normalization progress and thrust India and Pakistan back into a high-stakes contest of brinkmanship and escalation management.

CONSTRUCTING AN "INDO-PACIFIC" REGION AND MODI'S "ACT EAST" POLICY

For the United States, India is the critical linchpin in its new "Indo-Pacific" strategy, a conceptual and geographic reframing of what had previously been the "Asia–Pacific" region. Before it was inscribed in US official language for the unified combatant command in the region—with the United States Pacific Command (USAPACOM) renamed the Indo-Pacific Command (USINDOPACOM) in 2018—to indicate a greater emphasis on South Asia (and especially India), the term "Indo-Pacific" already had increasingly entered "the lexicon of official speeches, think-tank reports and government White Papers, as well as scholarly works."[107] In 2011, US Secretary of State Hillary Clinton referred to the "Indo-Pacific" as "the new 'Asia-Pacific,'" and in 2012 the prominent Indian strategic analyst C. Raja Mohan wrote that the seas of the western pacific and the Indian Ocean constitute "a single integrated geopolitical theater," the "Indo-Pacific."[108]

Nevertheless, the term has been criticized, with other analysts expressing skepticism about its conceptual coherence, or perceiving an American interest in instrumentalizing India in its competition with China. Australian-based scholar Chengxin Pan argues that rather than describing a natural geopolitical reality, the Indo-Pacific "is largely a product of geopolitical imaginations about the perceived 'rise of China'" that are "fueled by collective anxieties about China's growing influence in Asia." The framing, he argues, "has its roots first and foremost" in the American "geopolitical mindset of seeing its mirror image in the behaviour of other powers [which] sustains a perpetual state of fear," with China now its main source. The Indo-Pacific discourse, he argues, "is designed primarily to enable the USA and its regional allies to 'naturally' strengthen and expand their existing regional alliance networks in order to hedge against a perceived China-centric regional order in Asia."[109]

American perceptions and power may be largely driving the Indo-Pacific policy agenda, but that does not mean that American allies all view the region through the same lens. Cleo Paskal, a researcher at the British think tank Chatham House, surveyed Indo-Pacific strategies and perceptions in the US, UK, France, India, the Tonga microstate (population just over 100,000), and Japan. "At its most basic," Paskal observes,

> the region is where China's expansion is coming up against growing economic, political, and military resistance from the US, India, Japan, Australia, and others. However, those countries' resistance is not uniform, despite growing efforts to create and reinforce alliances and partnerships.[110]

The countries do not even hold the same understandings of the region's exact geographic boundaries. For example, Paskal notes, "India officially views it as meaning the area from the east coast of Africa to the west coast of the Americas"—a vast expanse—whereas "some in the US military take it to mean the area under the purview of the US Indo-Pacific Command, so [only] roughly as far west as the Maldives." (In 2020, the US and the Maldives signed a defense pact, to which India has extended its support.[111])

A recent analysis by the Brookings Institutions, a leading American think tank in Washington, DC, offered an extensive wish list for deepening US-India security cooperation "after the foundational agreements," including strengthening joint military exercises by prioritizing "high-end" activities and pursuing "low-end" activities with third countries "at risk of undue Chinese influence," continuing high technology cooperation and co-development, enhanced intelligence sharing, and so on. At the same time, author Joshua White acknowledged, there are "rising" concerns in the US about India's fiscal limitations and "drift toward illiberal majoritarian politics." Reflecting Democratic Party priorities, White predicts, the Biden administration "will likely seek, for good reason, to rebalance the bilateral relationship away from a disproportionate focus on security issues in order to address a wider array of topics including global health, energy and climate change, and technology cooperation."[112]

If the Indo-Pacific discourse is closely tied to the US–India relationship, a different sub-regional framing has more independent roots in India's recent foreign policy history. The Modi government announced a diplomatic initiative dubbed "Act East" shortly after taking office in 2014, expanding an earlier "Look East" policy, enacted after India's early 1990s economic reforms, of deepening its engagement with key countries and multilateral institutions in the Asia–Pacific region (particularly bilateral relations with Japan and South Korea, and multilateral relations with the Association of Southeast Asian Nations, ASEAN, and its ASEAN Regional Forum, in which India is an active member).

While the initial motivations for Look East were mainly economic, with Act East, the Modi government has sought to give "a new thrust to intensify economic, strategic and diplomatic relations with countries that share common concerns with India on China's growing economic and military strength and its implications for the evolving regional order."[113] Thus, despite some criticism to the contrary, Modi's Act East policy is "more than a rebranding" of Look East.[114] A key aim of Act East has been to improve infrastructure connectivity in key areas such as the Greater Mekong Subregion (Cambodia, Laos, Myanmar, Vietnam, and Thailand), and development of India's northeast as a "gateway" to Southeast Asia; it also seeks to develop a series of sea corridors spanning South and Southeast Asia and an Asia–Africa Growth Corridor (AAGC), with the particular support of Japan. To be sure, as analyst K. V. Kesavan of the Delhi-based Observer Research Foundation concedes, such initiatives "have a long way to go and it is still far-fetched to view AAGC [and by implication, the others] as a counter to China's ambitious Belt and Road Initiative (BRI)."[115]

Act East carries strategic implications for the Indian Ocean region, and specifically for maritime relations around the Bay of Bengal, as India has taken new initiatives to "in enhancing joint patrols and humanitarian assistance and disaster relief cooperation."[116] In these efforts, India is up against expanding Chinese influence in this region, with Myanmar (Burma) serving as a particular focus of competition between the two powers. India is often criticized for not doing more to promote democratization in Myanmar, in which the army again seized power in February 2021, ending a half-decade's fragile democratization and sharing of power between the military and Aung San Suu Kyi, the Nobel laureate who had spent most of the period since 1989 under house arrest during decades of the military's rule.

The political situation in Myanmar presents a difficult dilemma for India, which saw its earlier efforts to support democratization backfire, "as China strengthened ties with the Tatmadaw [the military] and turned Myanmar into a useful gateway into Southeast Asia."[117] India has found the Tatmadaw "a helpful ally" in its fight against insurgents in its northeast and relies on its cooperation to support its own infrastructure agenda for Southeast Asia. Following Myanmar's coup, Lt Gen Prakash Menon, a strategic analyst, counseled that India "must be smart" and not protest "too loudly,"[118] since China's interest in gaining overland access to the Indian Ocean via Myanmar made it all too easy for the generals to show disdain for any criticism from India. (China's infrastructure agenda in Myanmar predates its Belt and Road Initiative, focusing especially on oil and gas pipelines to provide alternative routes for Chinese energy imports.) On the other hand, analyst Mohamed Zeeshan argued that India's continued engagement with the Tatmadaw would "hurt its credibility," and that India should "distinguish itself from China and cut the Myanmar army loose."[119]

INDIA'S REGIONAL DIPLOMACY: SOFT POWER, HARD LINES, AND VACCINE NATIONALISM

The Modi government's hardline domestic policies may be undermining the "soft power" advantages India traditionally has brought to its external relations, especially with its (relatively) friendly South Asian neighbors. This interconnectedness was exhibited in November 2021 when Bangladesh experienced a nearly weeklong spasm of violence and property damage by mobs targeting the minority Hindu community during the Durga Puja festival. As the *New York Times* reported, the violence (which was set off by rumors that a Quran, the Muslim holy book, had been disrespected in a Hindu temple) "drew an outcry from politicians in neighboring India." But Bangladesh's Prime Minister Sheikh Hasina, generally a Modi ally, "had pointed words for India, even as she promised to hunt the culprits":

> We expect that nothing happens there [in India] which could influence any situation in Bangladesh affecting our Hindu community here.

As the *Times* observed,

> India is losing leverage in South Asia as its government tries to reshape the country into a Hindu state. In marginalizing and maligning its minority Muslims at home, Mr. Modi's government has weakened India's traditional leadership role of encouraging harmony in a region of many fault lines.

Yashwant Sinha, a former Indian foreign minister for the BJP-led NDA government in the early 2000s who has since resigned his party membership, told the newspaper,

> The openly partisan approach to communal issues has created a very peculiar situation for us as far as that moral high ground in

neighborhood policy is concerned. We can't say, "you stop it, this should not happen," because we ourselves are guilty of it.[120]

According to the *Times*, Hasina has suggested that India's hardening policies toward its Muslims have contributed to violence against Hindus in Bangladesh. Hindu minorities elsewhere in the region, from Pakistan to Sri Lanka, have also come under attack amid increasing extremism among sections of the majority communities (Muslims in Pakistan, ethnic Sinhalese in Sri Lanka). An action–reaction cycle may be setting in, with direct cross-border consequences: following the violence against Hindus in Bangladesh, right-wing Hindus in India's neighboring Tripura state organized large protests. At least one mosque and a number of Muslim-owned shops were vandalized, prompting police to deploy protection forces.

It wasn't supposed to be this way. Modi's first swearing-in ceremony, on May 26, 2014, was attended by his counterparts from the seven other states comprising the South Asian Association for Regional Cooperation (SAARC): Afghanistan, Bangladesh, Bhutan, Maldives, Nepal, Pakistan, and Sri Lanka. As a candidate, Modi had emphasized the centrality of South Asia in India's foreign policy, and in the months following the "largely symbolic curtain raiser" of his swearing-in ceremony, the new prime minister spoke of "reinvigorating" and "revitalizing" SAARC (established in 1985, and never especially vigorous nor vital). Modi promised to lead the region with cooperation "on issues of trade, transit, visas, investments, education, health, communication and space technologies."[121] There have been some positive results: in March 2015, Modi became the first Indian prime minister to visit Sri Lanka in 28 years, and the very first to visit the Tamil stronghold of Jaffna, marking a symbolic milestone in the postwar country's uneasy peace. He reached maritime and land boundary agreements with Bangladesh, the latter involving a dispute that dated back to India's Partition.[122]

But as in other areas of foreign policy, India's South Asia relations under Modi have been more reactive than visionary in practice, with bilateralism trumping regionalism as the government has responded to events ranging from natural disasters to terrorist attacks in its near abroad and has emphasized military–security relations over other areas of cooperation. British political scientist Scott Lucas characterizes Modi's regional approach as "confrontational rather than cooperative," with a "focus on military measures rather than social elements."[123] And, as analyst Aparna Pande told the *New York Times*,

> If you are pushing a nationalist narrative, it is difficult to then ask your neighbors not to do the same. You will then see every country in South Asia becoming more nationalist and, forget about anything else, that creates a strategic challenge for India.[124]

Modi's habit of oscillating between internationalist speechifying and nationalist action has been especially evident in India's vaccine diplomacy during the COVID-19 pandemic. As a leading exporter of low-cost pharmaceuticals (popularly dubbed "the world's pharmacy"), India's contribution to global vaccine supply has been indispensable, to be sure. A late 2020 estimate put the country's capacity to manufacture COVID-19 vaccine at well over 3 billion doses annually.[125] Most Indian vaccine manufacturers signed exclusive license agreements with foreign partners; in the largest of these, the Serum Institute of India (SII) makes an Indian version of the vaccine developed by Oxford University and AstraZeneca, called Covishield. On a more modest scale, India's first indigenously developed vaccine, called Covaxin, comes from the Indian company Bharat Biotech in collaboration with the Indian Council of Medical Research. Originally, the Indian government and SII struck an agreement that would have distributed about half of India's supply domestically. When India's winter 2020–21 case numbers were lower than public health experts had predicted, the Modi government made a great show of India's generosity and international standing by sending much of its purchased vaccine to other countries in South Asia and further abroad. High on his own supply and with characteristic panache, Modi proclaimed that India stood "ready to save humanity." Yet, as the *Diplomat* reported, citing Ministry of External Affairs figures, more than half of India's vaccine supplies to countries in South Asia "were delivered through commercial deals and not grants."[126]

The pandemic's next wave hit in spring 2021, driven by a more transmissible mutation of the virus dubbed the Delta variant, which was first identified in India amid relaxed social distancing practices for large gatherings like state-level election rallies and the giant Kumbh Mela religious festival along the Ganges River. Suddenly, "after having delivered 66 million doses to various developing countries, especially in the neighborhood," the Modi government imposed a vaccine export ban—even as it denied that it was doing so[127]—in a belated attempt to claw back supply for India's own population. The halt lasted from mid-April to October, nearly six months. "In India's absence, China filled the vacuum," and by late September 2021 it "had already delivered over 140 million doses across South Asia," from Afghanistan to Myanmar. Pakistan, Bangladesh, and Sri Lanka were among the top ten recipients of Chinese exports worldwide. Given concerns about cost, efficacy, and "the threat of Chinese political influence in strategic affairs," India's neighbors welcomed its resumption of vaccine exports in October 2021. But as the *Diplomat* noted at the time, "Much of New Delhi's vaccine diplomacy potential would depend on India's own vaccination rate—which is as yet extremely slow."[128]

Even during the halt on India's own vaccine exports, Indian officials still pointedly criticized developed countries, including the United States, for "vaccine nationalism" prioritizing their own populations—and pharmaceutical companies—ahead of developing countries.[129] In May 2021, with India reporting more than

200,000 cases and recording 4,000 deaths a day from COVID-19, External Affairs Minister Jaishankar visited the US—the first official visit by a senior Indian minister since President Joe Biden took office—to procure additional vaccine supply for India. An estimated one million Indians had already died in the pandemic, far exceeding the official death toll of 315,000.

Biden had recently pledged to ship 80 million doses of vaccine to countries in need, and as *Time* reported, India hoped to secure as many of those as it could. Having earlier rejected foreign-made vaccines, such as Pfizer's, the Modi government was now fast-tracking their import. The magazine observed, "India has come a long way in a short time—from the swaggering Vaccine Guru boasting about saving the world, to desperately scouring the globe for vaccines."[130]

Despite Modi's bravado, his government simply failed to order enough vaccine doses, preferring to believe forecasts by government-appointed scientists that were "tragically wrong" and reflected a politicized public health process that "would lull the country into a false sense of security."[131] Thus, "By the time India's first vaccination rolled out on Jan. 16"—four months before the Delta wave hit—"the Indian government had bought just 11 million doses from Serum Institute and 5.5 million from Bharat Biotech."[132] In February, it ordered another 21 million doses from SII, followed by another 110 million in March when infections started to rise. (By contrast, by November 2020, the US and EU had each pre-ordered 700 million doses, far more than needed.) As with vaccines, India had also exported supplies of oxygen, needed for hospitalized COVID-19 patients, even weeks into the Delta wave that led it to critical oxygen shortages, widespread price-gouging, and dangerous counterfeiting.

If developed countries could be accused of hoarding vaccine supplies, India's own vaccine nationalism took the opposite approach[133]—until it didn't. The Modi government's hubris compelled it to take a 180-degree turn, all while insisting that the pandemic was under control and that India had special capacities in the fight against the novel coronavirus. On June 21, 2021, Modi even touted yoga as a "protective shield" against COVID-19, citing testimony from Indian "frontline warriors" and doctors.[134] These remarks marked the eighth annual International Yoga Day, which Modi had persuaded the United Nations General Assembly to establish in 2014, his first year as prime minister. At the time, skeptics had seen the initiative as an effort to assert Indian—and specifically Hindu—ownership over globally popular yoga. As Modi's remarks now veered into pseudoscience, the value of this soft power initiative seemed even more dubious.

The Modi pattern that had emerged in 2016 with demonetization and continued in 2020 with the abrupt national lockdown in response to the first wave the pandemic was clearer than ever. Soaring rhetoric, sweeping gestures, and reactive fiats could not make up for the government's lack of foresight and the state's weak implementation capacity in an essential policy sphere. More than ever, India and the world would bear the consequences.

By fall, following a grim spring and summer, India's Delta wave had subsided. Significantly, the government's announcement that it intended to resume exporting COVID-19 vaccines "came shortly before Prime Minister Narendra Modi left for Washington to attend [the] Quad leaders' summit" in September.[135] Modi was back in his element: projecting strength and not looking back.

NOTES

1 Jasmine Wright, "Biden Commits to 'Free, Open, Secure' Indo-Pacific in Rare Op-Ed with 'Quad' Members," *CNNPolitics*, March 14, 2021, https://www.cnn.com/2021/03/14/politics/biden-modi-morrison-suga-quad-op-ed/index.html.
2 Guy Taylor, "Mike Pompeo Confronts 'Asian NATO' Hurdles in Asian Allies Meeting," *Washington Times*, October 5, 2020, sec. Security.

3. ANI, "US, European Officials Mulling to Create 'Asian NATO' to Contain China's Expansionist Ambitions," *Times of India / Asian News International*, October 1, 2020.
4. White House, "Quad Leaders' Joint Statement: 'The Spirit of the Quad,'" The White House, March 12, 2021, https://www.whitehouse.gov/briefing-room/statements-releases/2021/03/12/quad-leaders-joint-statement-the-spirit-of-the-quad/.
5. Joseph Biden et al., "Our Four Nations Are Committed to a Free, Open, Secure and Prosperous Indo-Pacific Region," *Washington Post*, March 13, 2021, sec. Opinion.
6. John Miller and Mike Shields, "Delta COVID Variant Becoming Globally Dominant, WHO Official Says," *Reuters*, June 18, 2021, sec. World, https://www.reuters.com/world/delta-covid-variant-becoming-globally-dominant-says-who-official-2021-06-18/.
7. Larry Diamond, "The Global Crisis of Democracy," *Wall Street Journal*, May 17, 2019, sec. Life.
8. Abhijnan Rej, "In 'Historic' Summit Quad Commits to Meeting Key Indo-Pacific Challenges," *The Diplomat*, March 13, 2021, https://thediplomat.com/2021/03/in-historic-summit-quad-commits-to-meeting-key-indo-pacific-challenges/.
9. Kishore Mahbubani, "The New Anti-China Alliance Will Fail," *Foreign Policy* (Foreign Policy, Spring 2021).
10. Sadanand Dhume, "Opinion | The Quad Enters the Ring with China," *Wall Street Journal*, September 30, 2021, sec. Opinion, https://www.wsj.com/articles/india-china-aukus-quad-japan-indo-pacific-australia-huawei-11633033358.
11. C. Raja Mohan, *Modi's World: Expanding India's Sphere of Influence* (HarperCollins India, 2015).
12. Sumit Ganguly, "Has Modi Truly Changed India's Foreign Policy?," *The Washington Quarterly* 40, no. 2 (April 3, 2017): 131–32, https://doi.org/10.1080/0163660X.2017.1328929.
13. Rajesh Basrur, "Modi's Foreign Policy Fundamentals: A Trajectory Unchanged," *International Affairs* 93, no. 1 (January 2017): 9, https://doi.org/10.1093/ia/iiw006. See also Surupa Gupta et al., "Indian Foreign Policy under Modi: A New Brand or Just Repackaging?," *International Studies Perspectives* 20, no. 1 (February 2019): 1–45, https://doi.org/10.1093/isp/eky008.
14. Manjari Chatterjee Miller and Kate Sullivan De Estrada, "Pragmatism in Indian Foreign Policy: How Ideas Constrain Modi," *International Affairs* 93, no. 1 (January 2017): 27, 28, https://doi.org/10.1093/ia/iiw001.

15 Ananth Krishnan, "'One-Third of Funding by AIIB Has Gone to India,'" *The Hindu*, September 25, 2020, sec. Industry.
16 Ibid.; see also Orange Wang, "China–India Border Clash 'First Major Test' for AIIB as Multilateral Lender," *South China Morning Post*, June 4, 2021, sec. Economy.
17 Ankit Panda, "What's Driving the India-China Standoff at Doklam?," *The Diplomat*, July 2017.
18 Panda.
19 Panda.
20 Jonah Blank, "What Were China's Objectives in the Doklam Dispute?," *The RAND Blog* (blog), September 8, 2017, https://www.rand.org/blog/2017/09/what-were-chinas-objectives-in-the-doklam-dispute.html.
21 Blank.
22 Kanti Bajpai, "Modi's China Policy and the Road to Confrontation," *Pacific Affairs* 91, no. 2 (June 1, 2018): 245–46, https://doi.org/10.5509/2018912245.
23 Bajpai, 231.
24 Sumit Ganguly, "India and China: On a Collision Course?," *Pacific Affairs* 91, no. 2 (June 1, 2018): 233, https://doi.org/10.5509/2018912231.
25 Bajpai, "Modi's China Policy and the Road to Confrontation," 246.
26 Bajpai, 253.
27 Bajpai, 246.
28 Bajpai, 254.
29 Bajpai, 255.
30 Bajpai, 255–56.
31 Bajpai, 260.
32 Ganguly, "India and China," 244.
33 Bajpai, "Modi's China Policy and the Road to Confrontation," 260.
34 Vinay Kaura, "India's Relations with China from the Doklam Crisis to the Galwan Tragedy," *India Quarterly: A Journal of International Affairs* 76, no. 4 (December 2020): 504, https://doi.org/10.1177/0974928420961768.
35 Kaura, 504.
36 Kaura, 505.
37 Archis Mohan, "In a First, PM Modi Comes Close to Acknowledging 'victory' at Doklam," *Business Standard*, October 5, 2017.
38 Ankit Panda, "A Skirmish in Galwan Valley: India and China's Deadliest Clash in More Than 50 Years," *The Diplomat*, June 2020.
39 BBC News, "India–China Clash: 20 Indian Troops Killed in Ladakh Fighting," June 16, 2020, sec. Asia.

40 Hannah Ellis-Petersen, "Indians Call for Boycott of Chinese Goods after Fatal Border Clashes," *Guardian*, June 18, 2020, http://www.theguardian.com/world/2020/jun/18/indians-call-for-boycott-of-chinese-goods-after-fatal-border-clashes.

41 Ellis-Petersen, "Indians Call for Boycott of Chinese Goods after Fatal Border Clashes."

42 Arshad Zargar, "India Bans TikTok and Dozens of Other Chinese Apps amid Border Standoff," *CBS News*, June 30, 2020, https://www.cbsnews.com/news/india-bans-tiktok-other-china-made-apps-as-border-dispute-drags-on-today-2020-06-30/.

43 Krishn Kaushik and Shubhajit Roy, Indian Express, "PMO Acknowledges: This Time, Chinese Came in Much Larger Strength to LAC," *Indian Express*, June 21, 2020, https://indianexpress.com/article/india/narendra-modi-india-china-border-dispute-galwan-all-party-meeting-6467932/.

44 Dinakar Peri, "Ladakh Standoff | India, China Agree to Stop Sending More Troops to Frontline," *The Hindu*, September 22, 2020, sec. National.

45 Ankit Panda, "India and China, One Year After the Galwan Clash," podcast, *The Diplomat*, June 2021, https://thediplomat.com/2021/06/india-and-china-one-year-after-the-galwan-clash/.

46 Simon Tisdall, "Narendra Modi's US Visa Secure despite Gujarat Riots Guilty Verdicts," *Guardian*, June 2, 2016, sec. World News.

47 James Mann, "Why Narendra Modi Was Banned From the US," *Wall Street Journal*, May 2, 2014, sec. Life and Style.

48 Shashank Bengali and Paul Richter, "US Eager to Forget about New India Premier's 2005 Visa Denial," *Los Angeles Times*, September 25, 2014, https://www.latimes.com/world/asia/la-fg-us-india-modi-20140925-story.html.

49 Annie Gowan, "Once Banned from the US, India's Modi Set for Historic Address to Congress," *Washington Post*, June 6, 2016, https://www.washingtonpost.com/news/worldviews/wp/2016/06/06/from-pariah-to-capitol-hill-narendra-modis-extraordinary-rise/.

50 Maggie Haberman, "Donald Trump Says He's a 'Big Fan' of Hindus," *New York Times*, October 16, 2016, sec. US.

51 Stuart Anderson, "The Story of How Trump Officials Tried to End H-1B Visas," *Forbes*, February 1, 2021, https://www.forbes.com/sites/stuartanderson/2021/02/01/the-story-of-how-trump-officials-tried-to-end-h-1b-visas/. See also Soutik Biswas, Soutik Biswas, "Why Trump's H-1B Visa Freeze Will Hurt India Most," *BBC News*, June 24, 2020, sec. India.

52 Devesh Kapur, "The Indian Prime Minister and Trump Addressed a Houston Rally. Who Was Signaling What?," *Washington Post*, September 29, 2019,

https://www.washingtonpost.com/politics/2019/09/29/prime-minister-modi-india-donald-trump-addressed-huge-houston-rally-who-was-signaling-what/.

53 Sukirti Dwivedi, "'We'll Be Peaceful Till Trump Leaves,' BJP Leader Kapil Mishra Warns Delhi Police," NDTV.com, February 24, 2020, https://www.ndtv.com/delhi-news/bjp-leader-kapil-mishras-3-day-ultimatum-to-delhi-police-to-clear-anti-caa-protest-jaffrabad-2184627.

54 Joanna Slater, "Trump's Second Day in India: Violence in Delhi and Support for Modi on 'Religious Freedom,'" *Washington Post*, February 25, 2020, sec. Asia.

55 Tanvi Madan, "The Dragon in the Room: The China Factor in the Development of US–India Ties in the Cold War," *India Review* 18, no. 4 (July 2019): 370, 378–79, https://doi.org/10.1080/14736489.2019.1662188.

56 Madan, 377.

57 Arijit Mazumdar and Erin Statz, "Democracy Promotion in India's Foreign Policy: Emerging Trends and Developments," *Asian Affairs: An American Review* 42, no. 2 (April 2015): 78, https://doi.org/10.1080/00927678.2015.1034611.

58 Brian P. Goldschmidt, "Making a US-India Strategic Partnership Work," Thesis (Peter R. Lavoy, advisor), The Naval Postgraduate School, Monterey, California, December 2001.

59 Harsh V. Pant and Julie M. Super, "India's 'Non-Alignment' Conundrum: A Twentieth-Century Policy in a Changing World," *International Affairs* 91, no. 4 (July 2015): 760, https://doi.org/10.1111/1468-2346.12336.

60 Sunil Khilnani et al., "NonAlignment 2.0: A Foreign and Strategic Policy for India in the Twenty First Century" (New Delhi, India: Centre for Policy Research, February 29, 2012).

61 Khilnani et al., iv.

62 Khilnani et al., 31–32.

63 Khilnani et al., 32.

64 Pant and Super, "India's 'Non-Alignment' Conundrum," 747.

65 Pant and Super, 761.

66 Pant and Super, 762.

67 Ravish Tiwari, "PM Narendra Modi Used 15% Fewer Words than Former PM Manmohan Singh in US Congress Speech," *The Economic Times*, June 10, 2016, https://economictimes.indiatimes.com/news/politics-and-nation/pm-narendra-modi-used-15-fewer-words-than-former-pm-manmohan-singh-in-us-congress-speech/articleshow/52681130.cms?from=mdr.

68 Pant and Super, "India's 'Non-Alignment' Conundrum," 763.

69 P.S. Raghavan, "The Making of India's Foreign Policy: From Non-Alignment to Multi-Alignment," *International Foreign Affairs Journal* 12, no. 4 (December 2017): 326–41.
70 Nayanima Basu, "India Is No Longer 'Non-Aligned', Says Foreign Secretary Vijay Gokhale," *The Print*, January 10, 2019, https://theprint.in/diplomacy/india-is-no-longer-non-aligned-says-foreign-secretary-vijay-gokhale/176222/.
71 Ashustosh Nagda, "India's Renewed Embrace of the Non-Aligned Movement," *The Diplomat*, May 11, 2020, https://thediplomat.com/2020/05/indias-renewed-embrace-of-the-non-aligned-movement/.
72 Zach Montague, "US-India Defense Ties Grow Closer as Shared Concerns in Asia Loom," *New York Times*, November 20, 2019, sec. World.
73 Maria Abi-Habib, "US and India, Wary of China, Agree to Strengthen Military Ties," *New York Times*, September 6, 2018, sec. World, https://www.nytimes.com/2018/09/06/world/asia/us-india-military-agreement.html.
74 Rajat Pandit, "India, US Defence Deals: How Defence Partnership Ringfences Ties between India, US," *The Economic Times*, February 23, 2020, https://economictimes.indiatimes.com/news/defence/how-defence-partnership-ringfences-ties-between-india-us/articleshow/74263597.cms.
75 Vikram Mahajan, "India-US: Defence Trade and Technology Initiative Is the Silent Enabler," *The Financial Express*, September 15, 2020. See also, Indian Express, "Explained: What Is US-India Defence Technology and Trade Initiative," *Indian Express*, October 19, 2019, https://indianexpress.com/article/explained/explained-us-india-defense-technology-and-trade-initiative-dtti-6077915/.
76 Javin Aryan, "The Defence Technology and Trade Initiative (DTTI): Lost in the Acronym Bowl," Observer Research Foundation, December 10, 2020.
77 Elizabeth Roche, "India, US Sign Pact for Cooperation in Development of Air-Launched UAV," *Mint*, September 3, 2021.
78 The Economist, "India Spends a Fortune on Defence and Gets Poor Value for Money," *The Economist*, March 28, 2018, https://www.economist.com/asia/2018/03/28/india-spends-a-fortune-on-defence-and-gets-poor-value-for-money.
79 The Economist.
80 Abi-Habib, "US and India, Wary of China, Agree to Strengthen Military Ties."
81 Krishn Kaushik, "India Third Highest Military Spender in 2020, States Data Published by Stockholm International Peace Research Institute," *Indian Express*, April 27, 2021.

82. Vivek Raghuvanshi, "India Releases Details of New Defense Budget," *Defense News*, February 2, 2021, sec. Asia Pacific, https://www.defensenews.com/global/asia-pacific/2021/02/02/india-releases-details-of-new-defense-budget/.
83. Armaan Bhatnagar, "India's Defence Spending in 7 Charts," *Times of India*, January 30, 2021, https://timesofindia.indiatimes.com/india/indias-defence-spending-in-7-charts/articleshow/80600625.cms.
84. The Economist, "India's Armed Forces Get Their Biggest Shake-Up in Decades," *The Economist*, January 18, 2020, https://www.economist.com/asia/2020/01/18/indias-armed-forces-get-their-biggest-shake-up-in-decades.
85. "India's Armed Forces Get Their Biggest Shake-Up in Decades."
86. Suhasini Raj and Mujib Mashal, "India's Top Military General Dies in Helicopter Crash," *New York Times*, December 8, 2021, sec. World.
87. Raj and Mashal.
88. ThePrint Team, "Pakistan-Based Social Media Accounts, Bots Spread Conspiracy Theories on CDS Rawat's Death," *ThePrint* (blog), December 16, 2021, https://theprint.in/defence/pakistan-based-social-media-accounts-bots-spread-conspiracy-theories-on-cds-rawats-death/782647/.
89. India tested its first nuclear device in 1974 but opted not to weaponize until 1998. It is now well accepted that China conducted a test on Pakistan's behalf of a 10-12 kt device at China's Lop Nur testing facility in 1990. Hans M. Kristensen and Robert S. Norris, "Pakistan's Nuclear Forces, 2011," *Bulletin of the Atomic Scientists* 67, no. 4 (2011): 92, https://doi.org/10.1177/0096340211413360.
90. For a summary and analysis, see Vinay Kaura, "India's Pakistan Policy: From 2016 'Surgical Strike' to 2019 Balakot 'Airstrike'," *The Round Table 109*, no. 3 (2020): 277–87.
91. Kaura, 279.
92. Kaura, 279.
93. TNN & Agencies, "'Terrorism Has Become Its Favourite Child': PM Modi Slams Pakistan at BRICS-BIMSTEC Outreach Summit," *Times of India*, October 16, 2016, https://timesofindia.indiatimes.com/india/terrorism-has-become-its-favourite-child-pm-modi-slams-pakistan-at-brics-bimstec-outreach-summit/articleshow/54882776.cms.
94. Kaura, "India's Pakistan Policy," 281.
95. See Chander Suta Dogra, "IAF Did Not Shoot Down Pak F-16 in Balakot Aftermath, Says US Scholar Christine Fair," *The Wire*, December 15, 2019, 2022, https://thewire.in/security/christine-fair-iaf-balakot-pakistan-f16.

96 See Lara Seligman, "Did India Shoot Down a Pakistani Jet? US Count Says No," *Foreign Policy* (blog), April 4, 2019, https://foreignpolicy.com/2019/04/04/did-india-shoot-down-a-pakistani-jet-u-s-count-says-no/; and "Analysis: Did India Shoot down a Pakistani F-16 in February? This Just Became a Big Deal," *Washington Post*, April 17, 2019, https://www.washingtonpost.com/politics/2019/04/17/did-india-shoot-down-pakistani-f-back-february-this-just-became-big-deal/.

97 Muzamil Jaleel, "Alert in J&K after Pakistan's Input to India and US on Threat of 'IED-Vehicle' Attack," *Indian Express*, June 16, 2019, https://indianexpress.com/article/india/alert-jk-pakistan-input-india-us-threat-ied-vehicle-attack-awantipora-pulwama-sco-summit-bishkek-5782710/.

98 Kaura, "India's Pakistan Policy," 281–82.

99 Rakesh Sood, "What Has Changed Post-Balakot?," *The Hindu*, March 20, 2019, sec. Lead, https://www.thehindu.com/opinion/lead/what-has-changed-post-balakot/article26583820.ece.

100 Kaura, "India's Pakistan Policy," 284.

101 Abhijnan Rej, "India–Pakistan Ceasefire Details Emerge—Along with Possibility of Joint Military Exercises," *The Diplomat*, March 23, 2021, https://thediplomat.com/2021/03/india-pakistan-ceasefire-details-emerge-along-with-possibility-of-joint-military-exercises/.

102 Indian Express, "Explained: What Are India's Investments in Afghanistan?," *Indian Express*, August 24, 2021, https://indianexpress.com/article/explained/explained-indias-afghan-investment-7406795/.

103 Nitish Pahwa, "The Taliban's Comeback Could Upend the Balance of Power Across Asia," *Slate*, August 23, 2021, https://slate.com/news-and-politics/2021/08/taliban-afghanistan-pakistan-india-china-power-balance.html.

104 United States Department of State, "Secretary Antony J. Blinken and Indian External Affairs Minister Dr. Subrahmanyam Jaishankar at a Joint Press Availability," United States Department of State, July 28, 2021, https://www.state.gov/secretary-antony-j-blinken-and-indian-external-affairs-minister-dr-subrahmanyam-jaishankar-at-a-joint-press-availability/.

105 Samaan Lateef Srinagar, "Kashmir: Minority Killings Increase amid Violent Demographic Tensions," DW.com, October 13, 2021, https://www.dw.com/en/kashmir-minority-killings-increase-amid-violent-demographic-tensions/a-59467733.

106 Khalid Shah, "Will the Ceasefire on India Pakistan Border Sustain?," ORF, September 29, 2021, https://www.orfonline.org/expert-speak/will-the-ceasefire-on-india-pakistan-border-sustain/.

107 The term has been attributed to the German general and political geographer Karl Haushofer as early as the 1920s, but it receded for nearly a century until suddenly appearing in American, Indian, and other sources in the early 2010s.
108 Quoted in Chengxin Pan, "The 'Indo-Pacific' and Geopolitical Anxieties about China's Rise in the Asian Regional Order," *Australian Journal of International Affairs* 68, no. 4 (August 8, 2014): 454, https://doi.org/10.1080/10357718.2014.884054.
109 Pan, 453, 456.
110 Cleo Paskal, "Introduction," *Indo-Pacific Strategies, Perceptions, and Partnerships*, Chatham House—International Affairs Think Tank, March 23, 2021, https://www.chathamhouse.org/2021/03/indo-pacific-strategies-perceptions-and-partnerships/01-introduction.
111 Amit Ranjan, "The Maldives' Geopolitical Dilemma: India–China Rivalry, and Entry of the USA," *Asian Affairs* 52, no. 2 (March 15, 2021): 375–95, https://doi.org/10.1080/03068374.2021.1911159.
112 Joshua T. White, "After the Foundational Agreements: An Agenda for US–India Defense and Security Cooperation," *Brookings.edu*, January 2021, 1.
113 K. V. Kesavan, "India's 'Act East' Policy and Regional Cooperation," Observer Research Foundation, February 14, 2020, https://www.orfonline.org/expert-speak/indias-act-east-policy-and-regional-cooperation-61375/.
114 Arijit Mazumdar, "From 'Look East' to 'Act East': India's Evolving Engagement with the Asia–Pacific Region," *Asian Affairs* 52, no. 2 (June 2021): 357–74, https://doi.org/10.1080/03068374.2021.1912467.
115 Kesavan, "India's 'Act East' Policy and Regional Cooperation."
116 Isabelle Saint-Mézard, "India's Act East Policy: Strategic Implications for the Indian Ocean," *Journal of the Indian Ocean Region* 12, no. 2 (December 2016): 177–90, https://doi.org/10.1080/19480881.2016.1226753.
117 Mohamed Zeeshan, "India's Approach Toward Myanmar Will Hurt Its Credibility," *The Diplomat*, April 5, 2021, https://thediplomat.com/2021/04/indias-approach-toward-myanmar-will-hurt-its-credibility/.
118 Lt. Gen. Prakash Menon, "India Must Be Smart in Supporting Myanmar, If Quad Won't Measure up," *The Print*, March 23, 2021, https://theprint.in/opinion/india-must-be-smart-in-supporting-myanmar-if-quad-wont-measure-up/626379/.
119 Zeeshan, "India's Approach Toward Myanmar Will Hurt Its Credibility."
120 Mujib Mashal, "In a Region in Strife, India's Moral High Ground Erodes," *New York Times*, November 6, 2021, sec. World, https://www.nytimes.com/2021/11/06/world/asia/india-region-muslim-hindu-strife.html.

121 W. P. S. Sidhu and Shruti Godbole, "Neighbourhood First: Bilateralism Trumps Regionalism," *Brookings India*, May 2015, 2.
122 Sidhu and Godbole.
123 "Is India's 'Neighbourhood First Policy' Unable to Win Regional Allies?," *TRT World*, October 5, 2021, https://www.trtworld.com/magazine/is-india-s-neighbourhood-first-policy-unable-to-win-regional-allies-50492.
124 Mashal, "In a Region in Strife, India's Moral High Ground Erodes."
125 Khan Sharun and Kuldeep Dhama, "India's Role in COVID-19 Vaccine Diplomacy," *Journal of Travel Medicine* 28, no. 7 (October 11, 2021), https://doi.org/10.1093/jtm/taab064.
126 Mohamed Zeeshan, "India Still Has an Opportunity with Vaccine Diplomacy," *The Diplomat*, October 1, 2021.
127 BS Web Team, "Haven't Imposed Any Export Ban on Covaxin, Covishield, Says Govt," *Business Standard India*, April 2, 2021, https://www.business-standard.com/article/current-affairs/have-not-imposed-any-export-ban-on-coronavirus-vaccines-says-govt-121040200726_1.html.
128 Zeeshan, "India Still Has an Opportunity with Vaccine Diplomacy."
129 Dipanjan Roy Chaudhury, "India Opposes Vaccine Nationalism; Calls for Greater Support to Joint Proposal with S Africa," *Economic Times*, April 16, 2021, https://economictimes.indiatimes.com/news/india/india-opposes-vaccine-nationalism-calls-for-greater-support-to-joint-proposal-with-s-africa/articleshow/82105063.cms?from=mdr.
130 Debasish Roy Chowdhury, "Modi Never Bought Enough COVID-19 Vaccines for India. Now the Whole World Is Paying," *Time,* May 28, 2021, https://time.com/6052370/modi-didnt-buy-enough-covid-19-vaccine/.
131 Karan Deep Singh, "As India's Lethal Covid Wave Neared, Politics Overrode Science," *New York Times*, September 14, 2021, sec. World, https://www.nytimes.com/2021/09/14/world/asia/india-modi-science-icmr.html.
132 Chowdhury, "Modi Never Bought Enough COVID-19 Vaccines for India."
133 Niladri Chatterjee, Zaad Mahmood, and Eleonor Marcussen, "Politics of Vaccine Nationalism in India: Global and Domestic Implications," *Forum for Development Studies*, May 9, 2021, http://www.tandfonline.com/doi/abs/10.1080/08039410.2021.1918238.
134 AFP, "India's Modi Hails Yoga as Covid-19 'Shield,'" *Agence France-Press*, June 21, 2021.
135 Zeeshan, "India Still Has an Opportunity with Vaccine Diplomacy."

SUGGESTED FURTHER READING

Ahamed, Meenakshi, *A Matter of Trust: India–US Relations From Truman to Trump* (HarperCollins India, 2021). ISBN: 978-9390327201

Hall, Ian, *Modi and the Reinvention of Indian Foreign Policy* (Bristol University Press, 2019). ISBN: 978-1-5292-0460-5

Jaishankar, S., *The India Way: Strategies for an Uncertain World* (HarperCollins India, 2020). 978-9353579791

Mohan, C. Raja, *Modi's World: Extending India's Sphere of Influence* (HarperCollins India, 2015). ISBN: 978-9351772057

Pant, Harsh V., *Indian Foreign Policy: The Modi Era* (Har-Anand Publications Pvt Ltd, 2019). ISBN: 978-9388409223

Paul, T.V., ed., *The China–India Rivalry in the Globalization Era* (Georgetown University Press, 2018). ISBN: 978-1626165991

CONCLUSION

One of the great scholars of pluralism, the late Robert Dahl, called India an "improbable democracy." He was observing India's post-1947 political development to the 1990s, and like many scholars he saw the country's democratic improbability in its low per capita income and myriad social divisions. But he reasoned,

> Although India is culturally diverse, it is the only country in the world where Hindu beliefs and practices are so widely shared.... Even though the caste system is divisive and Hindu nationalists are a standing danger to the Muslim minority, Hinduism does provide something of a common identity for a majority of Indians.

At the same time, Dahl said, "The sheer number of cultural fragments into which India is divided means that each is small, not only far short of a majority but far too small to rule over that vast and varied subcontinent." Dahl concluded, "for most Indians there is simply no realistic alternative to democracy."[1]

A quarter century later, democratization analysts observe an alarming decline in democracy and freedom worldwide—and especially in India. Freedom House, the Washington, DC-based research and advocacy organization, calls 2021 "the 15th consecutive year of decline in global freedom."[2] The decline is exhibited in both newer European democracies and in the United States, but as the world's largest democracy, India looms at a subcontinental scale in such assessments. In its 2021 annual report, Freedom House downgraded India from a free democracy to a "partly free democracy." In the same year, the Economist Intelligence Unit dropped India two places into 53rd position in its Democracy Index, calling it a "flawed democracy," and Sweden-based Varieties of Democracy (V-Dem) Institute called India an "electoral autocracy."[3]

Has India's relationship to democracy fundamentally changed since Dahl offered his assessment? India has come through a crisis of democracy before, in the Emergency (1975–77) under Indira Gandhi, but the trouble now may run deeper and has lasted longer. As we conclude our writing of this book, India stands more than halfway between the reelection of Narendra Modi and the BJP in 2019, to a stronger parliamentary majority and a second term of government, and the next general election expected in 2024. Were the Modi-led BJP to win reelection then, it would surpass the ten-year mark in power and the time in office held by the previous government, the Congress Party-led UPA (2004–14). Modi would be the longest-serving Indian prime minister since Indira Gandhi.

We began this book with a series of pressing puzzles:

1. Do the alternative governance models found in some of India's larger states have the potential to offset the rise of the BJP and "Hindu nationalism"?
2. Is India's high economic growth rate sustainable in a competitive global economy?
3. Given India's reluctance to project power, why has it been sought after (particularly by successive US administrations) as a counter-balance to a rising China?

In order to answer those questions, we noted several major changes since the Modi government came to power in 2014.

In terms of governance, the BJP has become the dominant national political party and effected a major realignment of the political system. The INC has been decimated but still remains the only significant opposition party at the national level. It currently holds 52 seats in the Lok Sabha (or 92 with coalition partners) compared to the BJP's 303 (353 with its allies) out of 545. The INC counts only three state chief ministers (Punjab, Rajasthan, and Chhattisgarh) among its ranks along with three allied chief ministers (Maharashtra, Jharkhand, Tamil Nadu). While a comeback for the INC is still possible, the chances appear slim as long as the party continues under the same listless leadership and without a strong policy agenda.

The BJP and allied parties have made significant "inroads" throughout northern India, even in left bastions like West Bengal. The advances of the BJP limit the prospects for alternative governance models found in large states like Bihar and West Bengal and perhaps even in Andhra Pradesh, though to a significantly lesser degree. The Trinamool Congress is registered as a national party, but outside of West Bengal it has established only toeholds in the northeastern states of Manipur, Assam, Tripura, and the plains state of Uttar Pradesh. The AITC is attempting to expand into Goa, Tamil Nadu, and Punjab—but so far does not have any electoral victories to show for its efforts. Nitish Kumar's Janata Dal (United) has only a small presence in the remote northeastern state of Arunachal Pradesh. Previously, the JD(U) successfully contested seats in Uttar Pradesh and the island territory of Lakshadweep. In any case, the JD(U) has returned to its alliance with the BJP and is unlikely to seek to mount a challenge. Finally, Y. S. Jaganmohan Reddy's YSR Congress, despite being tied with Trinamool as the fourth largest party in the Lok Sabha, is confined to Andhra Pradesh and Telangana—just like its archrival, Chandrababu Naidu's Telugu Desam Party. It would take a diverse coalition of regional and state-based parties—either joining forces with the Congress Party, or coming together as a third front—to topple Modi's BJP. The odds against such an effective electoral coalescing may look long, but the possibility cannot not be ruled out should the BJP experience a significant decline in voter approval, turnout, and support.

Meanwhile, sub-regional demands for statehood continue to be accommodated by the federal government as a part of the strategic calculus of ruling parties. However, if the BJP continues to expand its base, it is less likely to accommodate demands for creating new states in those areas where it stands to wrest control of the whole state.

In terms of internal security, the Naxalite insurgency is increasingly subdued, creating greater security but also limiting pressure to create greater equity in rural areas. Without an industrial base for labor-intensive industries, the plight of landless peasants and laborers will continue. Jammu and Kashmir has been reorganized, but it is unclear that the BJP's policies will bring greater stability or security in India's only Muslim majority polity state. The situation in Jammu and the Vale of Kashmir remains fraught.

Economically, while India is now a lower middle-income country with one of the fastest growing economies in the world, the long-term forecast for sustained growth is uncertain. India remains a crony-capitalist and mercantilist economy even as it distances itself from its quasi-socialist past. Economic policies are oriented toward populist theatrics (e.g., demonetization) and "pro-business" economic nationalism, as opposed to "pro-market" liberalism.

India is not becoming a major industrial hub in the global economy, and it is not well situated to provide the skill sets demanded by the global economy or labor-intensive industrial jobs needed for the overwhelming majority of its youthful population. Labor laws have been subverted by firms and politicians, but underlying issues constricting capital investment and encouraging firm expansion remain unresolved. India's IT service sector is well poised for global competition, but the skill sets needed by this sector are beyond the horizon of many in India's undereducated masses.

India's reliance on tariffs and subsidies will continue to provoke its partners in the global trade regime, resulting in frequent trade tensions. Nevertheless, as India learned from its socialist experiment during the Cold War and despite its vast market size, the country simply cannot prosper through autarchy. India needs a liberal posture to acquire world-class technology and resources. In this regard, the BJP is ill suited to steer the economy toward prosperity. While the BJP is geared toward climbing global rankings, it is temperamentally unsuited to fundamental reforms, particularly reforms that might threaten its vote base in the middle class.

In terms of international relations, India has attached itself to an emerging democratic bloc in the Quad, which also includes Australia, Japan, and the United States. But given America's own crisis of democracy and significant domestic challenges confronting the other members, it is less clear that this multilateral initiative is bound by deep and self-reflective democratic solidarity than it is by the rise of China as an unsettling force in the Indo-Pacific region and worldwide. Long-simmering tensions between China and India have erupted in conflict along their disputed border—amazingly, even as the two Asian giants deepen their economic cooperation through an institution like the Asian Infrastructure Development Bank (AIIB), in which China is the most powerful donor-member and India is the largest borrower-member.

China and India are also competing for regional influence and friendships in South Asia, India's traditional "near abroad" from Afghanistan to Bangladesh and Sri Lanka, and east to Myanmar. And of course, China's own non-democratic regime and its non-conditionality in economic assistance are contributing factors in the democratic recession both globally and in South Asia.

India's most vexing regional relationship is with Pakistan, a Chinese ally. While India's recent strategy of limited retaliation for Pakistan-related terrorism has been meant to call Pakistan's bluff in its nuclear weapons-backed policy of tying India's hands in a never-ending low-intensity conflict, India's responses instead have exposed weaknesses in its own military capabilities. Though it is loath to acknowledge these externally, India's efforts to increase military spending and reorganize its military leadership structure show that its leaders are well aware of deficits.

Finally, the Modi government's Hindu nationalism and anti-minority (especially anti-Muslim) policies at home are limiting its persuasive and "soft power" potential in South Asia and beyond. The region and the world have also been buffeted by India's "vaccine diplomacy" in the evolving COVID-19 pandemic, as its reactive policies have swung between grandiloquent generosity and cold self-interest.

Where does all of this put India's democracy today? Hindu nationalists, liberal secularists, religious Muslims, subnational regionalists, and many other constituencies would all offer different answers and assessments, no doubt. When each Indian general election is automatically the largest exercise of the voting franchise in world history—there were some 900 million voters, including 84 million first-time voters in 2019—it may seem strange even to raise the question, and to none more so than the BJP's most devoted followers.

We are reminded of a campaign in the last decade to raise awareness in India about the industrial waste and human remains that foul the Ganges River, considered by many Hindus to be India's most sacred. For many, the notion that Ma Ganga (Mother Ganges) is "polluted" is simply rejected. But, as advocates discovered, the idea that Ma Ganga is "suffering" may resonate deeply.

Indian democracy today is suffering. Its spirit still courses through India's institutions, but too many of these are corrupted or hamstrung and risk being turned to anti-minority purposes, if they have not been already. No issue is more important to India's democratic future than the dignity, rights, and basic safety of India's Muslims and other minorities.

The spirit of democracy still moves through India's people, but many have given themselves (or have been bystanders) to the "standing danger" of Hindu nationalism that Dahl perceived. Too many have been casualties of hate and violence, their bodies threatening to choke democracy's river like so many corpses thrown into the Ganges during the height of the COVID-19 pandemic.

India needs democracy's advocates and builders to prevail over its manipulators and subverters and to rally the bystanders to its deterioration. To paraphrase and multiply V. S. Naipul's famous formulation, India needs a billion mutinies now: mutinies of conscience, compassion, shared citizenship, and constructive solidarity.

The stakes suddenly seem very high, for India and the world. They have been, all along.

NOTES

1. Robert A. Dahl, *On Democracy* (New Haven: Yale University Press, 2000), 159.
2. Sarah Repucci and Amy Slipowitz, "Democracy under Siege," Freedom House, *Freedom in the World 2021*, accessed January 19, 2022, https://freedomhouse.org/report/freedom-world/2021/democracy-under-siege.
3. BBC News, "'Electoral Autocracy': The Downgrading of India's Democracy," March 16, 2021, sec. India, https://www.bbc.com/news/world-asia-india-56393944.

Bibliography

Abi-Habib, Maria. "US and India, Wary of China, Agree to Strengthen Military Ties." *New York Times*, September 6, 2018, sec. World. https://www.nytimes.com/2018/09/06/world/asia/us-india-military-agreement.html.

Abraham, Itty. *How India Became Territorial: Foreign Policy, Diaspora, and Geopolitics*. Studies in Asian Security. Stanford, CA: Stanford University Press, 2014.

ADB. "ADB Annual Report 2020." ADB, December 2020.

Adil, Masudul Hasan, and Neeraj R. Hatekar. "Demonetisation, Banking and Trust in 'Bricks' Or 'Clicks.'" *South Asia Research* 40, no. 2 (2020): 181–98. https://doi.org/10.1177/0262728020915566.

AFP. "India's Modi Hails Yoga as Covid-19 'Shield.'" *Agence France-Press*, June 21, 2021.

Agarwal, Namrata. "Mamata Banerjee Providing Protection to Terrorists, Naxalites in West Bengal: Kailash Vijayvargiya." *Zee News*, September 28, 2020.

Agarwala, Rina. "The Politics of India's Reformed Labor Model." In *Business and Politics in India*, edited by Christophe Jaffrelot, Atul Kohli, and Kanta Murali. Modern South Asia. New York: Oxford University Press, 2019.

AIIB. "AIIB Q1-2021 Financial-Statements." AIIB, March 2021.

Aiyar, Yamini. "Modi Consolidates Power: Leveraging Welfare Politics." *Journal of Democracy* 30, no. 4 (2019): 78–88. https://doi.org/10.1353/jod.2019.0070.

Anand, Rahul, Kalpana Kochhar, and Saurabh Mishra. *Make in India*. IMF Working Papers, WP/15/119. Washington, DC: International Monetary Fund, 2015.

Anderson, Edward, and Arkotong Longkumer. "'Neo-Hindutva': Evolving Forms, Spaces, and Expressions of Hindu Nationalism." *Contemporary South Asia* 26, no. 4 (2018): 371–77. https://doi.org/10.1080/09584935.2018.1548576.

Anderson, Stuart. "The Story of How Trump Officials Tried to End H-1B Visas." *Forbes*, February 1, 2021. https://www.forbes.com/sites/stuartanderson/2021/02/01/the-story-of-how-trump-officials-tried-to-end-h-1b-visas/?sh=60a1bac2173f.

ANI. "Mamata Banerjee Promises to Ensure Safety, Education for All." *Asian News International*, April 4, 2021.

———. "US, European Officials Mulling to Create 'Asian NATO' to Contain China's Expansionist Ambitions." *Times of India / Asian News International*, October 1, 2020.

Anonymous. "India: Behind the Farmers' Strike." *Against the Current* 35, no. 6 (2021): 10.

Apparasu, Srinivasa Rao. "After BJP Promises Special Status to Puducherry, Demands Rise for Andhra Pradesh." *Hindustan Times*, April 1, 2021.

Argade, Aashish, Arnab Kumar Laha, and Anand Kumar Jaiswal. "Connecting Smallholders' Marketplace Decisions to Agricultural Market Reform Policy in India—An Empirical Exploration." *Journal of Macromarketing* 41, no. 3 (2021): 471–83. https://doi.org/10.1177/0276146721997885.

Arun, M. G. "3 Years Later, Narendra Modi's Dream Make in India Plans Yet to Take Off." *India Today*, May 29, 2017.

Aryan, Javin. "The Defence Technology and Trade Initiative (DTTI): Lost in the Acronym Bowl." Observer Research Foundation, December 10, 2020.

Athukorala, Prema-chandra. "Trump's Trade War: An Indian Perspective." *Asian Economic Papers* 19, no. 1 (2020): 92–109. https://doi.org/10.1162/asep_a_00749.

Babu, Venkatsha. "Five Reasons Why Jagan Reddy Scuttled Amaravati as Andhra Pradesh's Capital." *Hindustan Times*, January 20, 2020. https://www.hindustantimes.com/opinion/five-reasons-why-jagan-reddy-scuttled-amaravati-as-andhra-pradesh-s-capital-opinion/story-5qepGlkZ4So2evcg9ihKBP.html.

Bagchi, Suvojit. "Bengal through the Decades: The More Things Change, Have They Stayed the Same?" Occasional Paper. Observer Research Foundation, April 2021.

Bajpai, Kanti. "Modi's China Policy and the Road to Confrontation." *Pacific Affairs* 91, no. 2 (June 1, 2018): 245–60. https://doi.org/10.5509/2018912245.

Baldwin, Richard E. *The Great Convergence: Information Technology and the New Globalization*. Cambridge, MA: The Belknap Press of Harvard University Press, 2016.

Banerjee, Abhijit. "Food for Thought: Parties Should Reward Their Foot Soldiers Amply." *Hindustan Times*, January 1, 2015.

Banerjee, Sayan, and Charles R. Hankla. "Party Systems and Public Goods: The Dynamics of Good Governance in the Indian States." *India*

Review 19, no. 5 (October 19, 2020): 496–522. https://doi.org/10.1080/14736489.2020.1855015.

Barman, Abheek. "Congress' Andhra Pradesh Policy Includes Weighing of Caste Equations." *Economic Times*, November 22, 2013.

Basrur, Rajesh. "Modi's Foreign Policy Fundamentals: A Trajectory Unchanged." *International Affairs* 93, no. 1 (January 2017): 7–26. https://doi.org/10.1093/ia/iiw006.

Basu, Nayanima. "India Is No Longer 'Non-Aligned', Says Foreign Secretary Vijay Gokhale." *The Print*, January 10, 2019. https://theprint.in/diplomacy/india-is-no-longer-non-aligned-says-foreign-secretary-vijay-gokhale/176222/.

BBC News. "'Electoral Autocracy': The Downgrading of India's Democracy." March 16, 2021, sec. India. https://www.bbc.com/news/world-asia-india-56393944.

———. "India–China Clash: 20 Indian Troops Killed in Ladakh Fighting." June 16, 2020, sec. Asia.

Bengali, Shashank, and Paul Richter. "US Eager to Forget about New India Premier's 2005 Visa Denial." *Los Angeles Times*, September 25, 2014, sec. World & Nation.

Bhatnagar, Armaan. "India's Defence Spending in 7 Charts." *Times of India*, January 30, 2021. https://timesofindia.indiatimes.com/india/indias-defence-spending-in-7-charts/articleshow/80600625.cms.

Bhattarai, Keshab, and Vipin Negi. "FDI and Economic Performance of Firms in India." *Studies in Microeconomics* 8, no. 1 (June 1, 2020): 44–74. https://doi.org/10.1177/2321022220918684.

Bhatty, Kiran, and Nandini Sundar. "Sliding from Majoritarianism toward Fascism: Educating India under the Modi Regime." *International Sociology* 35, no. 6 (2020): 632–50. https://doi.org/10.1177/0268580920937226.

Biden, Joseph, Narendra Modi, Scott Morrison, and Yoshihide Suga. "Our Four Nations Are Committed to a Free, Open, Secure and Prosperous Indo-Pacific Region." *Washington Post*, March 13, 2021, sec. Opinion.

Bird, Mike. "India's Stock Market Mania Defies Economic Reality; India's Stocks Are Outperforming Those in Similar Markets, Even as the Pandemic May Have Exacerbated Its Longer-Term Economic Challenges." *Wall Street Journal*, February 19, 2021, Eastern edition.

Biswas, Soutik. "Why Trump's H-1B Visa Freeze Will Hurt India Most." *BBC News*, June 24, 2020, sec. India.

Blank, Jonah. "What Were China's Objectives in the Doklam Dispute?" *The RAND Blog* (blog), September 8, 2017. https://www.rand.org/blog/2017/09/what-were-chinas-objectives-in-the-doklam-dispute.html.

Bond, Patrick. "BRICS Banking and the Debate over Sub-Imperialism." *Third World Quarterly* 37, no. 4 (2016): 611–29. https://doi.org/10.1080/01436597.2015.1128816.

Bose, Sumantra. *Kashmir at the Crossroads: Inside a 21st Century Conflict*. New Haven: Yale University Press, 2021.

BS Web Team. "Haven't Imposed Any Export Ban on Covaxin, Covishield, Says Govt." *Business Standard India*, April 2, 2021. https://www.business-standard.com/article/current-affairs/have-not-imposed-any-export-ban-on-coronavirus-vaccines-says-govt-121040200726_1.html.

Business Today. "Budget 2021: Banks Set for NPA Shock; What'll Govt Do?," February 1, 2021. https://www.businesstoday.in/union-budget-2021/expectations/budget-2021-banks-set-for-npa-shock-what-ll-govt-do/story/429746.html.

BW Online Bureau. "68% Of India Feels PM Narendra Modi Failed to Create Jobs, yet 64% Of India Feels He Will Be Re-Elected in May 2019, Says BW-Decode Survey." *Business World*, March 28, 2019.

Champine, Riley D. "The 'Cartographic Nightmare' of the Kashmir Region Explained." *National Geographic*, February 2021. https://www.nationalgeographic.com/magazine/graphics/the-cartographic-nightmare-of-the-kashmir-region-explained-feature.

Chatterjee Miller, Manjari, and Kate Sullivan De Estrada. "Pragmatism in Indian Foreign Policy: How Ideas Constrain Modi." *International Affairs* 93, no. 1 (January 2017): 27–49. https://doi.org/10.1093/ia/iiw001.

Chatterjee, Niladri, Zaad Mahmood, and Eleonor Marcussen. "Politics of Vaccine Nationalism in India: Global and Domestic Implications." *Forum for Development Studies*, May 9, 2021. http://www.tandfonline.com/doi/abs/10.1080/08039410.2021.1918238.

Chaudhury, Dipanjan Roy. "India Opposes Vaccine Nationalism; Calls for Greater Support to Joint Proposal with S Africa." *Economic Times*, April 16, 2021. https://economictimes.indiatimes.com/news/india/india-opposes-vaccine-nationalism-calls-for-greater-support-to-joint-proposal-with-s-africa/articleshow/82105063.cms?from=mdr.

Chhetri, Vivek. "Gorkhaland No Poll Plank." *Telegraph*, December 27, 2020.

Chin, Gregory T. "Asian Infrastructure Investment Bank: Governance Innovation and Prospects." *Global Governance* 22, no. 1 (2016): 11–25. https://doi.org/10.1163/19426720-02201002.

Chowdhury, Debaisish Roy. "Modi Never Bought Enough COVID-19 Vaccines for India. Now the Whole World Is Paying." *Time*, May 28, 2021. https://time.com/6052370/modi-didnt-buy-enough-covid-19-vaccine/.

Chowdhury, Santu. "Modi Targets Mamata: TMC Game of Corruption Over, Time for Real Change." *Indian Express*, March 8, 2021.

Corbridge, Stuart, John Harriss, and Craig Jeffrey. *India Today: Economy, Politics and Society*. Politics Today. Cambridge, UK; Malden, MA: Polity Press, 2013.

Crabtree, James. *The Billionaire Raj: A Journey through India's New Gilded Age*. Tim Duggan Books, 2018.

CRS, Shayerah Ilias Akhtar, and K Alan Kronstadt. "US–India Trade Relations." In Focus. Congressional Research Service, February 14, 2020. https://fas.org/sgp/crs/row/IF10384.pdf.

Dahl, Robert A. *On Democracy*. New Haven: Yale University Press, 2000.

Das, Arvind N. *The Republic of Bihar*. New Delhi; New York: Penguin Books, 1992.

Das, Madhuparna. "Mamata Govt Now in Trouble Over Amphan Relief 'Scam', After Cut-Money and PDS Corruption." *The Print*, June 30, 2020. https://theprint.in/india/mamata-govt-now-in-trouble-over-amphan-relief-scam-after-cut-money-and-pds-corruption/451774/.

Deb, Sandipan. "The Triumph of 'Bengali Pride' and the BJP's Mistakes." *Mint*, May 4, 2021, sec. Opinion. https://www.livemint.com/opinion/columns/the-triumph-of-bengali-pride-and-the-bjp-s-mistakes-11620072906394.html.

Demirgüç-Kunt, Asli, Leora Klapper, Dorothe Singer, Saniya Ansar, and Jake Hess. *The Global Findex Database, 2017: Measuring Financial Inclusion and the Fintech Revolution*. Washington, DC: World Bank, 2018.

Department for the Promotion of Industry and International Trade. "Quarterly Factsheet on FDI from April 2000 to March 2020." Factsheet. Government of India, n.d. https://dipp.gov.in/sites/default/files/FDI_Factsheet_March20_28May_2020.pdf.

Dhume, Sadanand. "Opinion | The Quad Enters the Ring with China." *Wall Street Journal*, September 30, 2021, sec. Opinion. https://www.wsj.com/articles/india-china-aukus-quad-japan-indo-pacific-australia-huawei-11633033358.

Diamond, Larry. "The Global Crisis of Democracy." *Wall Street Journal*, May 17, 2019, sec. Life.

Diwakar, Rekha. "The Origins and Consequences of Regional Parties and Subnationalism in India." *India Review* 20, no. 1 (January 1, 2021): 68–95. https://doi.org/10.1080/14736489.2021.1875701.

Dogra, Chander Suta. "IAF Did Not Shoot Down Pak F-16 in Balakot Aftermath, Says US Scholar Christine Fair." *The Wire*, December 15, 2019. https://thewire.in/security/christine-fair-iaf-balakot-pakistan-f16.

Dwivedi, Sukirti. "'We'll Be Peaceful Till Trump Leaves,' BJP Leader Kapil Mishra Warns Delhi Police." *NDTV.com*, February 24, 2020. https://www.ndtv.com/delhi-news/bjp-leader-kapil-mishras-3-day-ultimatum-to-delhi-police-to-clear-anti-caa-protest-jaffrabad-2184627.

Ellis-Petersen, Hannah. "Indians Call for Boycott of Chinese Goods after Fatal Border Clashes." *Guardian*, June 18, 2020, sec. World News.

European Commission. "India—Trade—European Commission." Countries and Regions—India, 2021. https://ec.europa.eu/trade/policy/countries-and-regions/countries/india/.

Evans, Jonathan. "In India, Hindu Support for Modi's Party Varies by Region and Is Tied to Beliefs about Diet and Language." *Pew Research Center* (blog), August 5, 2021. https://www.pewresearch.org/fact-tank/2021/08/05/in-india-hindu-support-for-modis-party-varies-by-region-and-is-tied-to-beliefs-about-diet-and-language/.

Fouillet, Cyril, Isabelle Guérin, and Jean-Michel Servet. "Demonetization and Digitalization: The Indian Government's Hidden Agenda." *Telecommunications Policy* 45, no. 2 (March 2021): 102079. https://doi.org/10.1016/j.telpol.2020.102079.

Ganguly, Sumit. "Has Modi Truly Changed India's Foreign Policy?" *The Washington Quarterly* 40, no. 2 (April 3, 2017): 131–43. https://doi.org/10.1080/0163660X.2017.1328929.

———. "India and China: On a Collision Course?" *Pacific Affairs* 91, no. 2 (June 1, 2018): 231–44. https://doi.org/10.5509/2018912231.

Garg, Reetika, and Pami Dua. "Foreign Portfolio Investment Flows to India: Determinants and Analysis." *World Development* 59 (July 2014): 16–28. https://doi.org/10.1016/j.worlddev.2014.01.030.

Gettleman, Jeffrey, and Kai Schultz. "India Locks Down 1.3 Billion People for 3 Weeks: Foreign Desk." *New York Times*, 2020, Late (East Coast) edition.

Ghosh, Saibal. "Financial Inclusion in India: Does Distance Matter?" *South Asia Economic Journal* 21, no. 2 (2020): 216–38. https://doi.org/10.1177/1391561420961649.

Goldschmidt, Brian P. "Making a US–India Strategic Partnership Work." Master's thesis, Naval Postgraduate School, January 2001.

Golwalkar, Madhavrao Sadashivrao. *We, or Our Nationhood Defined*. Nagpur, India: Bharat Publications, 1939.

Gordon, Nicholas. "'Sumantra Bose, "Kashmir at the Crossroads: Inside a 21st-Century Conflict" (Yale UP, 2021)'." New Books in South Asian Studies, n.d. newbooksnetwork.com.

Gordon, Sandy. "India's Power Realities beyond South Asia." *Widening Horizon: Australia's New Relationship with India.*" Australian Strategic Policy Institute, 2007. JSTOR. https://www.jstor.org/stable/resrep04164.8.

Government of India, Ministry of Commerce & Industry. "Trade Deficit between India and China." Press Release. Press Information Bureau, February 3, 2021. https://pib.gov.in/Pressreleaseshare.aspx?PRID=1575818.

Gowen, Annie. "Indian Kashmir Suffers Worst Violence in Years after Militant Leader's Death." *Washington Post*, July 12, 2016, sec. Asia & Pacific. https://www.washingtonpost.com/world/asia_pacific/indian-held-kashmir-suffers-worst-violence-in-years-after-militant-leaders-death/2016/07/12/c44ed4b8-482a-11e6-8dac-0c6e4accc5b1_story.html.

———. "Once Banned from the US, India's Modi Set for Historic Address to Congress." *Washington Post*, June 6, 2016.

Grover, Anju. "BJP's Doublespeak on Caste Census: Manoj Jha." *India Currents*, August 30, 2021.

Gupta, Prachi. "India Cuts China Imports by Half in a Year; Needs Measured Approach to Further Lower Dependence: SBI." *Financial Express*, July 8, 2020. http://search.proquest.com/docview/2421102086?pq-origsite=summon.

Gupta, Surupa, Rani D. Mullen, Rajesh Basrur, Ian Hall, Nicolas Blarel, Manjeet S. Pardesi, and Sumit Ganguly. "Indian Foreign Policy under Modi: A New Brand or Just Repackaging?" *International Studies Perspectives* 20, no. 1 (February 2019): 1–45. https://doi.org/10.1093/isp/eky008.

Haberman, Maggie. "Donald Trump Says He's a 'Big Fan' of Hindus." *New York Times*, October 16, 2016, sec. US.

Hansen, Thomas Blom. "Whose Public, Whose Authority? Reflections on the Moral Force of Violence." *Modern Asian Studies* 52, no. 3 (2018): 1076–87. https://doi.org/10.1017/S0026749X17000282.

Helleiner, Eric, and Hongying Wang. "Limits to the BRICS' Challenge: Credit Rating Reform and Institutional Innovation in Global Finance." *Review of International Political Economy* 25, no. 5 (September 3, 2018): 573–95. https://doi.org/10.1080/09692290.2018.1490330.

Hoelscher, Kristian. "The Evolution of the Smart Cities Agenda in India." *International Area Studies Review* 19, no. 1 (2016): 28–44. https://doi.org/10.1177/2233865916632089.

Hooijmaaijers, Bas. "Understanding Success and Failure in Establishing New Multilateral Development Banks: The SCO Development Bank, the NDB, and the AIIB." *Asian Perspective* 45, no. 2 (2021): 445–67.

Hurworth, Ella. "India to Overtake China as the World's Most Populous Country: UN." *CNN*, June 19, 2019. https://www.cnn.com/2019/06/19/health/india-china-world-population-intl-hnk/index.html.

IANS. "Saradha Scam: Salaries Paid from CM Relief Fund, Says CBI." *Business Standard*, December 27, 2020.

IBEF. "Bihar." PowerPoint. India Brand Equity Foundation, March 2021. https://www.ibef.org/download/Bihar-March-2021.pdf.

Illyas, Md. "Survey Finds Andhra Pradesh Did Better in GSDP Growth Compared to India." *Deccan Chronicle*, May 20, 2021, sec. Current Affairs.

ILO. "Women and Men in the Informal Economy, 3rd Edition." ILO, 2018. https://www.ilo.org/wcmsp5/groups/public/---dgreports/---dcomm/documents/publication/wcms_626831.pdf.

IMF. "IMF DataMapper." Database. IMF DataMapper, 2021. https://www.imf.org/external/datamapper/.

Indian Express. "Bypoll Wins Bolster TMC Strength in Bengal Assembly; Mamata Eyes 2024 with Return of 'Prodigal Sons', Import of New Faces." *Indian Express*, October 5, 2021.

———. "Explained: What Are India's Investments in Afghanistan?," August 24, 2021. https://indianexpress.com/article/explained/explained-indias-afghan-investment-7406795/.

———. "Explained: What Is US–India Defence Technology and Trade Initiative." *Indian Express*, October 19, 2019. https://indianexpress.com/article/explained/explained-us-india-defense-technology-and-trade-initiative-dtti-6077915/.

———. "Mamata to Give Rs 10k to Students Ahead of Polls; Here's What Her Counterparts Announced in Their States." *Indian Express*, December 23, 2020.

———. "PMO Acknowledges: This Time, Chinese Came in Much Larger Strength to LAC." *Indian Express*, June 21, 2020. https://indianexpress.com/article/india/narendra-modi-india-china-border-dispute-galwan-all-party-meeting-6467932/.

———. "This Puja, BJP Thinking of Slain Workers: Dilip Ghosh." *Indian Express*, October 10, 2021.

India News. "'He's Still Alive': TMC Justifies Assault on Slapper." *Hindustan Times*, January 6, 2015.

———. "Mamata's Nephew Slapped, TMC Sees BJP Hand." *Hindustan Times*, January 5, 2015.

"Is India's 'Neighbourhood First Policy' Unable to Win Regional Allies?" *TRT World*, October 5, 2021. https://www.trtworld.com/magazine/is-india-s-neighbourhood-first-policy-unable-to-win-regional-allies-50492.

Jaffrelot, Christophe. "Business-Friendly Gujarat under Narendra Modi: The Implications of a New Political Economy." In *Business and Politics in India*, edited by Christophe Jaffrelot, Atul Kohli, and Kanta Murali. Modern South Asia. New York, NY: Oxford University Press, 2019.

———. *Modi's India: Hindu Nationalism and the Rise of Ethnic Democracy*. Translated by Cynthia Schoch. Princeton: Princeton University Press, 2021.

Jaffrelot, Christophe, Atul Kohli, and Kanta Murali, eds. *Business and Politics in India*. Modern South Asia. New York: Oxford University Press, 2019.

Jaleel, Muzamil. "Alert in J&K after Pakistan's Input to India and US on Threat of 'IED-Vehicle' Attack." *Indian Express*, June 16, 2019. https://indianexpress.com/article/india/alert-jk-pakistan-input-india-us-threat-ied-vehicle-attack-awantipora-pulwama-sco-summit-bishkek-5782710/.

Jenkins, Rob. *Democracy and Economic Reform in India*. Cambridge, UK: Cambridge University Press, 2000.

———. "Business Interests, the State, and the Politics of Land Policy." In *Business and Politics in India*, edited by Christophe Jaffrelot, Atul Kohli, and Kanta Murali. Modern South Asia. New York: Oxford University Press, 2019.

Jha, Lata. "Modi's Address on Covid-19 Lockdown Draws 197 Million TV Viewers." *Mint*, March 27, 2020.

John, Juliette, Rushda Majeed, and Pallavi Nuka. "Modernizing the State, Connecting to the People: Bihar, India, 2005–2012." Innovations for Successful Societies. Princeton, NJ: Princeton University, 2015.

Joshi, Vijay. *India's Long Road: The Search for Prosperity*. New York: Oxford University Press, 2017.

Kanabar, Dinesh, and Ritesh Kanodia. "Column: FTP Boost for Brand India." *Financial Express*, April 3, 2015. 1669403760. ABI/INFORM Collection; ProQuest Central Essentials.

Kang, Bhavdeep. "Is the JD(U)-BJP Honeymoon in Bihar Over." *Free Press Journal*, August 5, 2021, Mumbai, India edition.

Kanungo, Pralay. "The Rise of the Bharatiya Janata Party in West Bengal." Edited by Christophe Jaffrelot. *Studies in Indian Politics* 3, no. 1 (2015): 50–68. https://doi.org/10.1177/2321023015575213.

Kapoor, Mudit, and Rahul Ahluwalia. "Part I: Andhra Pradesh." In *The Making of Miracles in Indian States*, edited by Arvind Panagariya and M. Govinda Rao. New York: Oxford University Press, 2015.

Kapur, Devesh. "The Indian Prime Minister and Trump Addressed a Houston Rally. Who Was Signaling What?" *Washington Post*, September 29, 2019, sec. Analysis.

Katzenstein, Mary Fainsod, Uday Singh Mehta, and Usha Thakkar. "The Rebirth of Shiv Sena: The Symbiosis of Discursive and Organizational Power." *The Journal of Asian Studies* 56, no. 2 (1997): 371–90. https://doi.org/10.2307/2646242.

Kaur, Ravinder. *Brand New Nation: Capitalist Dreams and Nationalist Designs in Twenty-First Century India*. South Asia in Motion. Stanford, California: Stanford University Press, 2020.

Kaura, Vinay. "India's Pakistan Policy: From 2016 'Surgical Strike' to 2019 Balakot 'Airstrike'." *The Round Table* 109, no. 3 (2020): 277–87.

———. "India's Relations with China from the Doklam Crisis to the Galwan Tragedy." *India Quarterly: A Journal of International Affairs* 76, no. 4 (December 2020): 501–18. https://doi.org/10.1177/0974928420961768.

Kaushik, Krishn. "India Third Highest Military Spender in 2020, States Data Published by Stockholm International Peace Research Institute." *Indian Express*, April 27, 2021.

Kesavan, K. V. "India's 'Act East' Policy and Regional Cooperation." Observer Research Foundation, February 14, 2020. https://www.orfonline.org/expert-speak/indias-act-east-policy-and-regional-cooperation-61375/.

Khilnani, Sunil, Rajiv Kumar, Pratap Bhanu Mehta, Prakash Menon, Nandan Nilekani, Srinath Raghavan, Shyam Saran, and Siddharth Varadarajan. "NonAlignment 2.0: A Foreign and Strategic Policy for India in the Twenty First Century." New Delhi, India: Centre for Policy Research, February 29, 2012.

Kohli, Atul. *Poverty Amid Plenty in the New India*. Cambridge; New York: Cambridge University Press, 2012.

———. "The NTR Phenomenon in Andhra Pradesh: Political Change in a South Indian State." *Asian Survey* 28, no. 10 (1988): 991–1017. https://doi.org/10.2307/2644703.

Krishna, Anirudh. *One Illness Away: Why People Become Poor and How They Escape Poverty*. New York: Oxford University Press, 2010.

Krishnan, Ananth. "'One-Third of Funding by AIIB Has Gone to India.'" *The Hindu*, September 25, 2020, sec. Industry.

Kristensen, Hans M., and Robert S. Norris. "Pakistan's Nuclear Forces, 2011." *Bulletin of the Atomic Scientists* 67, no. 4 (2011): 91–99. https://doi.org/10.1177/0096340211413360.

Kumar, Arun. "Bihar Plans Statewide Celebrations to Mark Its Economic Revival." *Hindustan Times*, March 16, 2010.

Kumar, Ashutosh. "Development Focus and Electoral Success at State Level: Nitish Kumar as Bihar's Leader." *South Asia Research* 33, no. 2 (July 1, 2013): 101–21. https://doi.org/10.1177/0262728013487630.

Kumar, Awanish. "Nitish Kumar's Honourable Exit: A Brief History of Caste Politics." *Economic and Political Weekly* 48, no. 28 (2013): 15–17.

Kumar, K. Ram. "Public Sector Banks Losing Market Share in Loans to Private Sector Rivals." *The Hindu Business Line*, May 7, 2021. https://www.thehindubusinessline.com/money-and-banking/public-sector-banks-losing-market-share-in-loans-to-private-sector-rivals/article34504920.ece.

Kumar, Shankar. "How India Is Quietly Resetting Its Economic Engagement with China." *Governance Now*. Noida: Athena Information Solutions Pvt. Ltd., June 29, 2020. 2418007810. Social Science Premium Collection.

Laborde, Cécile. "Minimal Secularism: Lessons for, and from, India." *The American Political Science Review* 115, no. 1 (2021): 1–13. https://doi.org/10.1017/S0003055420000775.

Madan, Tanvi. "The Dragon in the Room: The China Factor in the Development of US–India Ties in the Cold War." *India Review* 18, no. 4 (July 2019): 368–85. https://doi.org/10.1080/14736489.2019.1662188.

Mahajan, Anilesh S. "Assembly Election Results 2021: Lessons for the BJP." *India Today*, May 17, 2021.

Mahajan, Vikram. "India–US: Defence Trade and Technology Initiative Is the Silent Enabler." *Financial Express*, September 15, 2020.

Mahbubani, Kishore. "The New Anti-China Alliance Will Fail." *Foreign Policy*, Spring 2021.

Mann, James. "Why Narendra Modi Was Banned From the US." *Wall Street Journal*, May 2, 2014, sec. Life and Style.

Mashal, Mujib. "In a Region in Strife, India's Moral High Ground Erodes." *New York Times*, November 6, 2021, sec. World. https://www.nytimes.com/2021/11/06/world/asia/india-region-muslim-hindu-strife.html.

Mathew, Joe C., and Nidhi Singal. "Factory to the World?: The Production Linked Incentive Scheme Aims to Build an Indian Manufacturing Base across 13 Key Sectors. What Works. What Doesn't." *Business Today*. New Delhi: Living Media India, Limited, May 2, 2021. 2512662955. ABI/INFORM Collection; ProQuest Central Essentials.

Mazumdar, Arijit. "From 'Look East' to 'Act East': India's Evolving Engagement with the Asia–Pacific Region." *Asian Affairs* 52, no. 2 (June 2021): 357–74. https://doi.org/10.1080/03068374.2021.1912467.

Mazumdar, Arijit, and Erin Statz. "Democracy Promotion in India's Foreign Policy: Emerging Trends and Developments." *Asian Affairs: An American Review* 42, no. 2 (April 2015): 77–98. https://doi.org/10.1080/00927678.2015.1034611.

McDowell, Daniel. "Emergent International Liquidity Agreements: Central Bank Cooperation After the Global Financial Crisis." *Journal of International*

Relations and Development 22, no. 2 (2019): 441–67. https://doi.org/10.1057/s41268-017-0106-0.

McKinsey & Company. "India's Tuning Point: An Agenda for India's Economic Growth." McKinsey Global Institute, August 2020.

Mehrotra, Santosh. "Informal Employment Trends in the Indian Economy: Persistent Informality, but Growing Positive Development." Working Paper. Employment Policy Department. Geneva, CH: International Labor Organization, 2019. https://ilo.userservices.exlibrisgroup.com.

Mehta, Pratap Bhanu. "The Story of Indian Democracy Written in Blood and Betrayal." *Indian Express*, August 8, 2019. https://indianexpress.com/article/opinion/columns/jammu-kashmir-article-370-scrapped-special-status-amit-shah-narendra-modi-bjp-5880797/.

Menon, Lt. Gen. Prakash. "India Must Be Smart in Supporting Myanmar, If Quad Won't Measure Up." *The Print*, March 23, 2021. https://theprint.in/opinion/india-must-be-smart-in-supporting-myanmar-if-quad-wont-measure-up/626379/.

Miller, John, and Mike Shields. "Delta COVID Variant Becoming Globally Dominant, WHO Official Says." *Reuters*, June 18, 2021, sec. World. https://www.reuters.com/world/delta-covid-variant-becoming-globally-dominant-says-who-official-2021-06-18/.

Mitra, Atri, and G. Ananthakrishnan. "Saradha Scam: CBI Plea in SC on Mamata Govt 'Links', Says It Is Scuttling Probe." *Indian Express*, December 27, 2020.

Mitra, Subrata Kumar. *Politics in India: Structure, Process and Policy*. London; New York: Routledge, 2011.

Modi, Narendra. "Sabka Saath, Sabka Vikas, Sabka Vishwas and Now Sabka Prayas Are Vital for the Achievement of Our Goals: PM Modi on 75th Independence Day." Presented at the 75th Independence Day Speech, Red Fort, Delhi, India, August 15, 2021. https://www.narendramodi.in/text-of-prime-minnister-narendra-modi-s-address-from-the-red-fort-on-75th-independence-day-556737.

Mohan, Archis. "In a First, PM Modi Comes Close to Acknowledging 'Victory' at Doklam." *Business Standard*, October 5, 2017.

Mohan, C. Raja. *Modi's World: Expanding India's Sphere of Influence*. HarperCollins India, 2015.

Mohan, Rakesh, and Mohan Ray. "Indian Financial Sector: Structure, Trends and Turns." Washington, DC: IMF, January 2017.

Mohan, Rohini. *Amaravati: The Price of a Dream City*. YouTube video. The News Minute, 2017.

Mondaq Business Briefing. "Tax Street—June 2020." *Mondaq Business Briefing*, July 14, 2020. Business Insights: Essentials.

Montague, Zach. "US–India Defense Ties Grow Closer as Shared Concerns in Asia Loom." *New York Times*, November 20, 2019, sec. World.

Mooij, Jos. "Hype, Skill and Class: The Politics of Reform in Andhra Pradesh, India." *Commonwealth & Comparative Politics* 45, no. 1 (February 2007): 34–56. https://doi.org/10.1080/14662040601135771.

Mukherjee, Rohan. "Clearing the Jungle Raj: Bihar State, India, 2005–2009." Innovations for Successful Societies. Princeton, NJ: Princeton University, 2011.

Murali, Kanta. "Economic Liberalization and the Structural Power of Business." In *Business and Politics in India*, edited by Christophe Jaffrelot, Atul Kohli, and Kanta Murali. Modern South Asia. New York: Oxford University Press, 2019.

Nag, Jayatri. "Chaos Reigns in GJM as Top Leaders Float Own Parties." *Economic Times*, August 28, 2021.

Nagda, Ashutosh. "India's Renewed Embrace of the Non-Aligned Movement." *The Diplomat*, May 11, 2020.

Nair, Sthanu R. "Agrarian Suicides in India: Myth and Reality." *Development Policy Review* 39, no. 1 (2019): 3–21. https://doi.org/10.1111/dpr.12482.

Nam, Chang Woon, and Peter Steinhoff. "The 'Make in India' Initiative." *CESifo Forum; München* 19, no. 3 (Autumn 2018): 44–45.

Naqvi, Saba. "Delimitation Double Standards: One Rule for J&K, Another for South India." *Deccan Herald*, December 24, 2021. https://www.deccanherald.com/opinion/delimitation-double-standards-one-rule-for-jk-another-for-south-india-1064017.html.

Narlikar, Amrita, and Diana Tussie. "Breakthrough at Bali? Explanations, Aftermath, Implications." *International Negotiation* 21, no. 2 (2016): 209–32. https://doi.org/10.1163/15718069-12341331.

Nayar, Baldev Raj. *The Myth of the Shrinking State: Globalization and the State in India*. New Delhi: Oxford University Press, 2009.

NDB. "Annual Report 2020: Meeting Ever Evolving Development Challenges." New Development Bank, 2020. www.ndb.int/annual-report-2020/download.html.

OEC. "Economic Complexity Rankings (ECI)." Database. The Observatory of Economic Complexity, 2021. https://oec.world/en/rankings/eci/hs6/hs07.

OECD. "Trade in Value Added: India." Trade in Value Added—Country Notes. OECD, December 2018. https://www.oecd.org/industry/ind/TIVA-2018-India.pdf.

———. "Trade in Value Added (TIVA) Indicators: Guide to Country Notes." Guide. OECD, December 2018. https://www.oecd.org/sti/ind/tiva-2018-guide-to-country-notes.pdf.

O'Leary, Brendan. "Federalism and Federation." In *The Princeton Encyclopedia of Self-Determination*. Princeton University Press. Accessed August 17, 2021. https://pesd.princeton.edu/node/431.

Ollapally, Deepa M. "India and the International Order: Accommodation and Adjustment." *Ethics & International Affairs* 32, no. 1 (2018): 61–74. https://doi.org/10.1017/S0892679418000102.

Pahwa, Nitish. "The Taliban's Comeback Could Upend the Balance of Power Across Asia." *Slate*, August 23, 2021. https://slate.com/news-and-politics/2021/08/taliban-afghanistan-pakistan-india-china-power-balance.html.

Palit, Amitendu. "Will India's Disengaging Trade Policy Restrict It from Playing a Greater Global Role?" *World Trade Review* 20, no. 2 (May 2021): 203–19. https://doi.org/10.1017/S1474745620000518.

Pan, Chengxin. "The 'Indo-Pacific' and Geopolitical Anxieties about China's Rise in the Asian Regional Order." *Australian Journal of International Affairs* 68, no. 4 (August 8, 2014): 453–69. https://doi.org/10.1080/10357718.2014.884054.

Panagariya, Arvind. *Free Trade and Prosperity: How Openness Helps Developing Countries Grow Richer and Combat Poverty*. New York: Oxford University Press, 2019.

———. *New India: Reclaiming the Lost Glory*. New York: Oxford University Press, 2020.

Panagariya, Arvind, and M. Govinda Rao, eds. *The Making of Miracles in Indian States: Andhra Pradesh, Bihar, and Gujarat*. Oxford University Press, 2015. https://doi.org/10.1093/acprof:oso/9780190236625.001.0001.

Panda, Ankit. "A Skirmish in Galwan Valley: India and China's Deadliest Clash in More Than 50 Years." *The Diplomat*, June 2020.

———. "India and China, One Year After the Galwan Clash." *The Diplomat*, June 2021.

———. "What's Driving the India–China Standoff at Doklam?" *The Diplomat*, July 2017.

Pande, Aparna. *Making India Great: The Promise of a Reluctant Great Power*. Noida, Uttar Pradesh: HarperCollins India, 2020.

Pandit, Rajat. "How Defence Partnership Ringfences Ties between India, US." *Economic Times*, February 23, 2020. https://economictimes.indiatimes.com/news/defence/how-defence-partnership-ringfences-ties-between-india-us/articleshow/74263597.cms.

Pant, Harsh V., and Julie M. Super. "India's 'Non-Alignment' Conundrum: A Twentieth-Century Policy in a Changing World." *International Affairs* 91, no. 4 (July 2015): 747–64. https://doi.org/10.1111/1468-2346.12336.

Parkin, Benjamin. "Has the 'Make in India' Campaign Run out of Steam?" *Financial Times*, December 18, 2019. https://www.ft.com/content/3fbe1c46-0c7f-11ea-8fb7-8fcec0c3b0f9.

Paskal, Cleo. *Indo-Pacific Strategies, Perceptions and Partnerships: The View from Seven Countries.* Chatham House, March 23, 2021. https://www.chathamhouse.org/2021/03/indo-pacific-strategies-perceptions-and-partnerships/01-introduction.

———. "Introduction." *Indo-Pacific Strategies, Perceptions, and Partnerships*, Chatham House—International Affairs Think Tank, March 23, 2021. https://www.chathamhouse.org/2021/03/indo-pacific-strategies-perceptions-and-partnerships/01-introduction.

Patnaik, Ila, Ajay Shah, and Nirvikar Singh. "Foreign Investors under Stress: Evidence from India." *International Finance* 16, no. 2 (2013): 213–44. https://doi.org/10.1111/j.1468-2362.2013.12032.x.

Peri, Dinakar. "Ladakh Standoff | India, China Agree to Stop Sending More Troops to Frontline." *The Hindu*, September 22, 2020, sec. National.

Phillips, Matt, and Emily Schmall. "Stocks Soar in India, Luring Investors at Home and Abroad." *New York Times*, November 11, 2021.

Pingle, Gautam. "Reddys, Kammas and Telangana." *Economic and Political Weekly* 46, no. 46 (September 3, 2011): 19–21.

Planning Department. "Socio-Economic Survey 2016-17." Government of Andhra Pradesh, 2017.

Political Intelligence Morning Consult. "Global Leader Approval Tracker." Morning Consult, September 13, 2021. https://morningconsult.com/form/global-leader-approval/.

Prasad, N. Purendra. "Agrarian Class and Caste Relations in 'United' Andhra Pradesh, 1956–2014." *Economic and Political Weekly* 50, no. 16 (2015): 77–83.

PTI. "'Cut Money Means Chief Minister': Opposition Leaders' Protest On 'Scam.'" *NDTV.Com*, June 24, 2019.

Raghavan, P. S. "The Making of India's Foreign Policy: From Non-Alignment to Multi-Alignment." *International Foreign Affairs Journal* 12, no. 4 (December 2017): 326–41.

Raghuvanshi, Vivek. "India Releases Details of New Defense Budget." *Defense News*, February 2, 2021, sec. Asia Pacific. https://www.defensenews.com/global/asia-pacific/2021/02/02/india-releases-details-of-new-defense-budget/.

Raj, Suhasini, and Mujib Mashal. "India's Top Military General Dies in Helicopter Crash." *New York Times*, December 8, 2021, sec. World.

Rajan, Raghuram. "Make in India, Largely for India." *Indian Journal of Industrial Relations* 50, no. 3 (2015): 361–72.

Ramachandraiah, C. "Making of Amaravati: A Landscape of Speculation and Intimidation." *Economic and Political Weekly* 51, no. 17 (April 23, 2016): 68–75.

Ramanan, Sumana. "Why the Creation of Telangana Offers Maoists New Opportunities." *Scroll.In*, March 18, 2014. http://scroll.in/article/658486/why-the-creation-of-telangana-offers-maoists-new-opportunities.

Rana, Renu. "Asian Infrastructure Investment Bank, New Development Bank and the Reshaping of Global Economic Order: Unfolding Trends and Perceptions in Sino-Indian Economic Relations." *International Journal of China Studies* 10, no. 2 (2019): 273–90.

Rangarajan, C., and S. Mahendra Dev. "Poverty in India: Measurement, Trends and Other Issues." Mumbai: Indira Gandhi Institute of Development Research, December 2020. http://www.igidr.ac.in/pdf/publication/WP-2020-038.pdf.

Ranjan, Amit. "The Maldives' Geopolitical Dilemma: India–China Rivalry, and Entry of the USA." *Asian Affairs* 52, no. 2 (March 15, 2021): 375–95. https://doi.org/10.1080/03068374.2021.1911159.

Ray, Amlan, M. G. Deepika, and G. Badri Narayanan. "Analysis of India's Competitive Position in RCEP." *Vision (New Delhi, India)* 25, no. 3 (2021): 336–49. https://doi.org/10.1177/09722629211003699.

Reddy, Deepthi. "Telangana Statehood: A Timeline of Events." *The Hans India*, May 31, 2018, sec. Latest News. https://www.thehansindia.com/posts/index/Latest-News/2018-05-31/Telangana-statehood-A-timeline-of-events/385650.

Rehman, Shaikh Mujibur. "Subordinated Citizenship: Muslims in the Hindu Rashtra." *PS, Political Science & Politics* 54, no. 4 (2021): 634–35. https://doi.org/10.1017/S104909652100072X.

Rej, Abhijnan. "In 'Historic' Summit Quad Commits to Meeting Key Indo-Pacific Challenges." *The Diplomat*, March 13, 2021.

———. "India–Pakistan Ceasefire Details Emerge—Along with Possibility of Joint Military Exercises." *The Diplomat*, March 23, 2021. https://thediplomat.com/2021/03/india-pakistan-ceasefire-details-emerge-along-with-possibility-of-joint-military-exercises/.

Repucci, Sarah, and Slipowitz, Amy. "Democracy under Siege." Freedom House, *Freedom in the World 2021*. Accessed January 19, 2022. https://freedomhouse.org/report/freedom-world/2021/democracy-under-siege.

Roche, Elizabeth. "India, US Sign Pact for Cooperation in Development of Air-Launched UAV." *Mint*, September 3, 2021.

Roohi, Sanam. "Anticipating Future Capital: Regional Caste Contestations, Speculation and Silent Dispossession in Andhra Pradesh." *Journal of Contemporary Asia* 50, no. 5 (n.d.): 723–42.

Rosenbohm, Marc A. "The Impact on Domestic Prices and Government Costs of Limiting Wheat Procurement in India." *ProQuest Dissertations and Theses.* M.S., University of Missouri–Columbia, 2016. (2164291931).

Roy, Arundhati. "Opinion | The Silence Is the Loudest Sound." *New York Times*, August 15, 2019. https://www.nytimes.com/2019/08/15/opinion/sunday/kashmir-siege-modi.html.

Roy, Siddharthya. "Half a Century of India's Maoist Insurgency." *The Diplomat*, September 2017.

Ruparelia, Sanjay. "'Minimum Government, Maximum Governance': The Restructuring of Power in Modi's India." *South Asia: Journal of South Asian Studies* 38, no. 4 (October 2, 2015): 755–75. https://doi.org/10.1080/00856 401.2015.1089974.

Saghal, Neha, Jonathan Evans, Ariana Monique Salazar, Kelsey Jo Starr, and Manolo Corichi. "Religion in India: Tolerance and Segregation." Pew Research Center, June 29, 2021.

Sahoo, Niranjan. "From Bihar to Andhra, How India Fought, and Won, Its 50-Yr War with Left-Wing Extremism." *The Print*, June 26, 2019. https://theprint.in/opinion/from-bihar-to-andhra-how-india-fought-and-won-its-50-yr-war-with-left-wing-extremism/254462/.

Saint-Mézard, Isabelle. "India's Act East Policy: Strategic Implications for the Indian Ocean." *Journal of the Indian Ocean Region* 12, no. 2 (December 2016): 177–90. https://doi.org/10.1080/19480881.2016.1226753.

Sarkar, Pritha. "Patriarchy, 20th Century Bengal and the Naxalbari Movement: Tracing the Roots through Lives of Others." *Journal of International Women's Studies* 22, no. 9 (2021): 160–73.

Saxena, Rekha. "Constitutional Asymmetry in Indian Federalism." *Economic and Political Weekly* 56, no. 34 (June 5, 2015): 7–8.

Schelkle, Waltraud. *Constitution and Erosion of a Monetary Economy: Problems of India's Development since Independence.* GDI Book Series, no. 3. London: Frank Cass, 1994.

Schüller, Margot, and Jan Peter Wogart. "The Emergence of Post-Crisis Regional Financial Institutions in Asia—With a Little Help from Europe." Edited by Matthias Helble and Margot Schüller. *Asia Europe Journal* 15, no. 4 (2017): 483–501. https://doi.org/10.1007/s10308-017-0491-4.

Seligman, Lara. "Analysis: Did India Shoot down a Pakistani F-16 in February? This Just Became a Big Deal." *Washington Post*, April 17, 2019. https://www.washingtonpost.com/politics/2019/04/17/did-india-shoot-down-pakistani-f-back-february-this-just-became-big-deal

———. "Did India Shoot Down a Pakistani Jet? US Count Says No." *Foreign Policy* (blog), April 4, 2019. https://foreignpolicy.com/2019/04/04/did-india-shoot-down-a-pakistani-jet-u-s-count-says-no/.

Sen, Debarati. "Subnational Enterprise: Militarized Mothering, Women's Entrepreneurial Labour and Generational Dynamics in the Gorkhaland Struggle." *Journal of South Asian Development* 15, no. 3 (2020): 316–34. https://doi.org/10.1177/0973174120987094.

Sethi, Nidhi. "5 Reasons Why Chandrababu Naidu Exited NDA Government." *NDTV.Com*, March 16, 2018. https://www.ndtv.com/andhra-pradesh-news/5-reasons-why-chandrababu-naidu-pulled-out-of-nda-government-1824561.

Sethi, Nitin. "Electoral Bonds: Seeking Secretive Funds, Modi Govt Overruled RBI." *HuffPost*, November 17, 2019, sec. News. https://www.huffingtonpost.in/entry/rbi-warned-electoral-bonds-arun-jaitley-black-money-modi-government_in_5dcbde68e4b0d43931ccd200.

Shah, Khalid. "Will the Ceasefire on India Pakistan Border Sustain?" ORF, September 29, 2021. https://www.orfonline.org/expert-speak/will-the-ceasefire-on-india-pakistan-border-sustain/.

Sharma, Mihir. "The Change That Bengal Needs." *Indian Express*, May 21, 2011.

Sharma, Ruchir. "The Rise of the Rest of India: How States Have Become the Engines of Growth." *Foreign Affairs* 92, no. 5 (2013): 75–85.

Sharun, Khan, and Kuldeep Dhama. "India's Role in COVID-19 Vaccine Diplomacy." *Journal of Travel Medicine* 28, no. 7 (October 11, 2021). https://doi.org/10.1093/jtm/taab064.

Sidhu, W. P. S., and Shruti Godbole. "Neighbourhood First: Bilateralism Trumps Regionalism." *Brookings India*, May 2015, 2.

Singh, Bikash. "Mamata Banerjee Claims Achievement in Dealing with Naxalites." *Economic Times*, May 2, 2017.

Singh, Karan Deep. "As India's Lethal Covid Wave Neared, Politics Overrode Science." *New York Times*, September 14, 2021, sec. World. https://www.nytimes.com/2021/09/14/world/asia/india-modi-science-icmr.html.

———. "India Deaths from COVID May Exceed 3 Million." *New York Times*, July 21, 2021.

Singh, Prerna. *How Solidarity Works for Welfare: Subnationalism and Social Development in India.* Cambridge Studies in Comparative Politics. Cambridge: Cambridge University Press, 2015.

———. "Subnationalism and Social Development: A Comparative Analysis of Indian States." *World Politics* 67, no. 3 (2015): 506–62.

Singh, Vinay Kumar, and Rohit Prasad. "Diffusion of Banking Products in Financial Inclusion Linked Savings Accounts: A Case Study Based on Pradhan Mantri Jan Dhan Yojana in India." *Global Business Review* (2021): 97215092110068. https://doi.org/10.1177/09721509211006866.

Sinha, Aseema. "India's Porous State." In *Business and Politics in India*, edited by Christophe Jaffrelot, Atul Kohli, and Kanta Murali. Modern South Asia. New York: Oxford University Press, 2019.

Slater, Joanna. "Trump's Second Day in India: Violence in Delhi and Support for Modi on 'Religious Freedom.'" *Washington Post*, February 25, 2020, sec. Asia.

Sood, Rakesh. "What Has Changed Post-Balakot?" *The Hindu*, March 20, 2019, sec. Lead. https://www.thehindu.com/opinion/lead/what-has-changed-post-balakot/article26583820.ece.

Soz, Salman Anees. *The Great Disappointment: How Narendra Modi Squandered a Unique Opportunity to Transform the Indian Economy*. Gurgaon, Haryana, India: Ebury Press / Penguin Random House India, 2019.

Srinagar, Samaan Lateef. "Kashmir: Minority Killings Increase amid Violent Demographic Tensions." DW.com, October 13, 2021. https://www.dw.com/en/kashmir-minority-killings-increase-amid-violent-demographic-tensions/a-59467733.

Srinivasulu, K., and Overseas Development Institute. *Caste, Class and Social Articulation in Andhra Pradesh: Mapping Differential Regional Trajectories*. London: ODI, 2002.

Staniland, Paul. "Leftist Insurgency in Democracies." *Comparative Political Studies* 54, no. 3–4 (2020 2021): 518–52. https://doi.org/10.1177/0010414020938096.

Swamy, Rohini. "In Telangana, Naxal Poet Gaddar Embraces the Ballot & Old Foes to Fight 'Fundamentalists.'" *The Print*, December 4, 2018. https://theprint.in/politics/in-telangana-naxal-poet-gaddar-embraces-the-ballot-old-foes-to-fight-fundamentalists/157909/.

Taylor, Guy. "Mike Pompeo Confronts 'Asian NATO' Hurdles in Asian Allies Meeting." *Washington Times*, October 5, 2020, sec. Security.

Thakur, Joydeep. "Jobs, Subsidised Food in Mamata Manifesto." *Hindustan Times*, March 18, 2021.

The Economist. "How to Run a Continent." *The Economist*, May 21, 2015.

———. "India Spends a Fortune on Defence and Gets Poor Value for Money." *The Economist*, March 28, 2018. https://www.economist.com/asia/2018/03/28/india-spends-a-fortune-on-defence-and-gets-poor-value-for-money.

———. "India's Armed Forces Get Their Biggest Shake-Up in Decades." *The Economist*, January 18, 2020. https://www.economist.com/asia/2020/01/18/indias-armed-forces-get-their-biggest-shake-up-in-decades.

ThePrint Team. "Pakistan-Based Social Media Accounts, Bots Spread Conspiracy Theories on CDS Rawat's Death." *The Print*, December 16, 2021. https://theprint.in/defence/pakistan-based-social-media-accounts-bots-spread-conspiracy-theories-on-cds-rawats-death/782647/.

Tillin, Louise. *Remapping India: New States and Their Political Origins.* London: Hurst & Company, 2013.

———. "Statehood and the Politics of Intent." *Economic and Political Weekly* 46, no. 20 (2011): 34–38.

Times Now. "Fresh ED Summons to Mamata Banerjee's Nephew for Questioning in Coal Scam." *Times Now*, September 11, 2021.

Times of India. "Bihar Diwas at Pragati Maidan on Mar 22." *Times of India*, February 21, 2010.

———. "Formal Sector Much Bigger Than What You Thought All This While." *Times of India*, January 30, 2018. https://timesofindia.indiatimes.com/business/india-business/formal-sector-much-bigger-than-what-you-thought-all-this-while/articleshow/62706273.cms.

Tisdall, Simon. "Narendra Modi's US Visa Secure despite Gujarat Riots Guilty Verdicts." *Guardian*, June 2, 2016, sec. World News.

Tiwari, Ravish. "Manmohan Singh: PM Narendra Modi Used 15% Fewer Words than Former PM Manmohan Singh in US Congress Speech." *Economic Times*, June 10, 2016.

TNN & Agencies. "'Terrorism Has Become Its Favourite Child': PM Modi Slams Pakistan at BRICS-BIMSTEC Outreach Summit." *Times of India*, October 16, 2016. https://timesofindia.indiatimes.com/india/terrorism-has-become-its-favourite-child-pm-modi-slams-pakistan-at-brics-bimstec-outreach-summit/articleshow/54882776.cms.

UN. *World Social Report 2020: Inequality in a Rapidly Changing World.* United Nations, 2020. https://doi.org/10.18356/7f5d0efc-en.

UNDP. *Human Development Report 2019: Beyond Income, beyond Averages, beyond Today: Inequalities in Human Development in the 21st Century.* United Nations Development Programme, 2019.

United States Department of State. "Secretary Antony J. Blinken and Indian External Affairs Minister Dr. Subrahmanyam Jaishankar at a Joint Press Availability," July 28, 2021. https://www.state.gov/secretary-antony-j-blinken-and-indian-external-affairs-minister-dr-subrahmanyam-jaishankar-at-a-joint-press-availability/.

Unnithan, Sandeep. "Majority of the Maoist Leadership Hail from a Single District of Telangana, a Legacy That Haunts Its Demand for Statehood." *India Today*, July 29, 2013. https://www.indiatoday.in/magazine/india/telangana/story/20130729-maoist-leadership-hails-from-a-single-district-of-telangana-764751-1999-11-30.

———. "Policy Paralysis, Bureaucratic Lethargy Undoing Modi's Make in India Plan to Indigenise Weapons Production: With Strategic Partnerships Paving the Way for Joint Ventures between Indian and Foreign Firms, the Weak Link Is Slow Decision-Making in the Defence Ministry, Which Hands out the Contracts." *India Today*. New Delhi: Living Media India, Limited, March 6, 2017. 1872171816. ProQuest Central Essentials.

USTR. "2020 National Trade Estimate on Foreign Trade Barriers." United States Trade Representative, March 2020. https://ustr.gov/sites/default/files/2020_National_Trade_Estimate_Report.pdf.

Van der Veer, Peter. "What Transcends the Nation?" *Asian Ethnology* 80, no. 1 (2021): 19–30.

Van Dyke, Virginia. "State-Level Politics, Coalitions, and Rapid System Change in India." In *Routledge Handbook of South Asian Politics: India, Pakistan, Bangladesh, Sri Lanka, and Nepal*, edited by Paul Brass, 67–82. New York: Routledge, 2010.

Varshney, Ashutosh. "Populism and Nationalism: An Overview of Similarities and Differences." *Studies in Comparative International Development* 56, no. 2 (2021): 131–47. https://doi.org/10.1007/s12116-021-09332-x.

Varshney, Ashutosh, Srikrishna Ayyangar, and Siddharth Swaminathan. "Populism and Hindu Nationalism in India." *Studies in Comparative International Development* 56, no. 2 (2021): 197–222. https://doi.org/10.1007/s12116-021-09335-8.

Venkataramanan, K. "Explained | India's Asymmetric Federalism." *The Hindu*, August 11, 2019, sec. National. https://www.thehindu.com/news/national/the-forms-of-federalism-in-india/article28977671.ece.

Venugopal, Vasudha. "With Shah's Visit, BJP Hopes to Boost North Bengal Tally." *The Economic Times*, April 12, 2021.

Verma, H. K. "Rajnath Lauds Nitish Govt for Tackling Left-Wing Extremism." *Times of India*, 2018.

Verma, Rajiv, Saurabh Gupta, and Regina Birner. "Can Vigilance-Focused Governance Reforms Improve Service Delivery? The Case of Integrated Child Development Services (ICDS) in Bihar, India." *Development Policy Review* 36 (September 2, 2018): O786–802.

Wang, Orange. "China–India Border Clash 'First Major Test' for AIIB as Multilateral Lender." *South China Morning Post*, June 4, 2021, sec. Economy.

Wenner, Miriam. "Trajectories of Hybrid Governance: Legitimacy, Order and Leadership in India." *Development and Change* 52, no. 2 (2021): 265–88. https://doi.org/10.1111/dech.12624.

West Bengal, State Government of. "Bengal Surges Ahead—Agriculture." West Bengal Agriculture Department, January 2021. https://wb.gov.in/departments-details.aspx?id=D170907140022669&page=Agriculture.

White House. "Quad Leaders' Joint Statement: 'The Spirit of the Quad.'" The White House, March 12, 2021. https://www.whitehouse.gov/briefing-room/statements-releases/2021/03/12/quad-leaders-joint-statement-the-spirit-of-the-quad/.

White, Joshua T. "After the Foundational Agreements: An Agenda for US–India Defense and Security Cooperation." *Brookings.edu*, January 2021, 34.

WITS. "India Trade." Database. World Integrated Trade Solution (WITS) Data, 2021. https://wits.worldbank.org/countrysnapshot/en/IND.

World Bank. "Banks and Community Institutions Partner to Create an Ecosystem for Sustainable Financial Inclusion in Bihar, India." Text/HTML. World Bank, March 27, 2013. https://www.worldbank.org/en/news/feature/2013/03/27/banks-community-institutions-partner-create-sustainable-financial-inclusion-bihar-india.

———. "Debt Products FAQs." Text/HTML. World Bank. Accessed July 21, 2021. https://treasury.worldbank.org/en/about/unit/treasury/ibrd/debt-products-faqs.

———. "Doing Business—Data Irregularities Statement." World Bank, August 27, 2020. https://www.worldbank.org/en/news/statement/2020/08/27/doing-business---data-irregularities-statement.

———. "Enterprise Surveys: What Businesses Experience." Text/HTML. World Bank. Accessed June 8, 2021. https://www.enterprisesurveys.org/en/data/exploreeconomies.

———. "Global Findex Database." Database. World Bank Global Findex, 2017. https://globalfindex.worldbank.org/.

———. "Poverty & Equity Brief: South Asia." Poverty & Equity Brief. World Bank, April 2020.

———. "Poverty & Equity Brief: South Asia." World Bank, April 2021. https://databank.worldbank.org/data/download/poverty/987B9C90-CB9F-4D93-AE8C-750588BF00QA/SM2021/Global_POVEQ_IND.pdf.

———. "World Bank Group Statement on Doing Business Data Corrections and Findings of Internal Audit." World Bank, December 16, 2020. https://www.worldbank.org/en/news/statement/2020/12/16/world-bank-group-statement-on-doing-business-data-corrections-and-findings-of-internal-audit.

———. "World Bank Maps." Database. World Bank Maps, 2021. https://maps.worldbank.org/#.
———. "World Bank to Support Bihar Government's Initiative to Rebuild Flood-Affected Areas with $220 Million." Text/HTML. World Bank, January 12, 2011. https://www.worldbank.org/en/news/press-release/2011/01/12/world-bank-to-support-bihar-governments-initiative-to-rebuild-flood-affected-areas-with-220-million.
———. "World Development Indicators." Database. DataBank, 2021. https://databank.worldbank.org/.
World Bank, and Ernesto Sanchez-Triana. "Bihar Social and Environmental Analysis Concept Note." Concept Note. Bihar State Social and Environmental Analysis. Washington, DC: World Bank. Accessed July 7, 2021. https://documents1.worldbank.org/curated/en/718661468040753838/text/698510ESWoP1050t0Note0SanchezTriana.txt.
World Inequality Database. "India." WID—World Inequality Database. Accessed May 27, 2021. https://wid.world/country/india/.
Wright, Jasmine. "Biden Commits to 'Free, Open, Secure' Indo-Pacific in Rare Op-Ed with 'Quad' Members." *CNNPolitics*, March 14, 2021. https://www.cnn.com/2021/03/14/politics/biden-modi-morrison-suga-quad-op-ed/index.html.
WTO. "Concerns Grow about Slippage in Subsidy Notifications." World Trade Organization, April 25, 2017. https://www.wto.org/english/news_e/news17_e/scm_25apr17_e.htm.
Yaha, Anick, Nirvikar Singh, and Jean Paul Rabanal. "How Do Extreme Global Shocks Affect Foreign Portfolio Investment? An Event Study for India." *Emerging Markets Finance & Trade* 53, no. 8 (2017): 1923–38. https://doi.org/10.1080/1540496X.2016.1204599.
Yamunan, Sruthisagar. "They Gave up Farmland for New Andhra Capital. Now They Are Crippled with Uncertainty." *Scroll.In*, February 6, 2020. https://scroll.in/article/951454/they-gave-up-farmland-for-new-andhra-capital-now-they-are-crippled-with-uncertainty.
Zargar, Arshad. "India Bans TikTok and Dozens of Other Chinese Apps amid Border Standoff." *CBS News*. June 30, 2020. https://www.cbsnews.com/news/india-bans-tiktok-other-china-made-apps-as-border-dispute-drags-on-today-2020-06-30/.
Zarhani, Seyed Hossein. *Governance and Development in India: A Comparative Study on Andhra Pradesh and Bihar after Liberalization*. London; New York: Routledge, 2019.

Zeeshan, Mohamed. "India's Approach Toward Myanmar Will Hurt Its Credibility." *The Diplomat*, April 5, 2021. https://thediplomat.com/2021/04/indias-approach-toward-myanmar-will-hurt-its-credibility/.

———. "India Still Has an Opportunity with Vaccine Diplomacy." *The Diplomat*, October 1, 2021.